Lecture Notes in Computer Science 11457

Commenced Publication in 1973
Founding and Former Series Editors:
Gerhard Goos, Juris Hartmanis, and Jan van Leeuwen

More information about this series at http://www.springer.com/series/7407

Michał Pałka · Magnus Myreen (Eds.)

Trends in Functional Programming

19th International Symposium, TFP 2018
Gothenburg, Sweden, June 11–13, 2018
Revised Selected Papers

 Springer

Editors
Michał Pałka
Chalmers University of Technology
Gothenburg, Sweden

Magnus Myreen
Chalmers University of Technology
Gothenburg, Sweden

ISSN 0302-9743   ISSN 1611-3349   (electronic)
Lecture Notes in Computer Science
ISBN 978-3-030-18505-3   ISBN 978-3-030-18506-0   (eBook)
https://doi.org/10.1007/978-3-030-18506-0

LNCS Sublibrary: SL1 – Theoretical Computer Science and General Issues

This Springer imprint is published by the registered company Springer Nature Switzerland AG
The registered company address is: Gewerbestrasse 11, 6330 Cham, Switzerland

Preface

This volume contains a selection of the papers presented at TFP 2018: the Symposium on Trends in Function Programming 2018, held June 11–13, 2018, in Gothenburg, Sweden.

TFP is an international forum for researchers with interests in all aspects of functional programming, taking a broad view of current and future trends in the area. It aspires to be a lively environment for presenting the latest research results and other contributions, described in draft papers submitted prior to the symposium. This edition of the symposium is the first to adopt a new format for selecting articles for publication. In the new format, authors can choose to have their submissions formally reviewed either before or after the symposium. Four full papers were submitted for formal review before the symposium, out of which three were accepted by the Program Committee for presentation and later publication. Each submission was reviewed by at least three reviewers. For the remaining submissions, the Program Committee chairs only checked that the drafts were within the scope of TFP and thus relevant for presentation at TFP. Submissions appearing in the draft proceedings are not considered as peer-reviewed publications.

The TFP 2018 program consisted of two invited talks and 16 presentations. The invited talks were given by Simon Thompson (University of Kent, UK) on "Refactoring Reflected," and Neel Krishnaswami (University of Cambridge, UK) on "Retrofitting Purity with Comonads." Out of the 16 presentations, three full papers were accepted for publication before the symposium as mentioned earlier, whereas a further nine full papers were submitted to the formal post-refereeing process. The Program Committee selected four more papers for publication from these, which brings us to the total of seven that are included in these proceedings.

We are grateful to everyone at Chalmers University for their help in preparing and organizing TFP 2018, in particular Elisabeth Kegel Andreasson. We gratefully acknowledge the financial support of the Information and Communication Technology Area of Advance at Chalmers and Erlang Solutions, which allowed us to reduce registration costs. We also gratefully acknowledge the assistance of the TFP 2018 Program Committee and the TFP Steering Committee for their advice while organizing the symposium.

February 2019
Michał Pałka
Magnus Myreen

Organization

Program Committee

Soichiro Hidaka	Hosei University, Japan
Meng Wang	University of Bristol, UK
Sam Tobin-Hochstadt	Indiana University Bloomington, USA
Tiark Rompf	Purdue University, USA
Patricia Johann	Appalachian State University, USA
Neil Sculthorpe	Nottingham Trent University, UK
Andres Löh	Well-Typed LLP, UK
Tarmo Uustalu	Reykjavik University, Iceland
Cosmin E. Oancea	University of Copenhagen, Denmark
Mauro Jaskelioff	Universidad Nacional de Rosario, Argentina
Peter Achten	Radboud University, The Netherlands
Dimitrios Vytiniotis	Microsoft Research, UK
Alberto Pardo	Universidad de la República, Uruguay
Natalia Chechina	Bournemouth University, UK
Peter Sestoft	IT University of Copenhagen, Denmark
Scott Owens	University of Kent, UK
Michał Pałka (Chair)	Chalmers University of Technology, Sweden
Magnus Myreen (Chair)	Chalmers University of Technology, Sweden

Sponsoring Institutions

Chalmers ICT Area of Advance
Erlang Solutions

Contents

Colocation of Potential Parallelism in a Distributed Adaptive
Run-Time System for Parallel Haskell   1
  Evgenij Belikov, Hans-Wolfgang Loidl, and Greg Michaelson

Reversible Session-Based Concurrency in Haskell   20
  Folkert de Vries and Jorge A. Pérez

Intrinsic Currying for C++ Template Metaprograms   46
  Paul Keir, Andrew Gozillon, and Seyed Hossein Haeri

Towards Optic-Based Algebraic Theories: The Case of Lenses   74
  J. López-González and Juan M. Serrano

Saint: An API-Generic Type-Safe Interpreter   94
  Maximilian Algehed, Patrik Jansson, Sólrún Halla Einarsdóttir,
  and Alex Gerdes

Improving Haskell   114
  Martin A. T. Handley and Graham Hutton

High-Performance Defunctionalisation in Futhark   136
  Anders Kiel Hovgaard, Troels Henriksen, and Martin Elsman

Author Index   157

Colocation of Potential Parallelism in a Distributed Adaptive Run-Time System for Parallel Haskell

Evgenij Belikov$^{(\boxtimes)}$, Hans-Wolfgang Loidl, and Greg Michaelson

School of Mathematical and Computer Sciences, Heriot-Watt University,
Edinburgh EH14 4AS, Scotland, UK
{eb120,H.W.Loidl,G.Michaelson}@hw.ac.uk,
http://www.macs.hw.ac.uk

Abstract. This paper presents a novel variant of work stealing for load balancing in a distributed graph reducer, executing a semi-explicit parallel dialect of Haskell. The key concept of this load-balancer is *colocating* related *sparks* (potential parallelism) using maximum prefix matching on the encoding of the spark's ancestry within the computation tree, reconstructed at run time, in spark selection decisions. We evaluate spark colocation in terms of performance and scalability on a set of five benchmarks on a Beowulf-class cluster of multi-core machines using up to 256 cores. In comparison to the baseline mechanism, we achieve speedup increase of up to 46% for three out of five applications, due to improved locality and load balance throughout the execution as demonstrated by profiling data. For one less scalable program and one program with excessive amounts of very fine-grained parallelism we observe drops in speedup by 17% and 42%, respectively. Overall, spark colocation results in reduced mean time to fetch the required data and in higher degree of parallelism of finer granularity, which is most beneficial on higher PE numbers.

Keywords: Parallel functional programming · Graph reduction · Load balancing · Distributed-memory work stealing · Adaptive parallelism

1 Introduction

Exploiting modern distributed parallel architectures is key for improving application performance and scalability beyond a single machine, for instance for Large-Scale Data Analytics and High-Performance Computing. Additionally, using a high-level programming language is crucial for countering growing software complexity and for increasing programmer productivity by delegating most of the coordination and parallelism management to the run-time system (RTS). Functional Programming offers a high level of abstraction and advanced language features [1,14,16], e.g. higher-order functions, polymorphism, and type classes. In particular, functional languages appear suitable for exploitation of

© Springer Nature Switzerland AG 2019
M. Pałka and M. Myreen (Eds.): TFP 2018, LNCS 11457, pp. 1–19, 2019.
https://doi.org/10.1007/978-3-030-18506-0_1

fine-grained parallelism as independent sub-expressions can be evaluated in any order without changing the result (known as the Church-Rosser property [9]), facilitating incremental parallelisation and allowing for sequential debugging of parallel programs, whilst avoiding race conditions and deadlocks [13].

Work stealing [5] is a popular passive (i.e. receiver-initiated) decentralised load balancing mechanism, where idle processing elements (PEs) attempt to steal work from busy PEs. Important parameters in this mechanism are the target of the steal attempt and the choice of the (potential) parallel work units, or *sparks*. In our current parallel RTS the target is randomly selected, to avoid hotspots in the communication, and older sparks are preferred, because they typically represent work of larger granularity. Large granularity aims at offsetting the communication costs, especially in computations that use the Divide-and-Conquer (D&C) pattern or are nested and are run on distributed architectures with very high communication costs.

Note that in our system all parallelism is *advisory* rather than *mandatory*. This means that RTS policies can adaptively tune the amount of parallelism, deciding not to generate actual parallelism. This can effectively in-line work into other threads and thereby improve the granularity of the computation.

In this paper we investigate the effect of a modification to the spark (work) selection policy, namely *spark colocation* (SC), on performance and scalability. SC exports the spark that is, according to a specific metric, most closely related to the computation performed by the thief and is aimed at resolving the trade-off between data locality and load balance, instead of exporting the oldest spark. The chosen metric for proximity is the distance in the compute tree, and the RTS is extended to capture a trace of spark sites, representing the path in the tree leading to this spark. On selecting a spark to export to another PE, the one with the longest common prefix is used, as the one that is most closely related to recent work performed on the thief's PE. Compared to the baseline mechanism, SC achieves speedup increase of up to 46%, due to improved locality and load balance throughout the execution as demonstrated by profiling data, whilst for one less scalable application and one with excessive amount of overly fine-grained parallelism we observe drops in speedup of 17% and 42%, respectively.

Next we introduce the GUM RTS for Glasgow parallel Haskell in Sect. 2 and discuss the design and implementation of spark colocation in Sect. 3, followed by evaluation of empirical results for five applications based on means-based metrics from per-PE profiles gathered from runs on a 256-PE-cluster in Sect. 4. A brief discussion of related work follows in Sect. 5, before our conclusion and future work directions are presented in Sect. 6.

2   Distributed Graph Reduction in the GUM RTS

Here we briefly introduce the Glasgow parallel Haskell (GpH) language and the underlying GUM (Graph Reduction on a Unified Machine Model) RTS that implements distributed graph reduction [31], including most notably using global addresses to implement virtual shared memory, thread management using *sparks* that efficiently represent potential parallelism, and work stealing, or *fishing*, for passive load distribution.

2.1   Haskell Extension for Semi-explicit Parallelism

Glasgow parallel Haskell (GpH) [12] extends Haskell [15,24], a popular non-strict
purely functional language, by adding a sequential and a parallel combinator as
language primitives (pseq and par), which allow the specification of evaluation
order and identification of potential parallelism, respectively. This high-level
programming model is *semi-explicit*. The advisory parallelism identification and
optional application-level granularity control are explicit. All other coordination
aspects, such as communication and synchronisation, are implicitly controlled
by the RTS. Listing 1.1 provides an example.

```
1  fib 0 = 0                        -- sequential version
2  fib 1 = 1                        -- NB args of type Integer
3  fib n = fib (n−1) + fib (n−2)
4
5  pfib 0 _ = 0                     -- parallel version
6  pfib 1 _ = 1
7  pfib n t | n <= t = fib n        -- threshold for granularity control
8           | otherwise = x 'par' y 'pseq' x + y
9           where x = pfib (n−1) t
10                 y = pfib (n−2) t
```

Listing 1.1. GpH Example: Sequential and Parallel Fibonacci Functions

Using par, the programmer provides a hint to the RTS that the first argument
expression can be beneficially evaluated in parallel, thus creating a *spark*, and
the RTS decides at run time whether the spark will be turned into a lightweight thread increasing the actual degree of parallelism or ignored. Note that
in order to be useful the first expression should be unevaluated, represent a large-
enough amount of computation, and be shared with the rest of the program [21].
This mechanism can be viewed as implementing *lazy futures* similar to *lazy task
creation* [25]. To cleanly separate the computation and coordination concerns
Evaluation Strategies [22,30] were introduced on top of the basic primitives.

2.2   Memory Management

GUM implements GpH by supporting distributed graph reduction, where each
graph node represents a potentially shared computation, using a combination
of a *virtual shared memory* that holds the shared graph nodes and independent
local heaps associated with separate GUM instances that run on each PE in
parallel. Once a node has been evaluated it is replaced by the result, which is in
turn sent to all the PEs that require it.

This design, based on private heaps with some sharing across them, is scalable as most of garbage collection (GC) can be performed *locally* without the
need for communication and synchronisation. GUM uses a *generational* garbage
collector that is either *copying* or *compacting* depending on the RTS flags set,
thus avoiding a stop-the-world design (e.g. as used in GHC-SMP [23]). Heap
objects that survive for a long time are promoted from the initial and frequently
GC'd heap area (called *nursery*) to a different space that is GC'd less often. This
GC scheme assumes that most heap objects will expire after a short period of
time allowing the associated memory to be reclaimed. Additionally, GUM uses
distributed weighted reference counting [4] to manage the virtual shared heap.

2.3   Thread and Parallelism Management

GUM represents sub-computations using light-weight threads that are mapped to relatively few heavy-weight OS threads (often one per core) in an M-to-N fashion for scalability (similar to Green Threads). Each RTS instance maintains a local thread pool for runnable threads and blocked queues for threads waiting on a result of evaluation performed by another potentially remote thread[1].

GUM's scheduler is unfair and non-preemptive. It prioritises handling messages and implements the *evaluate-and-die* evaluation model [28]. In this model a thread picks up a thunk (an unevaluated expression) to evaluate and returns control to the scheduler once either the evaluation to weak-head normal form has completed or thread blocks waiting on another value under evaluation.

Sparks that represent potentially parallel work are created using the `par` primitive and kept in a separate local pool on each PE. Sparking is inexpensive, as it merely adds a pointer to a graph node representing the expression to be evaluated to the pool, which is implemented using an efficient lock-free dequeue [8], which allows the owner to use one end locally for pushing, whilst older sparks are stolen off the other end using a single atomic compare-and-swap operation (FIFO). The overhead is absent unless two threads happen to simultaneously operate on the same item of the dequeue. Sparks are discarded if they have been already evaluated or if the spark pool is full.

2.4   Workload Distribution

Load balancing across PEs is achieved through work stealing (also called *fishing*) and aims at reducing the overall idle time across PEs. The two main decisions include: (1) where to steal from (victim selection by the thief or selection of forwarding destination by victim with no sparks available for export) and (2) which spark to export (decision made by a victim that has exportable sparks). This work is focused on the latter decision.

Figure 1 illustrates the message types and the protocol. A FISH message is a request for work and is forwarded to randomly selected PEs until either some work was found or the FISH expires by reaching a maximum age (it is incremented with every hop). If the thief was successful, it receives a SCHEDULE message containing some work and potentially some related data. The thief responds by sending an ACK message with an updated list of pairs of old and new global addresses to the victim to update the virtual shared memory to reflect the change. If the FISH expires, it is sent back to the original PE, which then can then send out a new FISH.

The default mechanism selects a victim at random. A victim that receives a FISH, selects the oldest spark for donation and sends it back to the origin PE. This is where SC differs: it selects a spark from the same source of parallelism using *maximum prefix matching* on the encoding of the path of the spark within

---

[1] Parallelism is exploited over pure functions and I/O is handled orthogonally by a separate thread.

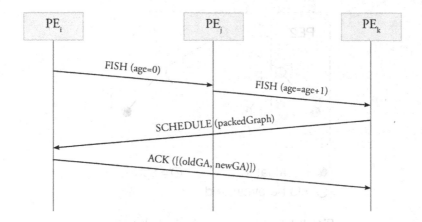

Fig. 1. Multi-Hop successful FISHing attempt

the computational graph, rather than using the age of the spark (as described in detail in Sect. 3).

Fish delay and delay factor as well as a limitation on the number of outstanding fishes (currently one) are used to avoid swamping the network with FISHes. Thread migration is not supported in the current implementation.

3   Spark Colocation

Spark Colocation is aimed at improving load balance and locality by exporting the spark that is most closely related to the computation performed by the thief.

3.1   Motivating Example

Consider the example from Fig. 2 that illustrates a situation where two PEs work on several tasks and one PE needs to decide which spark to donate.

The tree structure represents computational dependencies, whilst the dashed regions depict which tasks are located on which PE. In particular, both sparks ended up on PE1. As PE2 continues the evaluation it runs out of tasks and sends a FISH to PE1. In turn, PE1 can now decide which spark to donate. It would donate B, which we assume is older[2], in the baseline case. Then it would continue to execute the remaining spark A locally. However, the result of A is needed by PE2, which would require additional communication. Similarly, if spark B is exported and turned into a thread on PE2, communication is required to send the result to PE1. If Spark Colocation is used A would be donated as it is more related to the computation on PE2.

The main idea is to allocate computations to PEs that have worked on related computations. A related computation is located closely in the same computational sub-tree, because its result or produced data are likely to be required by

---

[2] This is reasonable as PE1 is the main PE and PE2 starts with no work.

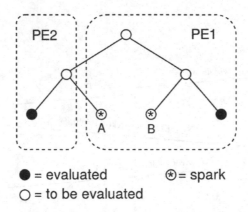

● = evaluated   ⊛ = spark
○ = to be evaluated

Fig. 2. Example of potential for colocation

the other computation. The concept of SC builds on the notion of proximity between computations. Two sparks are defined to be in close proximity if the path in the tree between their nodes is short. In particular, if the root node is on the path, the sparks can be considered unrelated.

3.2 Design

SC is an extension of the baseline work stealing mechanism, investigating the effect of favouring colocation of related sparks, rather than selecting a spark to export based on its age alone. The idea is to allocate computations to PEs that have worked on related computations, i.e. computation located closely in the same computational sub-tree likely to require the result of, or share some data with the other. Using SC, the information on the proximity between sparks that would normally be lost during compilation is forwarded to the RTS, where it can dynamically influence scheduling and load balancing decisions at run time.

Informally, the colocation algorithm behaves as follows: if a PE is idle, it will attempt to steal work from others that will respond with the spark on the path through the compute tree that is most related to the computation performed by the thief, rather than with the oldest. We use the *ancestry* relation with the *maximum prefix* function as the matching function for finding the best match between the encoding of the thief and of the sparks available to the victim. The baseline mechanism is used as a fallback.

Figure 3 illustrates the encoding for two sources of parallelism, thus base 2 is used for the encoding. For example, if spark A with the encoding 01 was turned into a thread and then had the choice between sparks B and C, the latter would be chosen as given its encoding 010 it has a longer common prefix of length two with A as opposed to B with encoding 00, which shares only one symbol with A. We can also see that A requires the result of computation C, whilst it does not require the result of B to proceed. An ancestor of a spark is recursively defined as either the direct creator of the spark (its parent), or as the ancestor of its parent.

The ancestry relation is encoded as a path in the computation represented by a string of symbols that encode the branch at each tree level.

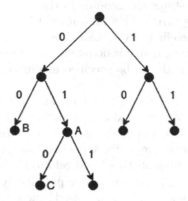

Fig. 3. Spark ancestry encoding example

We select *maximum prefix* as a matching function, because the resulting encoding mirrors closely the actual tree-like computational structure of the application. The ancestry relation defines the distance between a thread's encoding and the encoding of a given spark as the sum of edges traversed on the path from one encoding to the other in the tree. The smaller the distance the more closely related two sub-computations are deemed to be. Investigation of alternative encodings and matching functions remains for future work.

3.3 Implementation

SC is implemented as an explicit language primitive—a version of the **par** combinator we call **parEnc**—that takes additional encoding arguments that are passed to the RTS and used to tag the sparks. The path to the spark constitutes an encoding, where we start from the root and add a symbol for each sub-branch chosen at each level. The symbol corresponds to the **parEnc** site that leads to the creation of the spark and is appended to its inherited parent's encoding.

Spark Selection: In the baseline mechanism, the spark pool is implemented as a lock-free double-ended queue, so that the owning PE can add new sparks at the tail of the deque whilst sparks are exported off the head. This mechanism avoids most of the synchronisation cost as it is only incurred when threads attempt to dequeue the same spark, as the owner turns local sparks into threads by taking them from the tail, which is similar to the Breadth-first-Until-Saturation-then-Depth-first mechanism [6].

By contrast, SC uses spark encodings to select related sparks, if possible. Internally, we use hash tables to store and efficiently access the information on threads and sparks using their respective identifiers as lookup keys. This mechanism enables the RTS to distinguish sparks based on their source of parallelism and location within the compute tree of the application for a given input. Each time a spark is created it stores its encoding in the hash table. This encoding is compared to the encoding carried by an incoming FISH message, extended with information about the encoding of the thief. The spark pool is traversed and a spark with a maximum prefix match is donated. To trade precision for overhead, the maximum traversal length can be specified as an RTS option.

Matching Function: We have chosen to encode ancestry as a string of symbols to the base needed to encode the maximum number of branches at a level of the tree, reflecting the dynamic relationship that arises at run time.

As a natural choice, maximum prefix string matching is used to determine the spark for export, since it represents the closest relation between the computations in the graph. Nevertheless, the matching may potentially lead to more communication than in the baseline case and increased amount of inter-PE sharing as implicated by the number of global addresses. Therefore an empirical evaluation is needed.

Packet Format: To propagate ancestry information, the packet format is extended for the FISH and the SCHEDULE protocol messages. FISH is extended to carry the requesting PE's encoding, whilst SCHEDULE includes the exported spark and its encoding. When turned into a thread, the spark's encoding is used as the thread's encoding, which is in turn passed on to the sparks it may generate.

Profiling: To facilitate comparison between SC and the baseline mechanism, the event-based profiling sub-system is extended to record thread granularities, i.e. the run time elapsed from start to termination of a thread, and fetch times, i.e. run time spent in the state waiting for data to arrive, in addition to the already available profiling information such as per-PE load over time, message counts, and number of global addresses.

The extension is small as it requires mainly adding calls to a timer function in places where a thread enters a particular state (e.g. fetching) and recording the difference when a transition to another state occurs. The extension does not impede scalability as it only involves keeping an additional per-thread counter adding little to the existing profiling overhead, whilst the events are written out to file as they occur using a separate asynchronous thread responsible for buffered I/O.

4 Evaluation

We compare SC and the baseline mechanism using empirical measurements.

4.1 Methodology

We run each of the five applications five times for each PE-count both with and without event-based profiling and compare the median runs with and without SC[3]. The elapsed (wall-clock) run time is measured in milliseconds and includes both the mutation time and the garbage collection time. We don't have exclusive access to the cluster, so that although it is usually lightly loaded, we can't fully rule out some variation due to interference with other processes running on the machines. As PVM is used as a communication library [11], processes are placed onto nodes in a round robin fashion as specified in a hostfile that is read in top-to-bottom order.

Using ends-based metrics such as run time and speedup alone doesn't provide sufficient insight into why the observed effects of SC take place, for instance with respect to load balance over time. Therefore, we also collect profiling data for several means-based metrics: per-PE numbers of threads over time as a measure of load balance and degree of parallelism, thread sizes reflecting granularity, numbers of transmitted messages of different types, as well as the numbers inter-PE pointers to assess data locality, and fetch times and counts for data-carrying messages.

4.2 Target Platform

The applications are run on a 32-node Beowulf cluster of multi-cores using up to 256 PEs. The cluster comprises a mix of 8-core Xeon 5504 nodes with two sockets with four 2 GHz cores, 256 KB L2 cache, 4 MB shared L3 cache and 12 GB RAM, and 8-core Xeon 5450 nodes with two sockets with four 3 GHz cores, 6 MB shared L2 cache and 16 GB RAM. The machines are connected via Gigabit Ethernet with an average latency of 0.23 µs, measured using the Linux `ping` utility (average round-trip time of 100 packets). We use the CentOS 6.7 operating system, the GHC 6.12.3 Haskell compiler, the GCC 4.4.8 C compiler, and the PVM 3.4.6 communication library. The optimisations are turned on (`-O2`).

4.3 Applications

We use five D&C benchmark applications adopted from the parallel part of the established *nofib* benchmarking suite [26] and from a recent study of Evaluation Strategies [22]. In particular, we use `parfib` which is the standard parallelism microbenchmark, `parpair` with calls to `sumeuler` and `parfib` nested within the pair and evaluated in parallel, interval-based `sumeuler` version reformulated

---

[3] Median is used as it is more robust to outliers.

using the D&C pattern that calculates the sum of Euler Totient[4] functions in a given range, `worpitzky` that calculates the Worpitzky identity[5] and `minimax` that implements a game using alpha-beta pruning (Table 1).

Table 1. Applications overview

Application	Parallelism pattern	Regularity	Input parameters
`parfib`	D&C	Regular	50 35
`parpair`	Nested D&C	Irregular/regular	100000 10 50 35
`sumeuler`	D&C	Irregular	100000 10
`worpitzky`	D&C	Irregular	27 30 18
`minimax`	D&C	Irregular	4 8 2

4.4   Results

The results summarised in Table 2 demonstrate that substantial speedups can be reached for both the baseline and for the colocation case over sequential run time, achieving speedup improvement of up to 46% with SC over the baseline for three of the programs. However, we also observe a drop in speedup for SC, for the less scalable `minimax`, and for `worpitzky` with excessively fine-grained parallelism and parallelism degree of 17% and 42%, respectively. We focus on load balance and granularity profiles for `sumeuler` as they most clearly depict the differences between the mechanisms.

Table 2. Applications' speedups on 256 PEs

Application	Sequential run time (sec)	Baseline speedup	Colocation speedup	Change in %
`parfib`	1609	204	219	+7
`parpair`	2870	200	231	+16
`sumeuler`	1450	142	207	+46
`worpitzky`	3269	175	101	−42
`minimax`	160	95	79	−17

Load Balance: Figures 4 and 5 show the detailed per-PE profiling data for `sumeuler` indicating load balancing behaviour change resulting from SC use.

We visualise data using 128 PEs for readability, but the difference is stronger for higher numbers of PEs. Figure 4 visualises PEs 1–64 as horizontal bars, Fig. 5 PEs 65–128, baseline being on the left and SC on the right. A per-PE profile

---

[4] http://mathworld.wolfram.com/TotientFunction.html.
[5] http://mathworld.wolfram.com/WorpitzkysIdentity.html.

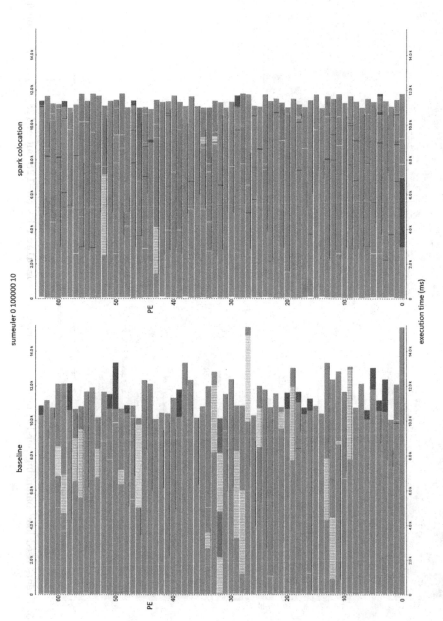

Fig. 4. Event-based load balancing per-PE profile comparison for sumeuler PEs 1–64 out of 128 (Color figure online)

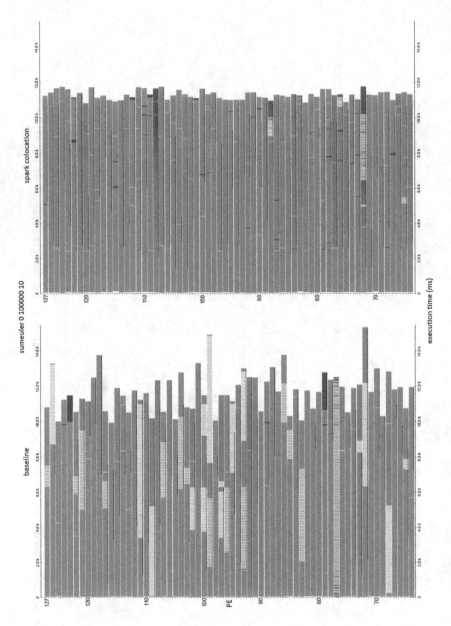

Fig. 5. Event-based load balancing per-PE profile comparison for **sumeuler PEs 65–128** out of 128 (Color figure online)

shows PEs on the y-axis and execution time in milliseconds on the x-axis, thus depicting load-balance across PEs over time. The darkness of the green value at each point in time shows the utilisation (i.e. the number of runnable threads) as an average over a fixed time window, whilst idle time is shown in red. Additionally, the small blue stripes embedded in the lines for each individual PE reflect the number of communicating (blocked-on-fetch) threads.

Overall, we observe better load balance for SC, as almost all of the bars are green, as opposed to the baseline case, where there are substantially more gaps and areas with a reduced number of threads visible. In particular, most of the blocking time is at the end of execution for the baseline (we can distinguish the execution and the waiting for termination as two distinct phases), but it is more spread out and more evenly distributed across more PEs for SC, which exhibits fewer blocking hotspots. We can see noticeably more short green stripes for baseline reflecting the need to fetch data, which appears less often for SC as either the data is readily available or the waiting can be overlapped with computation performed by another thread.

Additionally, the data show good load balance for SC, with very similar total run times on each PE, whilst for the baseline the run times are more variabile, with differences of over 30% of the total run time in some cases.

Granularity: We use event-based profiling to record execution time for each thread. Figure 6 depicts the granularity of `sumeuler` on 256 PEs, with number of threads on the y-axis and thread granularity in milliseconds on the x-axis. Light-red represents the baseline case, light-blue SC, and a darker shade shows the overlap between both. The granularity profiles are overlapping but distinct.

We observe fewer threads and coarser granularity for the baseline case[6], which results from exporting older and likely larger sparks, which are then turned into threads on arrival at the thief PE. Note that the RTS cannot re-balance threads, as opposed to sparks, between PEs, and therefore this behaviour can lead to load imbalance. By contrast, SC exports sparks that are closer to a thief's encoding, but of smaller granularity, which allows more flexibility in saturating larger number of PEs. Although finer granularity is associated with additional overhead, in this case the advantage of improved load balance out-weighs this overhead. Note that due to thread subsumption, which allows a thread to evaluate a potentially parallel child computation sequentially, not all of the fine-grained sparks will be turned into threads, thus reducing the overhead.

Degree of Parallelism: Complementing the granularity profiles, Tables 3 and 4 present the measured total (across PEs) and calculated median (per PE) spark and thread counts, representing the *potential* and *actual* degree of parallelism, respectively. We report data from the median run profiled on 256 PEs for each benchmark, comparing the baseline against SC.

Overall, we observe consistently higher potential parallelism in the range between 2% and 45% for SC, which translates into proportionally higher increase

---

[6] For other benchmarks SC consistently leads to more and smaller threads.

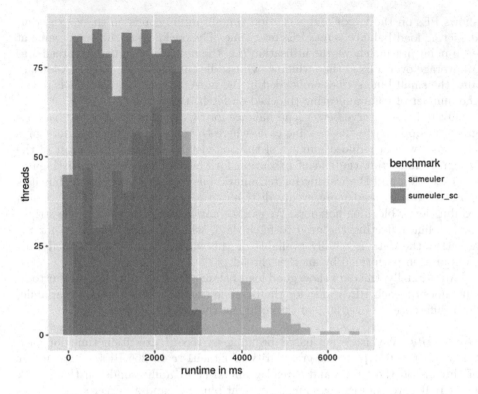

Fig. 6. Granularity of `sumeuler` on 256 PEs (Color figure online)

Table 3. Spark counts for benchmarks on 256 PEs

Application	Median		Total		Change in %
	Baseline	SC	Baseline	SC	
parfib	11	12	2755	3172	+15
parpair	14	19	3840	5045	+31
sumeuler	6	7	1854	1983	+7
worpitzky	1322	1927	337116	488550	+45
minimax	7	5	2466	2525	+2

in the number of threads of up to 197%. This can be attributed to the export of related sparks rather than the oldest, which may reduce potential for subsumption once the computation is shared across the PEs. Sparks are inexpensive as they are pointers to sub-graphs and can be maintained with low overhead and allow more flexibility for load balancing, potentially increasing utilisation. Threads are more expensive as they require the creation of data structures in the heap to hold thread state and related information, which may increase the memory management overhead.

Table 4. Thread counts for benchmarks on 256 PEs

Application	Median		Total		Change in %
	Baseline	SC	Baseline	SC	
parfib	4	6	1127	1584	+41
parpair	5	10	1195	2508	+110
sumeuler	3	4	802	955	+19
worpitzky	322	979	82065	243709	+197
minimax	4	4	1092	1055	−3

Using SC turns out to be particularly beneficial for larger numbers of PEs as the number of threads per PE is increased in all but one case, whilst the amount of total heap available grows with the number of PEs reducing the pressure on the garbage collector. The worpitzky benchmark is an example of worst-case behaviour, demonstrating that having a higher number of threads may become counterproductive when there are already more than enough threads in the baseline case, due to additional overhead, reducing scalability.

Fetching Behaviour: Another distinguishing characteristic and the *most direct indicator of SC's efficacy* is the *fetch time* threads spend waiting for data required by the computation to arrive. Table 5 compares the baseline and SC across applications for the median run on 256 PEs (no data available for minimax).

Table 5. Overview of fetching on 256 PEs (in ms)

Application	Baseline mean fetch time across PEs	Colocation mean fetch time across PEs	Mean fetch time change in % across PEs	Total fetch time change in %	Total fetch count change in %
parfib	829	637	−23	+8	+35
parpair	1109	566	−49	−5	+78
sumeuler	594	290	−51	−29	+49
worpitzky	19	12	−40	+81	+163

In some cases it is possible that the data is already available or fits into the same packet, resulting in fetch time of zero, as for many sumeuler threads, and in other cases the fetch time may exceed the time the thread spends performing the computation.

We observe that *SC has consistently a smaller mean fetch time across PEs* than the baseline, with drops in the range between 23% and 51%. This indicates that the threads in SC case are 'more useful' in the sense that they spend less time waiting on data to arrive. Thus, despite finer granularity, SC threads have higher average utilisation as can be seen from the load balancing results, and the degree of parallelism is increased, which allows more overlap between communication and computation. Although the total number of fetch messages is increased due to the larger number of threads, for `parpair` and `sumeuler`, the benchmarks that benefit most from SC, the total fetch times are still lower than for the baseline due to reduction in individual fetch times.

5   Related Work

Although popularised by Cilk [5], work stealing was used in earlier parallel implementations of functional languages [6,18,27], whilst remaining popular in contemporary implementations (e.g. [10]), as reviewed in a recent survey [32], with locality-awareness being a popular current research direction.

Table 6. Overview of GUM and related systems

RTS (Language)	Parallelism identification	Scheduling	Architecture	Synchronisation	Load balancing
Cilk [5] (C ext.)	Explicit (`cilk_spawn`)	LIFO	Shared	Explicit	Work stealing
GHC-SMP [23] (GpH)	Annotations (advisory)	FIFO unfair	Shared	Implicit	Work stealing
Manticore [10] (NESL/CML-alike)	Impl. data par. expl. task par	FIFO nestable	Shared	Implicit	Work pushing
X10 [7] (X10)	Impl. data par. expl. task par	PGAS	Shared	Implicit	Work stealing
GUM [31] (GpH)	Annotations (advisory)	FIFO unfair	Virtual shared	Implicit	Work stealing
DREAM [20] (Eden)	Explicit process instantiation	Round robinfair	Shared-nothing	Implicit	Work pushing

Table 6 provides an overview of GUM compared to the most related systems, which together span a wide spectrum of parallel language run-time systems. For more detailed and broader comparisons refer to further literature [2,3]. With respect to parallelism identification GUM and SMP occupy a unique place in the design space as the annotations provide hints that are advisory rather than mandatory, as is e.g. process instantiation performed in an Eden program, which will lead to a creation of a remote process. Eden and GUM are similar in the architectural respect that unlike other systems they enable distributed execution. On the other hand they differ in the implementation as GUM provides a Global Indirection Table for inter-PE pointers implementing the virtual shared memory abstraction, whilst DREAM uses shared-nothing design and sends data once it is in normal form. Manticore and X10 are somewhat similar in chosing to incorporate both implicit data parallelism and explicit task parallelism, whilst GUM makes no special arrangements for data parallelism and treats expressions requiring data as tasks. There is no agreement on the scheduling style among the systems, Manticore allowing nested schedulers and X10 following PGAS distribution style. GUM and SMP follow the evaluate-and-die model that leads to an unfair design, but helps improve performance by avoiding some overhead.

In all systems thread and memory management are implicit as well as synchronisation, with an exception of Cilk. This allows for a high level of expressiveness, compared to explicit synchronisation and parallelism management. Despite the popularity of work stealing, some systems have chosen to use work pushing to reduce the amount of communication. This diversity exacerbates the difficulty of directly comparing these systems and languages.

Granularity control is another key consideration for execution of non-strict parallel functional programs [19], both through thread subsumption [25] and explicit application-level specification using thresholding and sophisticated fuel-based algorithms [29] at application or library level. Moreover, work stealing was also shown to benefit from granularity awareness [17].

6   Conclusion

We have introduced *spark colocation,* a work stealing variant that maintains dynamic information about ancestry throughout the execution and uses this information to select sparks that are more closely related to a thief's computation, rather than picking the oldest spark. We report results from five Glasgow parallel Haskell benchmark programs running on a cluster of multi-cores using an extended version of the GUM RTS on up to 256 cores, showing speedup improvements of up to 46% for three of the programs. Examining profiling data suggests that the gain is due to improved load balance and reduced average fetching time, suggesting that related tasks were indeed colocated.

However, the drop in speedup for one less scalable application and one with excessive amounts of overly fine-grained parallelism, suggests that a heuristic could be developed to switch between the baseline and spark colocation depending on both application and architectural characteristics such as the number and computational capability of PEs.

Our mechanism requires minimal programmer overhead, and we argue that it is possible to automatically place annotations by enumerating pars and replacing each par with parEnc, with the corresponding encoding as an argument. As further future work, we would like to investigate different encodings and matching functions to effect granularity in the opposite direction towards a more coarse-grained setting, which becomes useful if the number of PEs is small or parallelism degree is excessive.

Acknowledgements. We are grateful to the anonymous reviewers for comments that have substantially improved the presentation of this paper.

References

1. Backus, J.: Can programming be liberated from the von Neumann style? A functional style and its algebra of programs. CACM **21**(8), 613–641 (1978)
2. Belikov, E.: Language run-time systems: an overview. In: Proceedings of Imperial College Computing Student Workshop, OpenAccess Series in Informatics (OASIcs), vol. 49, pp. 3–12. Leibniz-Zentrum fuer Informatik (2015)
3. Belikov, E., Deligiannis, P., Totoo, P., Aljabri, M., Loidl, H.-W.: A survey of high-level parallel programming models. Technical report HW-MACS-TR-0103, Department of Computer Science, Heriot-Watt University, December 2013
4. Bevan, D.: An efficient reference counting solution to the distributed garbage collection problem. Parallel Comput. **9**(2), 179–192 (1989)
5. Blumofe, R., Joerg, C., Kuszmaul, B., Leiserson, C., Randall, K., Zhou, Y.: Cilk: an efficient multithreaded runtime system. In: Proceedings of the Symposium on Principles and Practice of Parallel Programming (PPoPP 1995), pp. 207–216 (1995)
6. Burton, F.W., Sleep, M.R.: Executing functional programs on a virtual tree of processors. In: Proceedings of the 1981 Conference on Functional Programming Languages and Computer Architecture, pp. 187–194. ACM (1981)
7. Charles, P., et al.: X10: an object-oriented approach to non-uniform cluster computing. In: ACM SIGPLAN Notices, vol. 40, pp. 519–538. ACM (2005)
8. Chase, D., Lev, Y.: Dynamic circular work-stealing deque. In: Proceedings of the 17th ACM Symposium on Parallelism in Algorithms and Architectures, pp. 21–28 (2005)
9. Church, A., Rosser, J.B.: Some properties of conversion. Trans. Am. Math. Soc. **39**(3), 472–482 (1936)
10. Fluet, M., Rainey, M., Reppy, J., Shaw, A., Xiao, Y.: Manticore: a heterogeneous parallel language. In: Proceedings of the 2007 Workshop on Declarative Aspects of Multicore Programming, pp. 37–44. ACM (2007)
11. Geist, A., Beguelin, A., Dongarra, J., Jiang, W., Manchek, R., Sunderam, V.: PVM: Parallel Virtual Machine: A User's Guide and Tutorial for Networked Parallel Computing. MIT Press, Cambridge (1994)
12. Hammond, K.: Glasgow parallel Haskell (GpH). In: Padua, D. (ed.) Encyclopedia of Parallel Computing, pp. 768–779. Springer, Heidelberg (2011). https://doi.org/10.1007/978-0-387-09766-4_46
13. Hammond, K.: Why parallel functional programming matters: panel statement. In: Romanovsky, A., Vardanega, T. (eds.) Ada-Europe 2011. LNCS, vol. 6652, pp. 201–205. Springer, Heidelberg (2011). https://doi.org/10.1007/978-3-642-21338-0_17
14. Hu, Z., Hughes, J., Wang, M.: How functional programming mattered. Natl. Sci. Rev. **2**(3), 349–370 (2015)
15. Hudak, P., Hughes, J., Peyton Jones, S., Wadler, P.: A history of Haskell: being lazy with class. In: Proceedings of the Third ACM SIGPLAN Conference on History of Programming Languages, pp. 1–12. ACM (2007)
16. Hughes, J.: Why functional programming matters. Comp. J. **32**(2), 98–107 (1989)
17. Janjic, V., Hammond, K.: Granularity-aware work-stealing for computationally-uniform grids. In: 2010 10th IEEE/ACM International Conference on Cluster, Cloud and Grid Computing (CCGrid), pp. 123–134. IEEE (2010)
18. Kranz, D.A., Halstead Jr., R.H., Mohr, E.: Mul-T: a high-performance parallel Lisp. ACM SIGPLAN Not. **24**, 81–90 (1989)

19. Loidl, H.-W., Trinder, P., Butz, C.: Tuning task granularity and data locality of data parallel GpH programs. Parallel Process. Lett. **11**(04), 471–486 (2001)
20. Loogen, R., Ortega-Mallén, Y., Peña-Marí, R.: Parallel functional programming in Eden. J. Funct. Program. **15**(3), 431–475 (2005)
21. Marlow, S.: Parallel and Concurrent Programming in Haskell: Techniques for Multicore and Multithreaded Programming. O'Reilly, Sebastopol (2013)
22. Marlow, S., Maier, P., Loidl, H.-W., Aswad, M., Trinder, P.: Seq no more: better strategies for parallel Haskell. In: Proceedings of the 3rd ACM Symposium on Haskell, pp. 91–102 (2010)
23. Marlow, S., Peyton Jones, S.L., Singh, S.: Runtime support for multicore Haskell. ACM SIGPLAN Not. **44**, 65–78 (2009)
24. Marlow, S.: (Eds.) Haskell 2010 language report 2010. http://www.haskell.org/onlinereport/haskell2010
25. Mohr, E., Kranz, D., Halstead Jr., R., et al.: Lazy task creation: a technique for increasing the granularity of parallel programs. IEEE Trans. Parallel Distrib. Syst. **2**(3), 264–280 (1991)
26. Partain, W.: The NoFib benchmark suite of Haskell programs. In: Launchbury, J., Sansom, P. (eds.) Functional Programming, Glasgow 1992, pp. 195–202. Springer, Heidelberg (1993). https://doi.org/10.1007/978-1-4471-3215-8_17
27. Peyton Jones, S.L.: Parallel implementations of functional programming languages. Comput. J. **32**(2), 175–186 (1989)
28. Jones, S.L.P., Clack, C., Salkild, J.: High-performance parallel graph reduction. In: Odijk, E., Rem, M., Syre, J.-C. (eds.) PARLE 1989. LNCS, vol. 365, pp. 193–206. Springer, Heidelberg (1989). https://doi.org/10.1007/3540512845_40
29. Totoo, P., Loidl, H.-W.: Lazy data-oriented evaluation strategies. In: Proceedings of 3rd ACM Workshop on Functional High-Performance Computing, pp. 63–74 (2014)
30. Trinder, P., Hammond, K., Loidl, H.-W., Peyton Jones, S.L.: Algorithm + strategy = parallelism. J. Funct. Program. **8**(1), 23–60 (1998)
31. Trinder, P., Hammond, K., Mattson Jr., J., Partridge, A., Peyton Jones, S.: GUM: a portable parallel implementation of Haskell. In: Proceedings of PLDI, pp. 79–88 (1996)
32. Yang, J., He, Q.: Scheduling parallel computations by work stealing: a survey. Int. J. Parallel Prog. **46**(2), 173–197 (2018)

Reversible Session-Based Concurrency in Haskell

Folkert de Vries and Jorge A. Pérez[✉] [ID]

University of Groningen, Groningen, The Netherlands
j.a.perez@rug.nl

Abstract. A reversible semantics enables to undo computation steps. Reversing message-passing, concurrent programs is a challenging and delicate task; one typically aims at *causally consistent* reversible semantics. Prior work has addressed this challenge in the context of a process model of multiparty protocols (or *choreographies*). In this paper, we describe a Haskell implementation of this reversible operational semantics. We exploit algebraic data types to faithfully represent three core ingredients: a process calculus, multiparty session types, and forward and backward reduction semantics. Our implementation bears witness to the convenience of pure functional programming for implementing reversible languages.

Keywords: Reversibility · Message-passing concurrency ·
Session types · Haskell

1 Introduction

This paper describes a Haskell implementation of a *reversible semantics* for message-passing concurrent programs. Our work is framed within a prolific line of research, in the intersection of programming languages and concurrency theory, aimed at establishing semantic foundations for reversible computing in a concurrent setting (see, e.g., the survey [5]). When considering the interplay of reversibility and message-passing concurrency, a key observation is that communication is governed by *protocols* among (distributed) partners, and that those protocols may fruitfully inform the implementation of a reversible semantics.

In a language with a reversible semantics, computation steps can be undone. Thus, a program can perform standard *forward* steps, but also *backward* steps. Reversing a sequential program is not hard: it suffices to have a *memory* that records information about forward steps in case we wish to return to a prior state using a backward step. Reversing a concurrent program is much more difficult: since control may simultaneously reside in more than one point, memories should be carefully designed so as to record information about the steps performed in each thread, but also about the *causal dependencies* between steps from different threads. This motivates the definition of reversible semantics which are *causally consistent*. A causally consistent semantics ensures that backward steps lead to

© Springer Nature Switzerland AG 2019
M. Pałka and M. Myreen (Eds.): TFP 2018, LNCS 11457, pp. 20–45, 2019.
https://doi.org/10.1007/978-3-030-18506-0_2

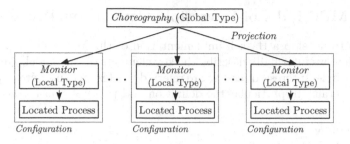

Fig. 1. The model of multiparty, reversible communications by Mezzina and Pérez [7].

states that could have been reached by performing forward steps only [5]. Hence, it never leads to states that are not reachable through forward steps.

Causal consistency then arises as a key correctness criterion in the definition of reversible programming languages. The quest for causally consistent semantics for (message-passing) concurrency has led to a number of proposals that use *process calculi* (most notably, the π-calculus [8]) to rigorously specify communicating processes and their operational semantics (cf. [7] and references therein). One common shortcoming in several of these works is that the proposed causally consistent semantics hinge on memories that are rather heavy; as a result, the resulting (reversible) programming models can be overly complex. This is a particularly notorious limitation in the work of Mezzina and Pérez [7], which addresses reversibility in the relevant context of π-calculus processes that exchange (higher-order) messages following *choreographies*, as defined by *multiparty session types* [3] that specify intended protocol executions. While their reversible semantics is causally consistent, it is unclear whether it can provide a suitable basis for the practical analysis of message-passing concurrent programs.

In this paper we describe a Haskell implementation of the reversible semantics by Mezzina and Pérez [7] (the MP model, in the following). As such, our implementation defines a Haskell interpreter of message-passing programs written in their reversible model. This allows us to assess in practice the mechanisms of the MP model to enforce causally consistent reversibility. The use of a functional programming language (Haskell) is a natural choice for developing our implementation. Haskell has a strong history in language design. Its type system and mathematical nature allow us to faithfully capture the formal reversible semantics and to trust that our implementation correctly preserves causal consistency. In particular, algebraic data types (sums and products) are essential to express the grammars and recursive data structures underlying the MP model.

Next, Sect. 2 recalls the key notions of the MP model, useful to follow our Haskell implementation, which we detail in Sect. 3. Section 4 explains how to run programs forwards and backwards using our implementation. Section 5 collects concluding remarks. The implementation is available at https://github.com/folkertdev/reversible-debugger.

2 The MP Model of Reversible Concurrent Processes

Our aim is to develop a Haskell implementation of the MP model [7], depicted in Fig. 1. Here we informally describe the key elements of the model, guided by a running example. Interested readers are referred to Mezzina and Pérez's paper [7] for further details, in particular the definition and proof of causal consistency.

2.1 Overview

Figure 1 depicts two of the three salient ingredients of the MP model: *configurations/processes* and the *choreography*, which represent the communicating partners (*participants*) and a description of their intended governing protocol, respectively. There is a configuration for each participant: it includes a *located process* that relies on asynchronous communication and is subject to a *monitor* that enables forward/backward steps at run-time and is obtained from the choreography. Choreographies are defined in terms of *global types* as in multiparty session types [3]. (We often use 'choreographies' and 'global types' as synonyms.) A global type is *projected* onto each participant to obtain its corresponding *local type*, which abstracts a participant's contribution to the protocol. Since local types specify the intended communication actions, they may be used as the monitors of the located processes.

The third ingredient of the MP model, not depicted in Fig. 1, is the *operational semantics* for configurations, which is defined by two reduction relations: forward ($\rightarrow$) and backward ($\rightsquigarrow$). We shall not recall these relations here; rather, we will introduce their key underlying intuitions by example—see Sect. 2.5 below.

2.2 Configurations and Processes

The language of processes is a π-calculus with labeled choice, communication of abstractions, and function application: while labeled choice is typical of session π-calculi [2], the latter constructs are typical of *higher-order* process calculi, which combine features from functional and concurrent languages [9]. The syntax of processes $P, Q, \ldots$ is as follows:

$$
\begin{aligned}
P, Q ::= &\ u!\langle V \rangle.P &&\text{send value } V \text{ on name } u, \text{ then run } P \\
&\mid u?(x).P &&\text{receive a value on name } u, \text{ bind it to } x, \text{ then run } P \\
&\mid u \triangleleft \{l_i.P_i\}_{i \in I} &&\text{select a label } l_j \ (j \in I), \text{ broadcast this choice, run } P_j \\
&\mid u \triangleright \{l_i : P_i\}_{i \in I} &&\text{receive a label } l_j \ (j \in I), \text{ run } P_j \\
&\mid P \parallel Q &&\text{parallel composition of } P \text{ and } Q \\
&\mid X \mid \mu X.P &&\text{variable and process recursion} \\
&\mid V\, u &&\text{function application} \\
&\mid (\nu n)P &&\text{name restriction: make } n \text{ local (or private) to } P \\
&\mid \mathbf{0} &&\text{terminated process}
\end{aligned}
$$

In $u \vartriangleleft \{l_i.P_i\}_{i \in I}$ and $u \vartriangleright \{l_i : P_i\}_{i \in I}$, we use I to denote some finite index set. The higher-order character of our process language may be better understood by considering that the syntax of values $(V, W, \ldots)$ includes *name abstractions* $\lambda x.P$, where P is a process. Formally we have:

$$u, w ::= n \mid x, y, z \qquad n, n' ::= a, b \mid s_{[\mathsf{p}]} \qquad v, v' ::= \mathtt{tt} \mid \mathtt{ff} \mid \cdots$$
$$V, W ::= a, b \mid x, y, z \mid v, v' \mid \lambda x.P$$

where $u, w, \ldots$ range over names $(n, n', \ldots)$ and variables $(x, y, \ldots)$. We distinguish between shared and session names, ranged over $a, b, c, \ldots$ and $s, s', \ldots$, respectively. Shared names are public names used to establish a protocol (see below); once established, the protocol runs along a session name, which is private to participants. We use $\mathsf{p}, \mathsf{q}, \ldots$ to denote participants, and use session names indexed by participants; we write, e.g., $s_{[\mathsf{p}]}$. We also use $v, v', \ldots$ to denote base values and constants. Values V include shared names, first-order values, and name abstractions. Notice that values need not include (indexed) session names: session name communication (*delegation*) is representable using abstraction passing [4].

The syntax of *configurations* $M, N, \ldots$ builds upon that of processes; indeed, we may consider configurations as compositions of located processes:

$$M, N ::= \ell \{a!\langle x \rangle.P\} \mid \ell \{a?(x).P\}$$
$$\mid M \parallel N \mid (\nu n)M \mid \mathbf{0}$$
$$\mid \ell_{[\mathsf{p}]} : \lparen C ; P \rparen \mid s_{[\mathsf{p}]} \lfloor H \cdot \widetilde{x} \cdot \sigma \rfloor^{\spadesuit} \mid s : (h_i \star h_o) \mid k \lfloor (V\, u), \ell \rfloor$$

Above, identifiers ℓ, ℓ' denote a *location* or *site*. The first two constructs enable protocol establishment: $\ell \{a!\langle x \rangle.P\}$ is the *request* of a service identified by shared name a implemented by P, whereas $\ell \{a?(x).P\}$ denotes service *acceptance*. Establishing an n-party protocol on service a then requires one configuration requesting a synchronizing with $n - 1$ configurations accepting a. Constructs for composing configurations, name restriction, and inaction, given in the second row, are standard. The third row above defines four constructs that appear only at run-time and enable reversibility:

- $\ell_{[\mathsf{p}]} : \lparen C ; P \rparen$ is a *running process*: location ℓ hosts a process P that implements participant p, and C records labeled choices enforced so far.
- $s_{[\mathsf{p}]} \lfloor H \cdot \widetilde{x} \cdot \sigma \rfloor^{\spadesuit}$ is a *monitor* where: $s_{[\mathsf{p}]}$ is the indexed session being monitored; H is a local type *with history* (see below); $\widetilde{x}$ is a set of free variables; and the *store* σ records their values. The *tag* $\spadesuit$ says whether the running process tied to the monitor is involved in a backward step ($\spadesuit = \blacklozenge$) or not ($\spadesuit = \lozenge$).
- $s : (h_i \star h_o)$ is the *message queue* of session s, composed of an input part h_i and an output part h_o. Messages sent by output prefixes are placed in the output part; an input prefix takes the first message in the output part and moves it to the input part. Hence, messages in the queue are not consumed but moved between the two parts of the queue.

– Finally, the *running function* $k \lfloor (V\,u)\,,\,\ell \rfloor$ serves to reverse the β-reduction resulting from the application $V\,u$. In $k \lfloor (V\,u)\,,\,\ell \rfloor$, ℓ is the location where the application resides, and k is a freshly generated identifier.

These intuitions are formalized by the operational semantics of the MP model, which we do not discuss here; see Mezzina and Pérez's papers [6,7] for details.

2.3   Global and Local Types

As mentioned above, multiparty protocols are expressed as global types $(G, G', \ldots)$, which can be *projected* onto local types $(T, T', \ldots)$, one per participant. The syntax of value, global, and local types follows [3]:

$$U, U' ::= \texttt{bool} \mid \texttt{nat} \mid \cdots \mid T \to \diamond$$

$$G, G' ::= \texttt{p} \to \texttt{q} : \langle U \rangle.G \mid \texttt{p} \to \texttt{q} : \{l_i : G_i\}_{i \in I} \mid \mu X.G \mid X \mid \texttt{end}$$

$$T, T' ::= \texttt{p}!\langle U \rangle.T \mid \texttt{p}?\langle U \rangle.T \mid \texttt{p} \oplus \{l_i : T_i\}_{i \in I} \mid \texttt{p} \& \{l_i : T_i\}_{i \in I} \mid \mu X.T \mid X \mid \texttt{end}$$

Value types U include first-order values, and type $T \to \diamond$ for higher-order values: abstractions from names to processes (where $\diamond$ denotes the type of processes).

Global type $\texttt{p} \to \texttt{q} : \langle U \rangle.G$ says that $\texttt{p}$ sends a value of type U to $\texttt{q}$, and then continues as G. Given a finite index set I and pairwise different labels l_i, global type $\texttt{p} \to \texttt{q} : \{l_i : G_i\}_{i \in I}$ specifies that $\texttt{p}$ may choose label l_i, send this selection to $\texttt{q}$, and then continue as G_i. In both cases, $\texttt{p} \neq \texttt{q}$. Recursive and terminated protocols are denoted $\mu X.G$ and $\texttt{end}$, respectively.

Global types are sequential, but may describe implicit parallelism. As a simple example, the global type $G = \texttt{p} \to \texttt{q} : \langle \texttt{bool} \rangle.\texttt{r} \to \texttt{s} : \langle \texttt{nat} \rangle.\texttt{end}$ is defined sequentially, but describes two independent exchanges (one involving $\texttt{p}$ and $\texttt{q}$, the other involving $\texttt{r}$ and $\texttt{s}$) which could be implemented in parallel. In this line, G may be regarded to be equivalent to $G' = \texttt{r} \to \texttt{s} : \langle \texttt{nat} \rangle.\texttt{p} \to \texttt{q} : \langle \texttt{bool} \rangle.\texttt{end}$.

Local types are used in the monitors introduced above. Local types $\texttt{p}!\langle U \rangle.T$ and $\texttt{p}?\langle U \rangle.T$ denote, respectively, an output and input of value of type U by $\texttt{p}$. Type $\texttt{p} \& \{l_i : T_i\}_{i \in I}$ says that $\texttt{p}$ offers different labeled alternatives; conversely, type $\texttt{p} \oplus \{l_i : T_i\}_{i \in I}$ says that $\texttt{p}$ may select one of such alternatives. Recursive and terminated local types are denoted $\mu X.T$ and $\texttt{end}$, respectively.

A distinguishing feature of the MP model are *local types with history* (H, H'). A type H is a local type equipped with a cursor (denoted $\frown$) used to distinguish the protocol actions that have been already executed (the past of the protocol) from those that are yet to be performed (the future of the protocol).

2.4   Projection

The projection of a global type G onto a participant $\texttt{p}$, denoted $G{\downarrow}_\texttt{p}$, is defined in Fig. 2. The definition is self-explanatory, perhaps except for choice. Intuitively, projection ensures that a choice between $\texttt{p}$ and $\texttt{q}$ should not implicitly determine different behavior for participants different from $\texttt{p}$ and $\texttt{q}$, for which any different

$$(p \to q : \langle U \rangle.G)\downarrow_r = \begin{cases} q!\langle U \rangle.(G\downarrow_r) & \text{if } r = p \\ p?\langle U \rangle.(G\downarrow_r) & \text{if } r = q \\ (G\downarrow_r) & \text{if } r \neq q, r \neq p \end{cases}$$

$$(p \to q : \{l_i : G_i\}_{i \in I})\downarrow_r = \begin{cases} q \oplus \{l_i : (G_i\downarrow_r)\}_{i \in I} & \text{if } r = p \\ p \& \{l_i : G_i\downarrow_r\}_{i \in I} & \text{if } r = q \\ (G_1\downarrow_r) & \text{if } r \neq q, r \neq p \text{ and} \\ & \forall i, j \in I.G_i\downarrow_r = G_j\downarrow_r \end{cases}$$

$$(\mu X.G)\downarrow_r = \begin{cases} \mu X.G\downarrow_r & \text{if } r \text{ occurs in } G \\ \text{end} & \text{otherwise} \end{cases}$$

$$X\downarrow_r = X \qquad \text{end}\downarrow_r = \text{end}$$

Fig. 2. Projection of a global type G onto a participant r [6,7].

behavior should be determined by some explicit communication. This is a condition adopted by the MP model but also by several other works, as it ensures decentralized implementability of multiparty session types. Our implementation relies on broadcasts to communicate choices to all protocol participants; this reduces the need for explicit communications in global types. Projection consistently handles the combination of recursion and choices in global types. In the particular case in which a branch of a choice in the global type may recurse back to the beginning, the local types for all involved participants will be themselves recursive; this ensures that participants will jump back to the beginning of the protocol in a coordinated way.

2.5 Example: Three-Buyer Protocol

We illustrate the forward and backward reduction semantics, denoted $\twoheadrightarrow$ and $\rightsquigarrow$, To this end, we recall the running example by Mezzina and Pérez [7], namely a reversible variant of the *Three-Buyer protocol* (cf., e.g., [1]) with abstraction passing (*delegation*).

The Protocol as Global and Local Types. The protocol involves three buyers (Alice (A), Bob (B), and Carol (C)) who interact with a Vendor (V) as follows:

1. Alice sends a book title to Vendor, which replies back to Alice and Bob with a quote. Alice tells Bob how much she can contribute.
2. Bob notifies Vendor and Alice that he agrees with the price, and asks Carol to assist him in completing the protocol. To delegate his remaining interactions with Alice and Vendor to Carol, Bob sends her the code she must execute.
3. Carol continues the rest of the protocol with Vendor and Alice as if she were Bob. She sends Bob's address (contained in the code she received) to Vendor.
4. Vendor answers to Alice and Carol (representing Bob) with the delivery date.

This protocol may be formalized as the following global type G:

$$G = \text{A} \to \text{V} : \langle \text{title} \rangle . \text{V} \to \{\text{A}, \text{B}\} : \langle \text{price} \rangle . \text{A} \to \text{B} : \langle \text{share} \rangle . \text{B} \to \{\text{A}, \text{V}\} : \langle \text{OK} \rangle .$$
$$\text{B} \to \text{C} : \langle \text{share} \rangle . \text{B} \to \text{C} : \langle \{\{\diamond\}\} \rangle . \text{B} \to \text{V} : \langle \text{address} \rangle . \text{V} \to \text{B} : \langle \text{date} \rangle . \text{end}$$

Above, $\text{p} \to \{\text{q}_1, \text{q}_2\} : \langle U \rangle . G$ stands for $\text{p} \to \text{q}_1 : \langle U \rangle . \text{p} \to \text{q}_2 : \langle U \rangle . G$ (and similarly for local types). We write $\{\{\diamond\}\}$ to denote the type $\text{end} \to \diamond$, associated to a *thunk* $\lambda x . P$ with $x \notin \text{fn}(P)$, written $\{\{P\}\}$. A thunk is an inactive process, which is activated by applying to it a dummy name of type end, denoted $*$. Also, price and share are base types treated as integers; title, OK, address, and date are base types treated as strings. The projections of G onto local types are as follows:

$$G{\downarrow}_\text{V} = \text{A}?\langle \text{title} \rangle . \{\text{A}, \text{B}\}!\langle \text{price} \rangle . \text{B}?\langle \text{OK} \rangle . \text{B}?\langle \text{address} \rangle . \text{B}!\langle \text{date} \rangle . \text{end}$$
$$G{\downarrow}_\text{A} = \text{V}!\langle \text{title} \rangle . \text{V}?\langle \text{price} \rangle . \text{B}!\langle \text{share} \rangle . \text{B}?\langle \text{OK} \rangle . \text{end}$$
$$G{\downarrow}_\text{B} = \text{V}?\langle \text{price} \rangle . \text{A}?\langle \text{share} \rangle . \{\text{A}, \text{V}\}!\langle \text{OK} \rangle . \text{C}!\langle \text{share} \rangle . \text{C}!\langle \{\{\diamond\}\} \rangle . \text{V}!\langle \text{address} \rangle . \text{V}?\langle \text{date} \rangle . \text{end}$$
$$G{\downarrow}_\text{C} = \text{B}?\langle \text{share} \rangle . \text{B}?\langle \{\{\diamond\}\} \rangle . \text{end}$$

Process Implementations and Their Behavior. We now give processes for each participant:

$$\text{Vendor} = d!\langle x : G{\downarrow}_\text{V} \rangle . x?(t) . x!\langle price(t) \rangle . x!\langle price(t) \rangle . x?(ok) . x?(a) . x!\langle date \rangle . \mathbf{0}$$
$$\text{Alice} = d?(y : G{\downarrow}_\text{A}) . y!\langle \text{`Logicomix'} \rangle . y?(p) . y!\langle h \rangle . y?(ok) . \mathbf{0}$$
$$\text{Bob} = d?(z : G{\downarrow}_\text{B}) . z?(p) . z?(h) . z!\langle ok \rangle . z!\langle ok \rangle . z!\langle h \rangle . z!\langle \{\{z!\langle \text{`9747'} \rangle . z?(d) . \mathbf{0}\}\} \rangle . \mathbf{0}$$
$$\text{Carol} = d?(w : G{\downarrow}_\text{C}) . w?(h) . w?(code) . (code *)$$

where $price(\cdot)$ returns a value of type price given a title. Observe how Bob's implementation sends part of its protocol to Carol as a thunk. The whole system, given below, is obtained by placing these processes in locations $\ell_1, \ldots, \ell_4$:

$$M = \ell_1 \{\text{Vendor}\} \parallel \ell_2 \{\text{Alice}\} \parallel \ell_3 \{\text{Bob}\} \parallel \ell_4 \{\text{Carol}\}$$

We now use configuration M to discuss the reduction relations $\twoheadrightarrow$ and $\rightsquigarrow$; below we shall refer to forward and backward reduction rules defined in Mezzina and Pérez's paper [7, Sect. 2.2.2].

From M, the session starts with an application of Rule (INIT), which defines a forward reduction that, by means of a synchronization on shared name d, initializes the protocol by creating running processes and monitors:

$$M \twoheadrightarrow (\nu s)\big(\ell_{1[\text{V}]} : \langle \mathbf{0} ; V_1\{s_{[\text{V}]}/x\}\rangle \parallel s_{[\text{V}]} \lfloor \widehat{} G{\downarrow}_\text{V} \cdot x \cdot [x \mapsto d] \rfloor^\diamond$$
$$\parallel \ell_{2[\text{A}]} : \langle \mathbf{0} ; A_1\{s_{[\text{A}]}/y\}\rangle \parallel s_{[\text{A}]} \lfloor \widehat{} G{\downarrow}_\text{A} \cdot y \cdot [y \mapsto d] \rfloor^\diamond$$
$$\parallel \ell_{3[\text{B}]} : \langle \mathbf{0} ; B_1\{s_{[\text{B}]}/z\}\rangle \parallel s_{[\text{B}]} \lfloor \widehat{} G{\downarrow}_\text{B} \cdot z \cdot [z \mapsto d] \rfloor^\diamond$$
$$\parallel \ell_{4[\text{C}]} : \langle \mathbf{0} ; C_1\{s_{[\text{C}]}/w\}\rangle \parallel s_{[\text{C}]} \lfloor \widehat{} G{\downarrow}_\text{C} \cdot w \cdot [w \mapsto d] \rfloor^\diamond \parallel s : (\epsilon \star \epsilon)\big) = M_1$$

where $V_1\{s_{[V]}/x\}$, $A_1\{s_{[A]}/y\}$, $B_1\{s_{[B]}/z\}$, and $C_1\{s_{[C]}/w\}$ stand for the continuation of processes Vendor, Alice, Bob, and Carol after the service request/accept. Observe that s is a fresh session name created after initialization; we write $\{s_{[V]}/x\}$ to denote a substitution of variable x with session name $s_{[V]}$.

From M_1 we could either undo this forward reduction (using Rule (RINIT)) or execute the communication from Alice to Vendor, using Rules (OUT) and (IN) as follows:

$$M_1 \twoheadrightarrow (\nu\,s)(\,\ell_{2[A]} : \lfloor 0 \; ; \; s_{[A]}?(p).s_{[A]}!\langle h\rangle.s_{[A]}?(ok).0 \rfloor$$

$$\parallel\, s_{[A]} \lfloor \mathsf{V}!\langle\mathrm{title}\rangle.\,\frown\! \mathsf{V}?\langle\mathrm{price}\rangle.\mathsf{B}!\langle\mathrm{share}\rangle.\mathsf{B}?\langle\mathrm{OK}\rangle.\mathrm{end} \cdot y \cdot [y \mapsto d] \rfloor^\Diamond$$

$$\parallel\, N_2 \parallel s : (\epsilon \star (\mathsf{A}\,,\,\mathsf{V}\,,\,\text{‘Logicomix’}))\,) = M_2$$

where N_2 stands for processes/monitors for Vendor, Bob, and Carol (not involved in the reduction). In M_2, the message from A to V now appears in the output part of the queue. An additional forward step completes the synchronization:

$$M_2 \twoheadrightarrow (\nu\,s)(\,\ell_{1[V]} : \lfloor 0 \; ; \; s_{[V]}!\langle price(t)\rangle.s_{[V]}!\langle price(t)\rangle.s_{[V]}?(ok).s_{[V]}?(a).s_{[V]}!\langle date\rangle.0 \rfloor$$

$$\parallel\, s_{[V]} \lfloor \mathsf{A}?\langle\mathrm{title}\rangle.\,\frown\!\{\mathsf{A},\mathsf{B}\}!\langle\mathrm{price}\rangle.T_{\mathsf{V}} \cdot x, t \cdot \sigma_3 \rfloor^\Diamond \parallel N_3$$

$$\parallel\, s : ((\mathsf{A}\,,\,\mathsf{V}\,,\,\text{‘Logicomix’}) \star \epsilon)\,) = M_3$$

where $\sigma_3 = [x \mapsto d], [t \mapsto \text{‘Logicomix’}]$, $T_{\mathsf{V}} = \mathsf{B}?\langle\mathrm{OK}\rangle.\mathsf{B}?\langle\mathrm{address}\rangle.\mathsf{B}!\langle\mathrm{date}\rangle.\mathrm{end}$, and N_3 stands for the rest of the system. Note that the cursors ($\frown$) in the local types with history of the monitors $s_{[V]}$ and $s_{[A]}$ have moved; also, the message from A to V is now in the input part of the queue.

We now illustrate reversibility: to return to M_1 from M_3 we need three backward reduction rules: (ROLLS), (RIN), and (ROUT). First, Rule (ROLLS) modifies the tags of monitors $s_{[V]}$ and $s_{[A]}$, from $\Diamond$ to $\blacklozenge$:

$$M_3 \rightsquigarrow (\nu\,s)(\,\ell_{1[V]} : \lfloor 0 \; ; \; s_{[V]}!\langle price(t)\rangle.s_{[V]}!\langle price(t)\rangle.s_{[V]}?(ok).s_{[V]}?(a).s_{[V]}!\langle date\rangle.0 \rfloor$$

$$\parallel\, s_{[V]} \lfloor \mathsf{A}?\langle\mathrm{title}\rangle.\,\frown\!\{\mathsf{A},\mathsf{B}\}!\langle\mathrm{price}\rangle.T_{\mathsf{B}} \cdot x, t \cdot \sigma_3 \rfloor^\blacklozenge$$

$$\parallel\, \ell_{2[A]} : \lfloor 0 \; ; \; s_{[A]}?(p).s_{[A]}!\langle h\rangle.s_{[A]}?(ok).0 \rfloor$$

$$\parallel\, s_{[A]} \lfloor \mathbb{T}_4\,[\,\frown\! \mathsf{V}?\langle\mathrm{price}\rangle.\mathsf{B}!\langle\mathrm{share}\rangle.\mathsf{B}?\langle\mathrm{OK}\rangle.\mathrm{end}] \cdot y \cdot [y \mapsto d] \rfloor^\blacklozenge$$

$$\parallel\, N_4 \parallel s : ((\mathsf{A}\,,\,\mathsf{V}\,,\,\text{‘Logicomix’}) \star \epsilon)\,) = M_4$$

where $\mathbb{T}_4\,[\bullet] = \mathsf{V}!\langle\mathrm{title}\rangle.\bullet$ is a *type context* (with hole $\bullet$) and, as before, N_4 represents the rest of the system.

M_4 has several possible forward and backward reductions. One particular backward reduction is the one that uses Rule (RIN) to undo the input at V:

$$M_4 \rightsquigarrow (\nu\, s)(\,\ell_{1\,[\mathsf{V}]} : \wr 0 \; ; s_{[\mathsf{V}]}?(t).s_{[\mathsf{V}]}!\langle price(t)\rangle.$$

$$s_{[\mathsf{V}]}!\langle price(t)\rangle.s_{[\mathsf{V}]}?(ok).s_{[\mathsf{V}]}?(a).s_{[\mathsf{V}]}!\langle date\rangle.0\wr$$

$$\| \; s_{[\mathsf{V}]}\lfloor \widehat{}\mathsf{A}?\langle title\rangle.\{\mathsf{A},\mathsf{B}\}!\langle price\rangle.T_{\mathsf{B}} \cdot x \cdot [x \mapsto d]\rfloor^{\diamond}$$

$$\| \; \ell_{2\,[\mathsf{A}]} : \wr 0 \; ; s_{[\mathsf{A}]}?(p).s_{[\mathsf{A}]}!\langle h\rangle.s_{[\mathsf{A}]}?(ok).0\wr$$

$$\| \; s_{[\mathsf{A}]}\lfloor T_4\,[\,\widehat{}\mathsf{V}?\langle price\rangle.\mathsf{B}!\langle share\rangle.\mathsf{B}?\langle OK\rangle.\mathsf{end}] \cdot y \cdot [y \mapsto d]\rfloor^{\blacklozenge}$$

$$\| \; N_4 \, \| \, s : (\epsilon \star (\mathsf{A}, \mathsf{V}, \text{'Logicomix'}))\,)\,) = M_5$$

As a result, the message from A to V is back again in the output part of the queue. The following backward reduction uses Rule (ROUT) to undo the output at A:

$$M_5 \rightsquigarrow (\nu\, s)(\,\ell_{1\,[\mathsf{V}]} : \wr 0 \; ; s_{[\mathsf{V}]}?(t).s_{[\mathsf{V}]}!\langle price(t)\rangle.s_{[\mathsf{V}]}!\langle price(t)\rangle.$$

$$s_{[\mathsf{V}]}?(ok).s_{[\mathsf{V}]}?(a).s_{[\mathsf{V}]}!\langle date\rangle.0\wr$$

$$\| \; s_{[\mathsf{V}]}\lfloor \widehat{}\mathsf{A}?\langle title\rangle.\{\mathsf{A},\mathsf{B}\}!\langle price\rangle.T_{\mathsf{B}} \cdot x \cdot [x \mapsto d]\rfloor^{\diamond}$$

$$\| \; \ell_{2\,[\mathsf{A}]} : \wr 0 \; ; s_{[\mathsf{A}]}!\langle\text{'Logicomix'}\rangle.s_{[\mathsf{A}]}?(p).s_{[\mathsf{A}]}!\langle h\rangle.s_{[\mathsf{A}]}?(ok).0\wr$$

$$\| \; s_{[\mathsf{A}]}\lfloor \widehat{}\mathsf{V}!\langle title\rangle.\mathsf{V}?\langle price\rangle.\mathsf{B}!\langle share\rangle.\mathsf{B}?\langle OK\rangle.\mathsf{end} \cdot y \cdot [y \mapsto d]\rfloor^{\diamond}$$

$$\| \; N_4 \, \| \, s : (\epsilon \star \epsilon)\,) = M_6$$

Clearly, $M_6 = M_1$. Summing up, the forward reductions $M_1 \twoheadrightarrow M_2 \twoheadrightarrow M_3$ can be reversed by the backward reductions $M_3 \rightsquigarrow M_4 \rightsquigarrow M_5 \rightsquigarrow M_6 = M_1$.

Abstraction Passing (Delegation). To illustrate abstraction passing, let us assume that M_3 above performs forward reductions until the configuration:

$$M_7 = (\nu\, s)(\,\ell_{3\,[\mathsf{B}]} : \wr 0 \; ; s_{[\mathsf{B}]}!\langle\{\!\{s_{[\mathsf{B}]}!\langle\text{'9747'}\rangle.s_{[\mathsf{B}]}?(d).0\}\!\}\rangle.0\wr$$

$$\| \; s_{[\mathsf{B}]}\lfloor T_7\,[\,\widehat{}\mathsf{C}!\langle\{\!\{\diamond\}\!\}\rangle.\mathsf{V}!\langle address\rangle.\mathsf{V}?\langle date\rangle.\mathsf{end}] \cdot z, p, h \cdot \sigma_7\rfloor^{\diamond}$$

$$\| \; \ell_{4\,[\mathsf{C}]} : \wr 0 \; ; s_{[\mathsf{C}]}?(code).(code \star)\wr$$

$$\| \; s_{[\mathsf{C}]}\lfloor T_8\,[\,\widehat{}\mathsf{B}?\langle\{\!\{\diamond\}\!\}\rangle.\mathsf{end}] \cdot w, h \cdot \sigma_8\rfloor^{\diamond} \; \| \; N_5 \, \| \, s : (h_7 \star \epsilon)\,)$$

where $\{\{s_{[B]}!\langle\text{`9747'}\rangle.s_{[B]}?(d).\mathbf{0}\}\}$ is a thunk (to be activated with the dummy value $*$) and $\mathbb{T}_7\,[\bullet]$, σ_7, $\mathbb{T}_8\,[\bullet]$, σ_8, and h_7 capture past interactions as follows:

$$\mathbb{T}_7\,[\bullet] = \mathsf{V}?\langle\text{price}\rangle.\mathsf{A}?\langle\text{share}\rangle.\{\mathsf{A},\mathsf{V}\}!\langle\text{OK}\rangle.\mathsf{C}!\langle\text{share}\rangle.\bullet$$

$$\sigma_7 = [z \mapsto d], [p \mapsto price(\text{`Logicomix'})], [h \mapsto 120]$$

$$\mathbb{T}_8\,[\bullet] = \mathsf{B}?\langle\text{share}\rangle.\bullet \qquad \sigma_8 = [w \mapsto d], [h \mapsto 120]$$

$$h_7 = (\mathsf{A},\mathsf{V},\text{`Logicomix'})$$

$$\circ\,(\mathsf{V},\mathsf{A},price(\text{`Logicomix'}))\circ(\mathsf{V},\mathsf{B},price(\text{`Logicomix'}))$$

$$\circ\,(\mathsf{A},\mathsf{B},120)\circ(\mathsf{B},\mathsf{A},\text{`ok'})\circ(\mathsf{B},\mathsf{V},\text{`ok'})\circ(\mathsf{B},\mathsf{C},120)$$

If $M_7 \twoheadrightarrow\;\twoheadrightarrow M_8$ to enable a (forward) synchronization we would have:

$$M_8 = (\nu\,s)(\ell_{3[B]} : \lceil\mathbf{0}\,;\,\mathbf{0}\rfloor$$

$$\|\;s_{[B]}\lfloor\mathbb{T}_7\,[\mathsf{C}!\langle\{\{\diamond\}\}\rangle.\,\overset{\frown}{}\mathsf{V}!\langle\text{address}\rangle.\mathsf{V}?\langle\text{date}\rangle.\text{end}]\cdot z,p,h\cdot\sigma_7\rfloor^{\diamond}$$

$$\|\;\ell_{4[C]} : \lceil\mathbf{0}\,;\,(code\,*)\rfloor\;\|\;s_{[C]}\lfloor\mathbb{T}_8\,[\mathsf{B}?\langle\{\{\diamond\}\}\rangle.\,\overset{\frown}{}\text{end}]\cdot w,h,code\cdot\sigma_9\rfloor^{\diamond}$$

$$\|\;N_5\;\|\;s : (h_7\circ(\mathsf{B},\mathsf{C},\{\{s_{[B]}!\langle\text{`9747'}\rangle.s_{[B]}?(d).\mathbf{0}\}\})\star\epsilon)\,)$$

where $\sigma_9 = \sigma_8[code \mapsto \{\{s_{[B]}!\langle\text{`9747'}\rangle.s_{[B]}?(d).\mathbf{0}\}\}]$. We now may obtain the actual code sent from B to C:

$$M_8 \twoheadrightarrow (\nu\,s)(\nu\,k)(\ell_{4[C]} : \lceil\mathbf{0}\,;\,s_{[B]}!\langle\text{`9747'}\rangle.s_{[B]}?(d).\mathbf{0}\rfloor\|\,N_6$$

$$\|\;s_{[B]}\lfloor\mathbb{T}_7\,[\mathsf{C}!\langle\{\{\diamond\}\}\rangle.\,\overset{\frown}{}\mathsf{V}!\langle\text{address}\rangle.\mathsf{V}?\langle\text{date}\rangle.\text{end}]\cdot z,p,h\cdot\sigma_7\rfloor^{\diamond}$$

$$\|\;k\lfloor(code\,*),\ell_4\rfloor\;\|\;s_{[C]}\lfloor\mathbb{T}_8\,[\mathsf{B}?\langle\{\{\diamond\}\}\rangle.k.\,\overset{\frown}{}\text{end}]\cdot w,h,code\cdot\sigma_9\rfloor^{\diamond}$$

$$\|\;s : (h_7\circ(\mathsf{B},\mathsf{C},\{\{s_{[B]}!\langle\text{`9747'}\rangle.s_{[B]}?(d).\mathbf{0}\}\})\star\epsilon)\,) = M_9$$

where N_6 is the rest of the system. Notice that this reduction has added a running function on a fresh k, which is also used in the type stored in the monitor $s_{[C]}$.

The reduction $M_8 \twoheadrightarrow M_9$ completes the code mobility from B to C: the now active thunk will execute B's protocol from C's location. Observe that Bob's identity B is "hardwired" in the sent thunk; there is no way for C to execute the code by referring to a participant different from B.

3 Implementing the MP Model in Haskell

We represent the process calculus, global types, local types, and the information for reversal as syntax trees. Local types are obtained by from the global type via projection, which we implement following Sect. 2.4, whereas processes and global types are written by the programmer. For this reason, we want to provide a convenient way to specify them as domain-specific languages (DSLs).

3.1 DSLs with the Free Monad

Free monads are a common way of defining DSLs in Haskell, mainly because they allow the use of do-notation to write programs in the DSL.

```
data Free f a
   = Pure a
   | Free (f (Free f a))
```

A simple practical example is a stack-based calculator:

```
data Operation next
   = Push Int next
   | Pop (Maybe Int -> next)
   | End
   deriving (Functor)
type Program next = Free Operation next
type TerminatingProgram = Program Void
```

We define a data type with our instructions, and make sure it has a Functor instance (i.e., there exists a function `fmap :: (a -> b) -> Operation a -> Operation b`). This instance is automatically derived using the `DeriveFunctor` language extension. Given an instance of `Functor`, `Free` returns the free monad on that functor. In this example, the free monad on `Operation` describes a list of instructions.

In general, a value of type 'Free Operation a' describes a program with holes: an incomplete program with placeholder values of type a in the position of some continuations. Composition allows filling in the holes with (possibly incomplete) subprograms. The holes are places where the `Pure` constructor occurs in the program. When evaluating, we want to have a tree without holes. We can leverage the type system to guarantee that `Pure` does not occur in the programs we evaluate by using `Void`.

`Void` is the data type with zero values (similar to the empty set). Thus, a value of the type `Free Operation Void` cannot be of the shape `Pure _`, because it requires a value of type `Void`. An alternative approach is to use existential quantification, which requires enabling a language extension.

We define wrappers around the constructors for convenience. The `liftF` function takes a concrete value of our program functor (`ProgramF a`) and turns it into a free value (`Free ProgramF a`, i.e., `Program a`). The helpers are used to write programs with do-notation:

```
-- specialized version of liftF for Free
liftF :: (Functor f) => f a -> Free f a
push :: Int -> Program ()
push v = liftF (Push v ())
pop :: Program (Maybe Int)
pop = liftF (Pop id)
terminate :: TerminatingProgram
```

```
terminate = liftF End
program :: TerminatingProgram
program = do
    push 5
    push 4
    Just a <- pop
    Just b <- pop
    push (a + b)
    terminate
```

Finally, we expose a function to evaluate the structure (but only if it is finite). Typically, a **Free** monad is transformed into some other monad, which in turn is evaluated. Here we can first transform into **State**, and then evaluate that.

```
interpret :: TerminatingProgram -> State [Int] ()
interpret instruction =
    case instruction of
        Pure _ ->
            -- cannot occur
            return ()
        Free End ->
            return ()
        Free (Push a next) -> do
            State.modify (\state -> a : state)
            interpret next
        Free (Pop toNext) -> do
            state <- State.get
            case state of
                x:xs -> do
                    State.put xs
                    interpret (toNext (Just x))
                [] ->
                    interpret (toNext Nothing)

evaluate :: TerminatingProgram -> [Int]
evaluate = flip execState [] . interpret
```

3.2   Implementing Processes

The implementation uses an algebraic data type to encode all the process constructors in the process syntax of P given in Sect. 2.2. Apart from the process-level recursion, **Program** is a direct translation of that process syntax:

```
type Participant = String
type Identifier = String

data ProgramF value next
```

```
-- communication primitives
= Send
    { owner :: Participant
    , value :: value
    , continuation :: next
    }
| Receive
    { owner :: Participant
    , variableName :: Identifier
    , continuation :: next
    }
-- choice primitives
    | Offer Participant [(String, next)]
    | Select Participant [(String, value, next)]
-- other constructors
    | Parallel next next
    | Application Identifier value
    | NoOp
    deriving (Functor)
```

As already discussed, processes exchange values. With respect to the syntax of values V, W discussed in Sect. 2.2, the `Value` type, given below, has some extra constructors which allow us to write more interesting examples: we have added integers, strings, and basic integer and comparison operators. We use `VReference` to denote the variables present in the formal syntax for V. The `Value` type also includes the label used to differentiate the different cases of offer and select statements.

```
data Value
    = VBool Bool
    | VInt Int
    | VString String
    | VUnit
    | VIntOperator Value IntOperator Value
    | VComparison Value Ordering Value
    | VFunction Identifier (Program Value)
    | VReference Identifier
    | VLabel String
```

We need some extra concepts to actually write programs with this syntax.

Delegation via Abstraction Passing. Delegation occurs when a participant can send (part of) its protocol to be fulfilled (i.e., implemented) by another participant. This mechanism was illustrated in the example in Sect. 2.5, where Carol acts on behalf of Bob by receiving and executing his code. For further illustration of the convenience of this mechanism, consider a load balancing server:

from the client's perspective, the server handles the request, but actually the load balancer delegates incoming requests to workers. The client does not need to be aware of this implementation detail. Recall the definition of `ProgramF`, given just above:

```
data ProgramF value next
    -- communication primitives
    = Send
        { owner :: Participant
        , value :: value
        , continuation :: next
        }
    | ...
```

The `ProgramF` constructors that move the local type forward (send/receive, select/offer) have an `owner` field that stores whose local type they should be checked against and modify. In the formal definition of the MP model, the connection between local types and processes/participants is enforced by the operational semantics. The `owner` field is also present in `TypeContext`, the data type we define for representing local types in Sect. 3.4.

As explained in Sect. 2.2, each protocol participant has its own monitor with its own store. Because these stores are not shared, all variables occurring in the arguments to operators and in function bodies must be dereferenced before a value can be safely sent over a channel.

A Convenient DSL. Many of the `ProgramF` constructors require an `owner`; we can thread the owner through a block with a wrapper around `Free`. We use `StateT` containing the owner and a counter to generate unique variable names.

```
newtype HighLevelProgram a =
    HighLevelProgram
        (StateT (Participant, Int)
        (Free (ProgramF Value)) a)
        deriving
            ( Functor, Applicative, Monad
            , MonadState (Participant, Int)
            , MonadFree (ProgramF Value))

uniqueVariableName :: HighLevelProgram String
uniqueVariableName = do
    (participant, n) <- State.get
    State.put (participant, n + 1)
    return $ "var" ++ show n

send :: Value -> HighLevelProgram ()
send value = do
```

```
      (participant, _) <- State.get
      liftF (Send participant value ())

receive :: HighLevelProgram Value
receive = do
      (participant, _) <- State.get
      variableName <- uniqueVariableName
      liftF (Receive participant variableName ())
      return (VReference variableName)

terminate :: HighLevelProgram a
terminate = liftF NoOp

-- other helpers omitted for brevity

compile :: Participant -> HighLevelProgram Void -> Program Value
compile participant (HighLevelProgram program) = do
      runStateT program (participant, 0)
```

We can now implement the Vendor from the three-buyer example as:

```
vendor :: HighLevelProgram a
vendor = do
      t <- H.receive
      H.send (price t)
      H.send (price t)
      ...
      terminate
```

3.3 Global Types

Following Fig. 1, our implementation uses a global type specification to obtain a local type (of type LocalType), one per participant, by means of projection. This is implemented as described in Sect. 2.4. Much like the process syntax, the specification of the global types discussed in Sect. 2.3 closely mimics the formal definition:

```
type GlobalType participant u a =
      Free (GlobalTypeF participant u) a

type TerminatingGlobalType participant u =
      GlobalType participant u Void

data GlobalTypeF participant u next
      = Transaction
            { from :: participant
            , to :: participant
```

```
      , tipe :: u
      , continuation ::  next
      }
  | Choice
      { from :: participant
      , to :: participant
      , options :: Map String next
      }
  | End
  | RecursionPoint next
  | RecursionVariable
  | WeakenRecursion next
  deriving (Functor)
```

where we use 'tipe' because 'type' is a reserved keyword in Haskell.

Constructors `RecursionPoint`, `RecursionVariable`, and `WeakenRecursion` are required to support nested recursion; they are taken from van Walree's work [10]. A `RecursionPoint` is a point in the protocol to which we can jump back later. A `RecursionVariable` triggers jumping to a previously encountered `RecursionPoint`. By default, it will jump to the closest and most recently encountered `RecursionPoint`, but `WeakenRecursion` makes it jump one `RecursionPoint` higher; encountering two weakens will jump two levels higher, etc.

We use `Monad.Free` to build a DSL for defining global types:

```
message :: participant -> participant -> tipe
        -> GlobalType participant tipe ()
message from to tipe = liftF (Transaction from to tipe ())

messages :: participant -> [participant]
         -> tipe -> GlobalType participant tipe ()
messages sender receivers tipe = go receivers
  where go [] = Pure ()
        go (x:xs) = Free (Transaction sender x tipe $ go xs)

oneOf :: participant -> participant
      -> [(String, GlobalType participant u a)]
      -> GlobalType participant u a
oneOf selector offerer options =
    Free (Choice selector offerer (Map.fromList options))

recurse :: GlobalType p u a -> GlobalType p u a
recurse cont = Free (RecursionPoint cont)

weakenRecursion :: GlobalType p u a -> GlobalType p u a
weakenRecursion cont = Free (WeakenRecursion cont)
```

```
recursionVariable :: GlobalType p u a
recursionVariable = Free RecursionVariable

end :: TerminatingGlobalType p u
end = Free End
```

Example 1 (Nested Recursion). The snippet below illustrates nested recursion. There is an outer loop that will perform a piece of protocol or end, and an inner loop that sends messages from A to B. When the inner loop is done, control flow returns to the outer loop:

```
import GlobalType as G

G.recurse $ -- recursion point 1
    G.oneOf A B
        [ ("loop"
        , G.recurse $ -- recursion point 2
                G.oneOf A B
                    [ ("continueLoop", do
                        G.message A B "date"
                        -- jumps to recursion point 2
                        G.recursionVariable
                      )
                    , ("endInnerLoop", do
                        -- jumps to recursion point 1
                        G.weakenRecursion G.recursionVariable
                      )
                    ]
          )
        , ("end", G.end)
        ]
```

Similarly, the global type for three-buyer example (cf. Sect. 2.5) can be written as:

```
-- a data type representing the participants
data MyParticipants = A | B | C | V
    deriving (Show, Eq, Ord, Enum, Bounded)
-- a data type representing the used types
data MyType = Title | Price | Share | Ok | Thunk | Address | Date
    deriving (Show, Eq, Ord)
-- a description of the protocol
globalType :: TerminatingGlobalType MyParticipants MyType
globalType = do
    message A V Title
    messages V [A, B] Price
    message A B Share
```

```
messages B [A, V] Ok
message B C Share
message B C Thunk
message B V Address
message V B Date
end
```

3.4   A Reversible Semantics

Having shown implementations for processes and global types, we now explain how to implement the reversible operational semantics for the MP model, which was illustrated in Sect. 2.5. We should define structures that allow us to move back to prior program states, reversing forward steps.

To enable backward steps, we need to store some information when we move forward, just as enabled by the configurations in the MP model (cf. Sect. 2.2). Indeed, we need to track information about the local type and the process. To implement local types with history, we define a data type called `TypeContext`: it contains the actions that have been performed; for some of them, it also stores extra information (e.g., `owner`). For the process, we need to track four things:

1. *Used variable names in receives.* Recall the process implementation for the vendor in the three-buyer example in Sect. 2.5:

   $$\text{Vendor} = d!\langle x : G\!\downarrow_V\rangle.x?(t).x!\langle price(t)\rangle.x!\langle price(t)\rangle.x?(ok).x?(a).x!\langle date\rangle.\mathbf{0}$$

   We can implement this process as:
   ```
   vendor :: HighLevelProgram a
   vendor = do
       t <- H.receive
       H.send (price t)
       H.send (price t)
       ...
       terminate
   ```
   The rest of the program depends on the assigned name. So, e.g., when we evaluate the `t <- H.receive` line (moving to configuration M_3, cf. Sect. 2.5), and then revert it, we must reconstruct a receive that assigns to `t`, because the following lines depend on name `t`.

2. *Function calls and their arguments.* Consider the reduction from configuration M_7 to M_8, as discussed in Sect. 2.5. Once the thunk is evaluated, producing configuration M_8, we lose all evidence that the code produced by the evaluation resulted from a function application. Without this evidence, reversing M_8 will not result in M_7. Indeed, we need to keep track of function applications. Following the semantics of the MP model, the function and its argument are stored in a map indexed by a unique identifier k. The identifier k itself is also stored in the local type with history to later associate the type with a specific function and argument. The reduction from M_8 to M_9, discussed in Sect. 2.5, offers an example of this tracking mechanism in the formal model.

Notice that a stack would seem a simpler solution, but it can give invalid behavior. Say that a participant is running in two locations, and the last-performed action at both locations is a function application. Now we want to undo both applications, but the order in which to undo them is undefined: we need both orders to work. Only using a stack could mix up the applications. When the application keeps track of exactly which function and argument it used the end result is always the same.

3. *Messages on the channel.* We consider again the implementation of the first three steps of the protocol:

```
alice :: HighLevelProgram a
alice = do
    H.send (VString "Logicomix" )
    ...

vendor :: HighLevelProgram a
vendor = do
    t <- H.receive
    ...
```

After Alice sends her message, it has to be stored to successfully undo the sending action. Likewise, when starting from configuration M_3 and undoing the receive, the value must be placed back into the queue.

Our implementation closely follows the formal semantics of the MP model. As discussed in Sect. 2.2, the message queue has an input and an output part. This allows to describe how a message moves from the sender into the output queue. Reception is represented by moving the message to the input queue, which serves as a history stack. When the receive is reversed, the queue pops the message from its stack and puts it at the output queue again. Reversing the send moves the message from the output queue back to the sender's program.

4. *Unused branches.* When a labeled choice is made and then reverted, we want all our options to be available again. In the MP model, choices made so far are stored in a stack denoted C, inside a running process (cf. Sect. 2.2).

The following code shows how we store these choices:

```
type Zipper a = ([a], a, [a])

data OtherOptions
    = OtherSelections (Zipper (String, Value, Program Value))
    | OtherOffers (Zipper (String, Program Value))
```

We need to remember which choice was made; the order of the options is important. We use a Zipper to store the elements in order and use the central 'a' to store the choice that was made.

3.5 Putting It All Together

With all the definitions in place, we can now define the forward and backward evaluation of our system. The reduction relations $\rightarrow$ and $\rightsquigarrow$, discussed and illustrated in Sect. 2.5, are implemented with the types:

```
forward  :: Location -> Session ()
backward :: Location -> Session ()
```

These functions take a `Location` (the analogue of the locations ℓ in the formal model) and try to move the process at that location forward or backward. The `Session` type contains the `ExecutionState`, the state of the session (all programs, local types, variable bindings, etc.). The `Except` type indicates that errors of type `Error` can be thrown (e.g., when an unbound variable is used):

```
type Session a = StateT ExecutionState (Except Error) a
```

The configurations of the MP model (cf. Sect. 2.2) are our main reference to store the execution state. Some data is bound to its location (e.g., the current running process), while other data is bound to its participant (e.g., the local type). The information about a participant is grouped in a type called `Monitor`:

```
data Monitor value tipe =
    Monitor
        { _localType :: LocalTypeState tipe
        , _recursiveVariableNumber :: Int
        , _recursionPoints :: [LocalType tipe]
        , _usedVariables :: [Binding]
        , _applicationHistory :: Map Identifier (value, value)
        , _store :: Map Identifier value
        }
        deriving (Show, Eq)

data Binding =
    Binding
        { _visibleName :: Identifier
        , _internalName :: Identifier
        }
    deriving (Show, Eq)
```

Some explanations follow:

- `_localType` contains `TypeContext` and `LocalType` stored as a tuple. This tuple gives a cursor into the local type, where everything to the left is the past and everything to the right is the future.
- The next two fields keep track of recursion in the local type. We use the `_recursiveVariableNumber` is an index into the `_recursionPoints` list: when a `RecursionVariable` is encountered we look at that index to find the new future local type.
- `_usedVariables` and `_applicationHistory` are used in reversal. As mentioned in Sect. 3.4, used variable names must be stored so we can use them when reversing. We store them in a stack keeping both the original name given by the programmer and the generated unique internal name. For function applications we use a `Map` indexed by unique identifiers that stores function and argument.

- _store is a variable store with the currently defined bindings. Variable shad-
  owing (when two processes of the same participant define the same variable
  name) is not an issue: variables are assigned a name that is guaranteed unique.

We can now define ExecutionState: it contains some counters for generating
unique variable names, a monitor for every participant, and a program for every
location. Additionally, every location has a default participant and a stack for
unchosen branches:

```
data ExecutionState value =
    ExecutionState
        { variableCount :: Int
        , locationCount :: Int
        , applicationCount :: Int
        , participants :: Map Participant (Monitor value String)
        , locations :: Map Location
                    (Participant , [OtherOptions], Program value)
        , queue :: Queue value
        , isFunction :: value -> Maybe (Identifier,Program value)
        }
```

The message queue is global and thus also lives in the ExecutionState. Finally,
we need a way of inspecting values, to see whether they are functions and if so,
to extract their bodies for application.

3.6 Causal Consistency?

As mentioned in Sect. 1, causal consistency is a key correctness criterion for
a reversible semantics: this property ensures that backward steps always lead
to states that could have been reached by moving forward only. The global
type defines a partial order on all the communication steps. The relation of this
partial order is a causal dependency. Stepping backward is only allowed when
all its causally dependent actions are undone.

The reversible semantics of the MP model, summarized in Sect. 2, enjoys
causal consistency for processes running a single global protocol (i.e., a single
session). Rather than typed processes, the MP model describes *untyped* processes
whose (reversible) operational semantics is governed by local types. This suffices
to prove causal consistency, but also to ensure that process reductions correspond
to valid actions specified by the global type. Given this, one may then wonder,
does our Haskell implementation preserve causal consistency?

In the semantics and the implementation, this causal dependency becomes a
data dependency. For instance, a send can only be undone only when the queue
is in a state that can only be reached by first undoing the corresponding receive.
Only in this state is the appropriate data of the appropriate type available. Being
able to undo a send thus means that the corresponding receive has already been
reversed, so it is impossible to introduce causal inconsistencies.

Because of the encoding of causal dependencies as data dependencies, and the fact that these data dependencies are preserved in the implementation, we claim that our Haskell implementation respects the formal semantics of the MP model, and therefore that it preserves the causal consistency property.

4   Running and Debugging Programs

Finally, we want to be able to run our programs. Our implementation offers mechanisms to step through a program interactively, and run it to completion.

We can step through the program interactively in the Haskell REPL environment. When the `ThreeBuyer` example is loaded, the program is in a state corresponding to configuration M_1 from Sect. 2.5. We can print the initial state of our program:

```
> initialProgram
locations: fromList [("l1",("A",[],Free (Send {owner = "A", ...
```

Next we introduce the `stepForward` and `stepBackward` functions. They use mutability, normally frowned upon in Haskell, to avoid having to manually keep track of the updated program state like in the snippet below:

```
state1 = stepForwardInconvenient "l1" state0
state2 = stepForwardInconvenient "l1" state1
state3 = stepForwardInconvenient "l1" state2
```

Manual state passing is error-prone and inconvenient. We provide helpers to work around this issue (internally, those helpers use `IORef`). We must first initialize the program state:

```
> import Interpreter
> state <- initializeProgram initialProgram
```

We can then use `stepForward` and `stepBackward` to evaluate the program: we advance Alice at l_1 to reach M_2 and then the vendor at l_4 to reach M_3:

```
> stepForward "l1" state
locations: fromList [("l1",("A",[],Free (Receive {owner = "A", ...
> stepForward "l4" state
locations: fromList [("l1",("A",[],Free (Receive {owner = "A", ...
```

When the user tries an invalid step, an error is displayed. For instance, in state M_3, where l_1 and l_4 have been moved forward once (like in the snippet above), l_1 cannot move forward (it needs to receive but there is nothing in the queue) and not backward (l_4, the receiver, must undo its action first).

```
> stepForward "l1" state
*** Exception: QueueError "Receive" EmptyQueue
CallStack (from HasCallStack):
  error, called at ...
> stepBackward "l1" state
*** Exception: QueueError "BackwardSend" EmptyQueue state
CallStack (from HasCallStack):
  error, called at ...
```

Errors are defined as:

```
data Error
    = UndefinedParticipant Participant
    | UndefinedVariable Participant Identifier
    | SynchronizationError String
    | LabelError String
    | QueueError String Queue.QueueError
    | ChoiceError ChoiceError
    | Terminated
```

To fully evaluate a program, we use a round-robin scheduler that calls forward on the locations in order. A forward step can produce an error. There are two error cases that we can recover from:

- **blocked on receive**, either QueueError _ InvalidQueueItem or Queue
  Error _ EmptyQueue: the process wants to perform a receive, but the
  expected item is not at the top of the queue yet. In this case we proceed
  evaluating the other locations so they can send the value that the faulty location expects. Above, '_' means that we ignore the String field used to provide
  better error messages. Because no error message is generated, that field is not
  needed.
- **location terminates** with Terminated: the execution has reached a NoOp.
  In this case we do not want to schedule this location any more.

Otherwise we continue until there are no active (non-terminated) locations left.
    Running until completion (or error) is also available in the REPL:

```
> untilError initialProgram
Right locations: fromList [("l1",("A",[],Free NoOp)), ...
```

Note that this scheduler can still get into deadlocks, for instance consider these two equivalent global types:

```
globalType1 = do
    message A V Title
    message V B Price
    message V A Price
    message A B Share
```

```
globalType2 = do
    message A V Title
    message V A Price
    message V B Price
    message A B Share
```

Above, the second and third messages (involving `Price`) are swapped. The communication they describe is the same, but in practice they are very different. The first example will run to completion, whereas the second can deadlock because A can send a `Share` before V sends the `Price`. B expects the price from V first, but the share from A is the first in the queue. Therefore, no progress can be made.

In general, a key issue is that a global type is written sequentially, while it may represent implicit parallelism, as explained in Sect. 2.3. Currently, our implementation just executes the global type with the order given by the programmer. It should be possible to execute communication actions in different but equivalent orders; these optimizations are beyond the scope of our current implementation.

5   Discussion and Concluding Remarks

5.1   Benefits of Pure Functional Programming

It has consistently been the case that sticking closer to the formal model gives better code. The abilities that Haskell gives for directly specifying formal statements are invaluable. A key invaluable feature is algebraic data types (ADTs, also known as tagged unions or sum types). Compare the formal definition given in Sect. 2.3 and the Haskell data type for global types.

$$G, G' ::= \mathsf{p} \to \mathsf{q} : \langle U \rangle.G \mid \mathsf{p} \to \mathsf{q} : \{l_i : G_i\}_{i \in I} \mid \mu X.G \mid X \mid \mathsf{end}$$

```
data GlobalTypeF u next
    = Transaction {..} | Choice {..}  | RecursionPoint next
    | RecursionVariable | End
    | WeakenRecursion next
```

The definitions correspond almost directly: the `WeakenRecursion` constructor is added to support nested recursion, which the formal model does not explicitly represent. Moreover, we know that these are all the ways to construct a value of type `GlobalTypeF` and can exhaustively match on all the cases. Functional languages have had these features for a very long time. Secondly, purity and immutability are very useful in implementing and testing the reversible semantics.

In a pure language, given functions `f :: a -> b` and `g :: b -> a` to prove that f and g are inverses it is enough to prove that `f` $\cdot$ `g` and `g` $\cdot$ `f` both compose to the identity. In an impure language, even if these equalities are observed we cannot be sure that there were no side-effects. Because we do not need to consider a context (the outside world) in a pure language, checking that reversibility works is as simple as comparing initial and final states for all backward reduction rules.

5.2   Concluding Remarks

We presented a functional implementation of the (reversible) MP model [7] using Haskell. By embedding this reversible semantics we can now execute our example programs automatically and inspect them interactively.

We have seen that the MP model can be split into three core components: (i) a process calculus, (ii) multiparty session types (global and local types), and (iii) forward and backward reduction semantics. The three components can be cleanly represented as recursive Haskell data types. We are confident that other features developed in Mezzina and Pérez's work [7] (in particular, an alternative semantics for decoupled rollbacks) can easily be integrated in the development described here. Relatedly, the implementation process has shown that sticking to the formal model leads to better code; there is less space for bugs to creep in. Furthermore, Haskell's mathematical nature means that the implementation inspired by the formal specification is easy (and often idiomatic) to express. Finally, we have discussed how Haskell allows for the definition of flexible embedded domain-specific languages, and makes it easy to transform between different representations of our programs (using among others `Monad.Free`).

Acknowledgments. Many thanks to the anonymous reviewers and to the TFP'18 co-chairs (Michał Pałka and Magnus Myreen) for their useful remarks and suggestions, which led to substantial improvements. Pérez is also affiliated to CWI, Amsterdam, The Netherlands and to the NOVA Laboratory for Computer Science and Informatics (supported by FCT grant NOVA LINCS PEst/UID/CEC/04516/2013), Universidade Nova de Lisboa, Portugal.

This research has been partially supported by the Undergraduate School of Science and the Bernoulli Institute of the University of Groningen. We also acknowledge support from the COST Action IC1405 "Reversible computation – Extending horizons of computing".

References

1. Coppo, M., Dezani-Ciancaglini, M., Padovani, L., Yoshida, N.: A gentle introduction to multiparty asynchronous session types. In: Bernardo, M., Johnsen, E.B. (eds.) SFM 2015. LNCS, vol. 9104, pp. 146–178. Springer, Cham (2015). https://doi.org/10.1007/978-3-319-18941-3_4. http://www.di.unito.it/~dezani/papers/cdpy15.pdf
2. Honda, K., Vasconcelos, V.T., Kubo, M.: Language primitives and type discipline for structured communication-based programming. In: Hankin, C. (ed.) ESOP 1998. LNCS, vol. 1381, pp. 122–138. Springer, Heidelberg (1998). https://doi.org/10.1007/BFb0053567
3. Honda, K., Yoshida, N., Carbone, M.: Multiparty asynchronous session types. In: Necula, G.C., Wadler, P. (eds.) POPL 2008, pp. 273–284. ACM (2008). https://doi.org/10.1145/1328438.1328472
4. Kouzapas, D., Pérez, J.A., Yoshida, N.: On the relative expressiveness of higher-order session processes. In: Thiemann, P. (ed.) ESOP 2016. LNCS, vol. 9632, pp. 446–475. Springer, Heidelberg (2016). https://doi.org/10.1007/978-3-662-49498-1_18

5. Lanese, I., Mezzina, C.A., Tiezzi, F.: Causal-consistent reversibility. Bull. EATCS 114 (2014). http://eatcs.org/beatcs/index.php/beatcs/article/view/305
6. Mezzina, C.A., Pérez, J.A.: Causally consistent reversible choreographies. CoRR abs/1703.06021 (2017). http://arxiv.org/abs/1703.06021
7. Mezzina, C.A., Pérez, J.A.: Causally consistent reversible choreographies: a monitors-as-memories approach. In: Vanhoof, W., Pientka, B. (eds.) Proceedings of the 19th International Symposium on Principles and Practice of Declarative Programming, Namur, Belgium, 09–11 October 2017, pp. 127–138. ACM (2017). https://doi.org/10.1145/3131851.3131864
8. Milner, R., Parrow, J., Walker, D.: A calculus of mobile processes, parts I and II. Inf. Comput. **100**(1), 1–40 (1992)
9. Sangiorgi, D.: Asynchronous process calculi: the first-and higher-order paradigms. Theor. Comput. Sci. **253**(2), 311–350 (2001). https://doi.org/10.1016/S0304-3975(00)00097-9
10. van Walree, F.: Session types in Cloud Haskell. Master's thesis, University of Utrecht (2017). https://dspace.library.uu.nl/handle/1874/355676

Intrinsic Currying for C++ Template Metaprograms

Paul Keir[1]([⊠])[iD], Andrew Gozillon[1][iD], and Seyed Hossein Haeri[2][iD]

[1] University of the West of Scotland, Paisley, UK
{paul.keir,andrew.gozillon}@uws.ac.uk
[2] Université catholique de Louvain, Louvain-la-Neuve, Belgium
hossein.haeri@uclouvain.be

Abstract. C++ template metaprogramming is a form of strict functional programming, with a notable absence of intrinsic support for elementary higher-order operations. We describe a variadic template metaprogramming library which offers a model of implicitly curried, left-associative metafunction application through juxtaposition; inspired by languages such as Haskell, OCaml and F$^\sharp$. New and existing traits and metafunctions, constructed according to conventional idioms, seemlessly take advantage of the framework's features. Furthermore, a distinctive versatility is exposed, allowing a user to define higher-order metafunction classes using an equational definition syntax; without recourse to elaborate nested metafunctions. The primary type expression evaluator of the library is derived from a single application of an elementary folding combinator for type lists. The definition of the fold's binary operator argument is therefore a focal point; and constructed mindful that substitution failure of a template parameter's deduced type produces no compilation error. Two distinctive features of C++ metafunctions require particular consideration: zero argument metafunctions; and variadic metafunctions. We conclude by demonstrating characteristics of the library's main evaluation metafunction in conjunction with the universal property of an updated *right-fold* combinator, to compose a range of metafunctions including *map*, *reverse*, *left-fold*, and the *Ackermann function*.

Keywords: Types · Templates · Metaprogramming · Currying

1 Introduction

C++ template metaprogramming is a form of strict functional programming, with a notable absence of intrinsic support for elementary higher-order operations. Having no canonical representation of metafunctions, authors of template metaprogramming libraries are left to endlessly reinvent the wheel. In this paper we argue that the development of C++ metaprogramming requires a further component: implicit currying.

© Springer Nature Switzerland AG 2019
M. Pałka and M. Myreen (Eds.): TFP 2018, LNCS 11457, pp. 46–73, 2019.
https://doi.org/10.1007/978-3-030-18506-0_3

Beyond basic parametric polymorphism, interesting template metaprograms make fullsome use of a Turing complete language, and rely on *explicit* recursion for full expressivity; yet the advantages of *structured* recursion schemes such as catamorphisms (folds) are widely understood [24].

Considering the high profile of C++, and template metaprogramming, it is surprising that substantial use of template metaprogramming is so rare. Despite notable exceptions [12,14,20,21,33,39], the opportunity to enforce program correctness at compile-time, through embedded domain-specific languages, is underexplored.

Template metaprogramming libraries certainly exist [4,9,10,17,27] and are utilised widely. Many basic templates offered by these libraries were added to the C++11 [2] version of the language standard; including for example a simple type wrapper for integral constants. Prior to this, libraries such as the Boost Metaprogramming Library (MPL) [4] were an obvious choice. Boost itself is a pre-eminent collection of over 150 open-source C++ libraries. Of these, over 40 make use of MPL including: Proto, for creating embedded domain-specific libraries (EDSLs); Spirit, a parser framework; Fusion, a tuple library; Phoenix, a functional programming interface; Metaparse, for parsing strings at compile time; Graph, a generic graph-traversal library; and Hana [9], a more recent metaprogramming library, which is itself now used by Boost Yap, a C++14 expression template library. So, as elementary idioms become included within successive C++ standards, new concepts blossom in fresh libraries. Nevertheless, obstacles inhibit wider adoption; including the apparent complexity of the discipline.

There are likely a number of reasons for this. Poor syntax is often cited; for example dependent name disambiguation via the `template` and `typename` keywords. So too, while metaprogramming libraries provide structured recursion operators[1] such as *map* and *fold*, standard C++ library support is regrettably absent. Idiomatic functional programs will of course also utilise the higher order nature of such operators, and yet no standard C++ representation exists for metafunctions; nor even a standard approach for *returning* a metafunction.

Finally on this point, consider the effort of translating a sizable functional program into a C++ metaprogram without currying. Even the simplest tutorial on recursive combinators such as *map* will soon introduce code such as: *(map (1+) xs)*; yet notice the use of implicit currying within the *section* of the infix addition operator in *(1+)*. Such missing features are a significant inhibiting factor in the pursuit of good practice, including *reuse*, in C++ metaprogramming. The *Curtains* library has been developed to address such concerns; facilitating an embedded domain-specific language for C++ template metaprograms, with support for implicit currying. The Curtains equivalent of the Haskell expression *(const map () (1+) [0,1,2])* is shown below:

```
eval<const_q,map_q,void,eval<add_q,ic<1>>,ilist<0,1,2>>
```

---

[1] Often *map* is named `transform` after the standard C++ runtime function. A *fold* is more often named `fold`; with `accumulate` provided as an alias.

We present *three* implementations, each built upon a single recursive combinator: a left-fold; and while each implementation is purposefully distinct, differences are accounted for entirely by the choice of higher-order, binary combining operation used with the fold. Of the three approaches, our preferred is accomplished in just 30 lines of code, and handles fixed arity metafunctions. The second approach handles idiomatic variadic and nullary metafunctions; while the third treatment finds a middle way, by asking the user to select a single arity, for an otherwise possibly variadic metafunction. Each implementation supports implicit currying.

2   Elementary Metaprogramming

In C++ a user-defined type is referred to as a *class*, yet may be declared using either the `class` keyword, or the `struct` keyword. The difference between the two forms relates only to the default access permission of the class. For ease of exposition we will use the latter, more permissive form throughout; so avoiding verbose usage of the `public` access specifier. Following the class declaration shown below, the type expression `int_wrap::type` becomes synonymous with `int`.

`struct int_wrap { using type = int; };`

A class may also be parameterised, and so declared as a *class template*. The class template `add_pointer`, shown below, is parameterised with a single *type* template parameter[2] named `T`. Providing `add_pointer` with a type argument *instantiates* the template; so forming a *type*. The resulting type, say `add_pointer<int>`, may then be used wherever a type is expected; say to declare a runtime variable, or as an argument for another template.

`template <class T> struct add_pointer { using type = T*; };`

A common metaprogramming idiom can then be explained. A class template with a single member type definition, conventionally names the member: `type`. Compile-time class template parameters can then be understood as isomorphic to common run-time function parameters; with the relevant member type definition analogous to the return value. A class template so equipped is often referred to as a *metafunction*.

From this perspective, the `add_pointer` *type trait* class template from the standard C++ type support library is a *unary* metafunction. Given an `int` argument, the metafunction returns a *first order* type; an `int*`, within the `type` member of the instantiated `add_pointer` template. The application of such a metafunction will involve the familiar angle-bracket syntax: `add_pointer<int>`; with the result obtained via `typename add_pointer<int>::type`[3].

---

[2] This is a second, distinct usage of the `class` keyword. The `struct` keyword is not permitted in this context; though `typename` is.

[3] The `typename` disambiguator informs the compiler that a dependent name following the `::` operator, refers to a *type* [37, p. 228].

Template metaprograms are untyped; though various mechanisms exist to allow ad-hoc treatment of particular types, or type patterns, via class template *specialisation*. For example, the specialisation on the second line of the following possible implementation of the standard C++ library type trait, `remove_const`, handles types which are `const` qualified; so matching the type pattern: `const T`.

```
template <class T> struct remove_const          { using type = T; };
template <class T> struct remove_const<const T> { using type = T; };
```

A crucial component of elementary first-order template metaprogramming is recursion. One or more class template specialisations can represent the *base cases*. Meanwhile each *recursive step* includes an instantiation of the class template being defined. We demonstrate recursion using integers at the type level; with the assistance of the `ic` *alias template* defined below[4]. Akin to a C++ `typedef`, or a Haskell type synonym, an alias template defines a new name for an existing template: `std::integral_constant` in this case. On *this* occasion, `ic` specifies a *non-type* parameter; and the `auto` specifier ensures the argument's type is inferred. Consequently, the *type* `ic<42>`, for example, can concisely represent the word-sized compile-time integer constant: 42.

```
template <auto I> using ic = std::integral_constant<decltype(I),I>;
```

Using our integer representation, the code below defines a recursive template metafunction, `fact`, which calculates the factorial of its argument[5]. For example `fact<ic<3>>::type` $\equiv$ `ic<6>`.

```
template <class T> struct fact;
template <        > struct fact<ic<0>> : ic<1> {};
template <auto  N> struct fact<ic<N>> :
                          ic<N*typename fact<ic<N-1>>::type{}> {};
```

The standard C++ type support library defines an alias template for each type trait, providing a convenient syntax to access the `type` member of the associated class template. For example, `add_pointer_t<int>` evaluates to `int*` using the `add_pointer_t` alias template shown below:

```
template <class T> using add_pointer_t = typename add_pointer<T>::type;
```

Specialisation of alias templates is not possible; and neither is *recursion*. Consequently, alias templates have limited capability, and are typically used to provide *syntactic sugar* to existing class template definitions. Alias templates can nevertheless themselves be interpreted as metafunctions.

Lastly, *variadic templates* facilitate a variable quantity of template arguments. For example, the variadic alias template `ct_tail` below accepts one or

---

[4] `decltype` is a keyword used to query the type of an expression.

[5] The type expression `typename fact<ic<N-1>>::type` will evaluate to a type; an instantiation of `ic`, and hence also of `std::integral_constant`. The `{}` braces which follow this expression will aggregate-initialise a `constexpr std::integral_constant` object before using its conversion operator member to provide an `int` value as the multiplier, with `N` the multiplicand.

more arguments: e.g. `ct_tail<char*,int,long>` ≡ `long`. The standard library's
`std::common_type_t` obtains a common type from its parameter pack argument[6].

```
template <class T, class... Ts> using ct_tail = std::common_type_t<Ts...>;
```

2.1 Higher Order Metaprogramming

A basic challenge for higher-order template metaprogramming is how a metafunction should be *returned*. Metafunctions can certainly be passed as template
arguments. Considering the class template definition `ho`, below, `ho<add_pointer>`
and `ho<add_pointer_t>` are both valid template instantiations.

```
template <template <class> class> struct ho {};
```

Given that a metafunction can be defined *either* using an alias template;
or a class template, it is reassuring that either approach can also represent the
return types: a metafunction can either "return" a nested class template; or an
alias template. The code below defines a unary metafunction, `ct`, which returns
another metafunction; as the member alias template `m_invoke`. Applying the `ct`
metafunction to a type argument, will thus return a metafunction which itself
determines the common type among the arguments that it is provided *and* the
single argument already provided to `ct`.

```
template <class T>
struct ct {
  template <class... Ts>
  using m_invoke = std::common_type_t<T,Ts...>;
};
```

Applying the metafunction returned by `ct` to a `long` argument, might involve
syntax such as the following: `typename ct<long>::template m_invoke<int>`[7]; a
type expression which evaluates to `long`. The verbosity of such nested metafunction invocations can be reduced through a helpful combinator:

```
template <class F, class... Ts>
using invoke = typename F::template m_invoke<Ts...>;
```

The `invoke` combinator offers improved syntax when applying a nested metafunction member named `m_invoke`; with the previous example represented as
`invoke<ct<long>,int>`. Applying a returned metafunction can thus both be tran-
scribed more concisely; while clearly articulating the separation of a nested metafunction from its arguments. Without further treatment, however, *non-nested*
metafunctions, such as type traits, are incompatible. The first argument of the
`invoke` combinator, expects a *type*; not a *template*. A combinator to envelop
the functionality of an arbitrary type trait template, within the `m_invoke` alias
template member of a proxy class, would be useful. Consider `quote` below:

---

[6] Regarding a template parameter pack: note that its *declaration* is *preceded* by an
ellipsis; while its *expansion* is *followed* by one [37, p. 188].

[7] The `template` disambiguator informs the compiler that a dependent name following
a `::`, `->`, or `.` operator, refers to a *template* [37, p. 230].

```
template <template <class...> class M>
struct quote {
  template <class... Ts>
  using m_invoke = M<Ts...>;
};
```

Instantiating `quote` with a suitable class template argument, `M`, will produce a type with an `m_invoke` member metafunction, and equivalent functionality to the `M` argument. Given a type trait *template* such as `std::common_type_t`, for example, the `quote<std::common_type_t>` *type* is a suitable first argument for the `invoke` combinator; and the following equivalency between types holds:

`invoke<quote<common_type_t>,int,long> ≡ long`

Alas, instantiating `quote` with a *non-variadic* template argument, as in `quote<std::add_pointer_t>`, will produce a compilation error; relating to the provision of a pack argument to a non-pack template parameter list. The interface and functionality of `quote` can nevertheless be constructed in unambiguous C++ using an alternative approach.

Expanding a parameter pack into a fixed length template parameter list is problematic *only* within the context of an *alias* template[8]; as with the `m_invoke` member of `quote`. By ensuring the parameter pack is instead expanded within a *class* template, this problematic and byzantine corner case can be evaded. An additional class template, `iv1430`[9], is therefore introduced:

```
template <class, template <class...> class, class...>
struct iv1430 {};
```

```
template <template <class...> class M, class... Ts>
struct iv1430<void_t<M<Ts...>>,M,Ts...> { using type = M<Ts...>; };
```

A final version of `quote`[10] can then be defined, using `iv1430`, as shown below. With this version, no compilation errors are encountered when `quote` is provided with non-variadic template arguments, as pack expansion now occurs within a class template rather than an alias template. For example, non-variadic traits such as `std::add_pointer_t` or `std::is_object`; as well as variadic ones such as

---

[8] Discussion regarding the virtue of this restriction remains an active topic within the ISO C++ Standards Committee; identified as core issue 1430 [25].

[9] The `iv1430` class template makes use of a powerful C++ feature wherein template substitution failure is not an error (SFINAE). Furthermore, `iv1430` is defined as "SFINAE-friendly". For example, as `int` and `int*` have no *common type*, neither `common_type<int,int*>`, nor the equivalent `iv1430<void,common_type_t,int,int*>`, has a `type` member. The failed instantiation of the `iv1430` specialisation with `iv1430<void,common_type_t,int,int*>` resolves to the primary template; leaving subsequent access to the absent `type` member *only* a substitution error. The alternative is a hard error. C++17's `std::void_t` is an alias template helpful in such contexts; provided with zero or more *valid* type template arguments, the aggregate instantiates to `void` [37, p. 420].

[10] A variant, `quote_c`, accepting class template arguments, is defined in Appendix A.1.

`std::conjunction` or `std::is_constructible` can each be converted, using `quote`, into a form suitable for use with the `invoke` combinator. Such a type, suitably equipped with an `m_invoke` alias template member, either by the use of the `quote` combinator, or by elementary design, is known as a *metafunction class*.

```
template <template <class...> class M>
struct quote {
  template <class... Ts>
  using m_invoke = typename iv1430<void,M,Ts...>::type;
};
```

The following two equivalences demonstrate the use of `invoke` along with the non-variadic metafunctions, `std::add_pointer` and `std::add_pointer_t`:

```
invoke<quote<std::add_pointer_t>,int> ≡ int*
invoke<quote<std::add_pointer  >,int> ≡ add_pointer<int>
```

The intermediate reduction steps for the first of these is shown below:

```
invoke<quote<std::add_pointer_t>,int>
   ≡ {invoke alias template}
quote<std::add_pointer_t>::m_invoke<int>>
   ≡ {m_invoke alias template member of quote template}
iv1430<void,std::add_pointer_t,int>::type
   ≡ {type member of iv1430 template specialisation}
std::add_pointer_t<int>
   ≡ {standard C++ alias template add_pointer_t}
std::add_pointer<int>::type
   ≡ {standard C++ template add_pointer}
int*
```

2.2   The Identity Metafunction

A metafunction which returns its argument, is a central component throughout the Curtains implementation. The `id` metafunction, shown below, utilised as a *mix-in* class template, can specify a base class, facilitating the common requirement within metaprogramming for a class to include a member type definition named `type`; introduced orthogonally here via inheritance.

```
template <class T>  struct id { using type = T; };
```

A possible implementation of `std::add_volatile`, constructed using this idiom, is shown below. Seen as a metafunction, such syntax can be interpreted as highlighting the *type* which will be provided as the return "value"; located to the right of the colon, within the angle brackets of the id template.

```
template <class T> struct add_volatile : id<volatile T> {};
```

With routine application of the `invoke` combinator, providing a type trait as an argument to the `quote` combinator can become as common as accessing a `type` member. We adopt the "_q" suffix here in deference to the "_t" suffix convention

of the standard C++ type support library's alias templates. The relevant pair
for the `add_volatile` type trait are shown in the code below:

```
template <class T>
using add_volatile_t = typename add_volatile<T>::type;
using add_volatile_q = quote<add_volatile_t>;
```

3 Curried Template Evaluation

This section presents our implicitly currying evaluation mechanism: the metafunction `eval`.

Function application in Haskell [22] is written *e1 e2*; where *e2* is an arbitrary
Haskell expression, and *e1* is a Haskell expression which reduces to a value with
a function type. Application associates to the left, and so the parentheses may
be omitted in *(f x) y*. Hence function application is implicitly curried within
Haskell. We aim to create a comparable evaluation environment within the context of C++ metaprogramming. Given a C++ variadic template evaluator, *eval*,
we would like metafunction application to be written *eval<e1,e2[,...]>*, where
the ellipsis represents an optional trailing list of type arguments. Metafunction
application should also associate to the left, and hence the omission of the inner
template instantiation of `eval` within `eval<eval<F,X>,Y>` would be permitted;
and denoted as `eval<F,X,Y>`.

A basic expectation is that a quoted metafunction, provided to `eval`, together
with a full set of valid template arguments, should produce the same result as
with the traditional metafunction alone. For an arbitrary metafunction *M*, and
parameter pack *Ts*, where *M<Ts...>* is well formed; *eval<quote<M>,Ts...>* is also
well formed. Furthermore, the following equality holds:

$$M\texttt{<}Ts...\texttt{>} \equiv eval\texttt{<}quote\texttt{<}M\texttt{>},Ts...\texttt{>}$$

For example, given `add_pointer_q`, defined as `quote<std::add_pointer_t>`, we
find that `eval<add_pointer_q,int>` ≡ `std::add_pointer_t<int>` ≡ `int*`. Class
templates are also suitable metafunctions; and so `eval<quote<std::is_pod>,int>`
≡ `std::is_pod<int>`. Note that the equality assumes a valid left-hand side; for
curried applications of *quote<M>*, only the right-hand side will be valid.

3.1 Components of Implicit Currying

Given such conditions, it follows that a method for managing the partial evaluation of a metafunction is required. The `curry` class template below can help
here: given a metafunction class F as its *first* argument, and *n* further type
arguments, `curry` will instantiate to a new metafunction class; equivalent to F
partially applied to those *n* arguments. Additional arguments can be provided
using `curry` again; or `invoke` (page 5) may be used to instantiate the full metafunction application, and optionally also supply any remaining arguments.

```
template <class F, class... Ts>
struct curry {
  template <class... Us>
  using m_invoke = invoke<F,Ts...,Us...>;
};
```

The equivalences below demonstrate uses of `curry` with a metafunction class `common_type_q`; constructed via `quote` from the type trait: `std::common_type_t`. Note `invoke`'s accommodation of nested instantiations of `curry`, here; and referenced later in Sect. 4.2.

```
invoke<curry<common_type_q,char>,int>              ≡ int
invoke<curry<common_type_q,char,int>,long>         ≡ long
invoke<curry<curry<common_type_q,char>,int>,long>  ≡ long
```

The C++ compiler will issue a helpful error if the first argument to `curry` is not a metafunction class; due to the instantiation of `invoke` within `curry`'s `m_invoke` member. Error checking is nevertheless incidental; and providing "too many" arguments for `curry`'s template parameter pack *is* accepted, at least until its application through `invoke`.

Note that the absence of currying within the simple `invoke`, will manifest itself in a compilation error, and *not only* with metafunctions applied to "too few" arguments; as in say `invoke<quote<is_same>,int>`. In Haskell *(id id 42)* ≡ *((id id) 42)*; and either expression thus evaluates to 42. Consider the definition of `id_q` below, a simple preparation of the earlier `id` template class:

```
using id_q = quote_c<id>;
```

A comparable C++ template expression, `invoke<id_q,id_q,ic<42>>`, will also result in an error; as `invoke` attempts to apply its first argument, to all those that remain; "too many" arguments. So too the issue may not be as conspicuous; while the Haskell expression *(foldr id 42 [id])* presents *foldr* with its full quota of three arguments, reduction will nevertheless require evaluation of the familiar *(id id 42)*.

One may briefly consider the remedy of prescribing thorough use of the `curry` class template. However, while explicit invocation of an occasional application of `curry` may be tolerable, *systematic* integration within a larger system would be tedious; and error prone as a consequence. This is the explicit currying seen in other systems.

3.2 Folding with Types

The creation of a C++ metafunction expression evaluator, with *implicit* currying, can be achieved by defining both: a generic folding combinator; and a specific combining operation. Adopting Haskell's model of function application involves the left-associative currying operator, denoted by the space between operands; i.e. their *juxtaposition*. Given the elementary binary function *const*, which returns its first argument, the Haskell-like expression *(const 1 2)* is parsed as *((const 1) 2)*, with *(const 1)* returning a function equivalent to the partial application of *const*. Operationally, this can be processed as a *left-fold*, with currying as the binary combining operation. A definition for a similar fold over a homogeneous list in Haskell is shown below:

foldl f z []   = z
foldl f z (x:xs) = foldl f (f z x) xs

Evaluating an expression such as *(const 1 2)* can then be understood intuitively as a left-fold on a heterogeneous list of three elements: the binary function *const*; the numeric literal *1*; and the numeric literal *2*.

The code below defines a C++ left-fold metafunction class[11] through two specialisations of a class template `ifoldl`; one for the base case; and one for the recursive step. The type template parameter `F`, which expects a metafunction class, is seen applied to two arguments, `Z` and `T`, at the `invoke<F,Z,T>` instantiation within the recursive `ifoldl` specialisation. Finally, the `quote_c` alias template is used to produce a metafunction class suitable for use with `invoke`: `ifoldl_q`.

```
template <class, class Z, class...>
struct ifoldl             : id<Z> {};

template <class F, class Z, class T, class... Ts>
struct ifoldl<F,Z,T,Ts...> : ifoldl<F,invoke<F,Z,T>,Ts...> {};

using ifoldl_q = quote_c<ifoldl>;
```

The left-fold above is defined recursively according to conventional metaprogramming idioms. As a simple example of its operation, the code below performs a compile-time calculation of $((0 - 1) - 2)$.

```
template <class T, class U> using sub = ic<T::value - U::value>;

invoke<ifoldl_q,quote<sub>,ic<0>,ic<1>,ic<2>> ≡ ic<-3>
```

It is noteworthy that an implementation utilising C++17's *fold expressions*, with an equivalent interface and functionality is also possible, though no more concise, by overloading an arbitrary binary operator. Such a version is provided in Appendix A.11.

While considering the definition of a combining operation for use with the folding metafunction class, `ifoldl_q`, and with which to facilitate an implicitly currying evaluator, it can be worthwhile to examine the limitations of naively providing `ifoldl_q` with a suitably *quoted* version of either `invoke`; or `curry`. Corresponding evaluators, `eval_i` and `eval_c`, are shown below:

```
template <class F, class... Ts>
using eval_i = invoke<ifoldl_q,quote<invoke>,F,Ts...>;

template <class F, class... Ts>
using eval_c = invoke<ifoldl_q,quote<curry>, F,Ts...>;
```

---

[11] A template parameter pack `Ts` is used by `ifoldl` rather than a type list; and hence it is not strictly isomorphic to the Haskell fold above; this is however only part of the implementation, *not* of the public API.

The `eval_i` combinator will apply `invoke`, two arguments at a time, starting from the leftmost pair. Of course as `invoke` has no support for currying, this only succeeds for unary functions. For example, `eval_i<id_q,id_q,ic<42>>`, akin to the Haskell expression, *(id id 42)*, *will* reduce to `ic<42>` as expected. However, `eval_i<const_q,int,bool>`, in attempting to instantiate `invoke<const_q,int>`, instead produces a compilation error; `const_q` is defined below:

```
template <class T, class> using const_t = T;
                         using const_q = quote<const_t>;
```

The `eval_c` combinator will instantiate nested `curry` classes instead; ever deeper with recursive step. A final application of `invoke` may then be useful, to convert the nested `curry` classes, into the expected result type. For example, `eval_c<const_q,int,bool>` will reduce to `curry<curry<const_q,int>,bool>`, which *is* a valid metafunction class; providing it to `invoke`, with no further arguments, will produce the anticipated result: `int`. The `eval_c` combinator, combined with the final application of `invoke`, thus behaves exactly as `invoke` alone. Consequently, it encounters the same restrictions regarding currying; for example `eval_c<id_q,id_q,ic<42>>` fails to compile as `id_q` is provided with two arguments; `id_q` and `ic<42>`. Another approach is required.

A *suitable* binary combining operation for use with the left-fold of `ifoldl_q` makes conditional use of both `curry` *and* `invoke`. Algorithm 1 illustrates in pseudocode the operation of this metafunction; with the C++ definition provided below. Intuitively, `curry_invoke_q` will use `invoke` to apply its first argument to its second, when possible; otherwise it returns the application in curried form.

```
template <class F, class T, class = void_t<>>
struct curry_invoke                            : id<curry<F,T>>  {};

template <class F, class T>
struct curry_invoke<F,T,void_t<invoke<F,T>>> : id<invoke<F,T>> {};

using curry_invoke_q = quote_c<curry_invoke>;
```

With `curry_invoke_q` as the combining operation of `ifoldl_q`, and the elementary `id_q` as a starting value, an implicitly currying evaluation metafunction, `eval`, can be defined; as shown below.

```
template <class... Fs>
using eval = invoke<ifoldl_q,curry_invoke_q,id_q,Fs...>;
```

As `eval` is defined by a conventional catamorphism, `eval<>` simply returns the "zero" value of the defining left-fold; the identity metafunction class: `id_q`. Likewise, for an arbitrary type *T*, *eval<T>* evaluates to *T*; consequently `eval<int>` and `eval<id_q>` reduce to `int` and `id_q` respectively. Demonstrations of the utility of `eval` are explored in Sect. 5; while the intermediate steps involved in reducing a sample expression, `eval<const_q,id_q,int,char>`, to `char` are listed in Appendix A.12.

Algorithm 1. Invocation with conditional currying

Precondition: f is a possibly curried metafunction class
Precondition: t is an arbitrary type
Postcondition: g is a curried metafunction class

1: **function** CURRY-INVOKE(f, t)
2:     **if** ISVALIDEXPRESSION$(f(t))$ **then**
3:         $g \leftarrow f(t)$
4:     **else**
5:         $g \leftarrow$ CURRY(f, t)
6:     **end if**
7:     **return** g
8: **end function**

---

4   Variadic and Nullary Metafunctions

Section 3's `eval` metafunction accommodates a domain-specific language of expressions involving curried evaluation of *fixed arity* metafunctions. C++ templates also support idiomatic *nullary* and *variadic* metafunctions. Variadic templates were introduced in C++11. While the argument count and values of the instantiated template may be unknown to a template's author, such aspects are of course resolved at compile-time. Meanwhile, nullary metafunctions arise when either the template parameters of a class are specified with default values; or a variadic class template has a template parameter pack, optionally with preceding defaulted template parameters. For an arbitrary nullary metafunction, `N`, angle brackets remain necessary during instantiation; as in `N<>`. We propose that a modified evaluation combinator, `eval_v`, support the following syntax for such eventualities: `eval_v<N>`. Our implementation will continue to operate as a left-fold, but more intricacy and heuristics is required for the combining operation.

4.1   An Antidetection Idiom

Now is an opportune moment to introduce a novel metafunction: `invalid`; a combinator aligned with the SFINAE *detection idiom* [7], which provides a useful form of inverse to the idiomatic application of C++17's `std::void_t`.

An elementary enquiry, facilitated easily using `std::void_t`, is whether or not a class has a member named `type`. Instantiating the `xt` class template shown below using a type which *does* have such a member, will create a type which *does not*; and vice versa: instantiating `xt` with an argument which *does not* have a `type` member, will produce a type which does.

```
template <class, class = void_t<>>
struct xt : id<void>                    {};

template <class T>
struct xt<T,void_t<typename T::type>> {};
```

For an arbitrary metafunction class *F*, and type arguments *Ts...*, where *void_t<invoke<F,Ts...>>* instantiates to void, we can interpret the argument to void_t as being *valid*. Using the invalid combinator, shown below, with *F* and *Ts* arguments as before, will see *void_t<invoke<invalid<F>,Ts...>>* *fail* to instantiate; where *invoke<F,Ts...>* is valid, *invoke<invalid<F>,Ts...>* is *invalid*.

```
template <class F>
struct invalid {
  template <class... Us>
  using m_invoke =
    typename xt<iv1430<void,F::template m_invoke,Us...>>::type;
};
```

Considering the potential for multiple arguments to std::void_t, the idea emerges to combine requirements for valid instantiations of invoke with those which are invalid. For example, for arbitrary types *T* and *U*, *void_t<invoke<F,T>,invoke<invalid<F>,U>>* could help specify that a class template specialisation should be selected when *invoke<F,T>*, but *not invoke<F,U>*, is valid.

4.2   The Combining Operation

A new binary combining operation for use with Sect. 3.2's left-fold again makes conditional use of curry *and* invoke; with additional SFINAE guidance from the invalid class template. Algorithm 2 illustrates in pseudocode the operation of this recursive metafunction. On line 2, the first argument of *Curry-invoke-peek*, a function *f*, perhaps already with curried arguments, has its potential for application determined, both: (1) with no further arguments; and (2) with *t* as a single argument. Having the first condition true, with the second false, allows for *f* to be evaluated, with the resulting function *f'* passed alongside *t*, via a recursive call to *Curry-invoke-peek* on line 4. Alternatively, the *Curry-invoke-peek* function will conclude on line 6 simply by returning *f*, curried with the type *t*. The C++ definition, curry_invoke_peek_q, is shown below.

```
template <class F, class T, class = void_t<>>
struct curry_invoke_peek : id<curry<F,T>> {};

template <class F, class T>
struct curry_invoke_peek<F,T,void_t<invoke<F>,invoke<invalid<F>,T>>>
    : curry_invoke_peek<invoke<F>,T> {};

using curry_invoke_peek_q = quote<curry_invoke_peek>;
```

Algorithm 2 differs from Algorithm 1 in two ways. Firstly, invoke may be used *either* to evaluate the application of *f* to *t*; *or*, to evaluate *f* itself. This supports variadic metafunctions, through the incremental consideration of additional arguments. Secondly, Algorithm 2 is recursive; accommodating nullary metafunctions, which too may return nullary metafunctions.

Algorithm 2. Conditional invocation of a function and argument

Precondition: f is a possibly curried metafunction class
Precondition: t is an arbitrary type
Postcondition: g is a curried metafunction class

1: **function** CURRY-INVOKE-PEEK(f, t)
2:     **if** ISVALIDEXPRESSION($f()$) $\wedge \neg$ISVALIDEXPRESSION($f(t)$) **then**
3:         $f' \leftarrow f()$
4:         $g \leftarrow$ CURRY-INVOKE-PEEK(f', t)
5:     **else**
6:         $g \leftarrow$ CURRY(f, t)
7:     **end if**
8:     **return** g
9: **end function**

Given a metafunction class F, and a template parameter pack Fs, the type expression `invoke<ifoldl_q,curry_invoke_peek_q,F,Fs...>` will produce a *curried* representation of a metafunction application. Consider the invocation of `invoke` below; comparable to the Haskell *(const id 42 'a')*.

`invoke<ifoldl_q,curry_invoke_peek_q,const_q,id_q,int,char>`

The expression reduces to `curry<id_q,char>`. Applying `invoke` to this, once again, with no further arguments, can produce the sought `char`. A curried metafunction application, with fewer arguments than required by the metafunction, is also a valid output of the fold; say `curry<const_q,int>`. Applying `invoke` to this, however, produces a compilation error. A metafunction combinator is thus defined, which applies `invoke` to a curried metafunction application *only* when this can be achieved without error.

The `invoke_if` metafunction combinator defined below will apply `invoke` conditionally to its `F` parameter whenever possible; otherwise, `F` is simply returned. Furthermore, should such an invocation be achieved, the attempt will be repeated; by passing the result, `invoke<F>`, recursively to `invoke_if`. By this route, the uncommon scenario of a nullary metafunction returning a possibly nullary metafunction is also handled.

```
template <class F, class = void_t<>>
struct invoke_if                        : id<F>                   {};

template <class F>
struct invoke_if<F,void_t<invoke<F>>> : invoke_if<invoke<F>> {};

template <class F> using invoke_if_t = typename invoke_if<F>::type;
```

Consequently, `eval_v` can be defined as shown below. As discussed, the fold produces a curried result; hence the `invoke_if` combinator, via `invoke_if_t`, is utilised to conditionally apply `invoke` upon it.

```
template <class... Fs>
using eval_v =
  invoke_if_t<invoke<ifoldl_q,curry_invoke_peek_q,id_q,Fs...>>;
```

Evaluating metafunction applications involving nullary metafunctions can produce surprising results. Consider the `zero_constv_q` metafunction class below:

```
template <class...> struct zero_constv : id<const_q> {};
```

```
using zero_constv_q = quote_c<zero_constv>;
```

Applied to *zero* arguments, the type expression `eval<zero_constv_q>`, reduces to `const_q`. In fact for an arbitrary pack of types *Ts*, the expression *eval<zero_constv_q,Ts...>* will *always* reduce to `const_q`: the fold's combining operation curries successive arguments until an invalid set is formed; or until there are no more.

To define a metafunction which is valid *only* for nullary invocations, class template specialisation is necessary. Line 1 in the code below *declares* a primary variadic class template, `zero_const`; which is then specialised on line 2 to return `const_q` for zero arguments. In this scenario, the operational semantics of `eval_v`'s underlying fold will evaluate `zero_const_q` rather than curry further arguments; ensuring `const_q` is now the active metafunction. Hence, `eval<zero_const_q,int,bool>` will reduce to `int`.

```
1  template <class...> struct zero_const;
2  template <        > struct zero_const<> : id<const_q> {};
3
4  using zero_const_q = quote_c<zero_const>;
```

4.3 Explicit Fixed Arity

Our third implementation of the expression evaluator, `eval_n`, allows the user to curate a selection of variadic metafunctions, or metafunction classes; but requires that each is annotated with a chosen arity.

The class template `bases`, defined below, allows an existing variadic metafunction class *F*, to be paired with an arity type *N*, as a fellow base class, as in *bases<F,N>*. For example, `constv_q` (Appendix A.5) could be given an arity of 7 using `bases<constv_q,ic<7>>`.

```
template <class... Ts> struct bases   : Ts... {};
template <>            struct bases<>        {};
```

Expression evaluation is then undertaken through the `eval_n` combinator shown below. The binary metafunction classes `curry_invoke_peekn_q` and `invoke_ifn_t` are defined in Appendices A.2 and A.3. Intuitively, the operation of `curry_invoke_peekn_q` is much like `curry_invoke_peek_q`. Now, however, the decision to apply `invoke` rather than `curry` is determined simply: the arity of a metafunction's representation is decremented with each curried argument. If that arity becomes zero, use `invoke`.

```
template <class... Fs>
using eval_n =
  invoke_ifn_t<invoke<ifoldl_q,curry_invoke_peekn_q,id_q,Fs...>>;
```

A disadvantage of this approach is that the user is burdened with the task of manually adding rank values. Certainly a future iteration of Curtains could infer the rank attribute with fixed arity metafunctions. Nevertheless, it is likely that more extensive benefits of this approach will stay muted while template metaprograms remain *untyped*. C++ Concepts [3] should shed light here, and further work will seek to explore Curtains' relationship with dependent types [23]; allowing for example, fixed length vectors, and the generic *zipWith* family of combinators.

5   Using the Curtains API

The method of evaluating a type expression involving metafunction classes and other types was introduced via the `eval` combinator in Sects. 3 and 4. We now consider examples from the perspective of the end user of the *Curtains* API.

5.1   Defining Metafunctions Using Equations

Notably, the application of a metafunction class via `eval` will be curried *implicitly*. For example, `eval<const_q,char>` produces a curried, unevaluated metafunction class, which can then be applied to a second type argument; producing the final result: `eval<eval<const_q,char>,bool>` $\equiv$ `char`. We can then comfortably define a metafunction for the composition of two metafunctions; as shown below.

```
template <class F, class G>
struct compose_t
{
  template <class T>
  using m_invoke = eval<F,eval<G,T>>;
};
using compose_q = quote<compose_t>;
```

Thanks to the implicit currying of the `eval` combinator, the composition will *also* work when given non-unary metafunctions *F* and *G*. For example, a comparable C++ template metaprogram expression to Haskell's *((.) const id 1 2)* is `eval<compose_q,const_q,id_q,int,char>`; which reduce to *1* and `int` respectively.

We now highlight a new factor in the definition of higher-order metafunctions, concerning a flexibility in the syntax. The definition of `compose_t` shown above is a *binary* metafunction which returns a *unary* metafunction via a nested alias template named `m_invoke`. This is analogous to the Haskell definition of the composition operator *(.)* shown below:

```
(.) f g = \x -> f (g x)
```

As with the C++ metafunction `compose_t`, syntactically this defines a binary function which returns a unary lambda function. Note that it is also sometimes convenient to define such functions using a shorter, "equational syntax":

```
(.) f g x = f (g x)
```

This flexibility is found in most languages with lambda expressions; though C++ metaprogramming does not support the latter form. Curtains' support for implicit currying *does* however permit such equational definitions. The alternative definition for `compose_t` is shown below:

```
template <class F, class G, class T>
using compose_t = eval<F,eval<G,T>>;


using compose_q = quote<compose_t>;
```

This is especially convenient for C++ metaprogramming. Firstly, the "lambda syntax" for C++ higher-order metafunctions is verbose. Secondly, while Curtains uses the name `m_invoke`, there is no standard naming convention for this; the returned metafunction.

5.2   Structured Recursion

This integration of currying facilitates a direct transfer of functional programming idioms to C++ template metaprogramming; especially when manipulating higher-order metafunctions. The derivation of functionality from structure can be demonstrated by the use of recursion schemes including catamorphisms and anamorphisms to create metaprogram equivalents of many familiar functions. A Curtains right-fold definition is shown below, along with a simple type list[12].

```
template <class...> struct list {};

template <class, class, class> struct foldr;
using foldr_q = quote_c<foldr>;

template <class F, class Z, class T, class... Ts>
struct foldr<F,Z,list<T,Ts...>>
    : id<eval<F,T,eval<foldr_q,F,Z,list<Ts...>>>> {};

template <class F, class Z>
struct foldr<F,Z,list<>> : id<Z>                      {};
```

The `foldr` metafunction is constructed from two class template specialisations; corresponding to the traditional pair of defining equations. A Haskell expression such as *(foldr id 42 [id])* reduces to *(id id 42)* ≡ *(42)*. Such an operation is accomplished through the elementary treatment of all functions as unary, with left-associative application; possibly returning another function through

---

[12] A `std::tuple` would do, though the minimal `list` class template shown is sufficient for compile-time calculations.

currying. Given *id*, the type of the second argument, $(a \rightarrow b \rightarrow b)$, resolves with a as a function type $(c \rightarrow c)$. Curtains makes no interpretation of the types/kinds of a metafunction's arguments, but here usefully places no demand on the fold's binary combining operation to be provided with two arguments. Ultimately, an isomorphic Curtains expression, such as `eval<foldr_q,id_q,char,list<id_q>>`, reduces similarly to `char`.

With the simple list-forming metafunction `cons_q` provided in Appendix A.4, metafunctions constructed from `foldr_q` can be defined; with varying levels of effort. For example `eval<foldr_q,cons_q,list<>>` behaves as the identity metafunction when provided with a list argument. A fold can also produce the familiar *map* function in Haskell:

$$map\ f = foldr\ ((:)\ .\ f)\ []$$

The only difference required for a Curtains definition of *map* is for the infix composition operator to be applied prefix:

```
template <class F>
using map_t = eval<foldr_q,eval<compose_q,cons_q,F>,list<>>;
using map_q = quote<map_t>;
```

A Haskell function to reverse a list using a right-fold is shown below:

$$reverse\ xs = foldr\ (\lambda x\ y \rightarrow y\ .\ ((:)\ x))\ id\ xs\ []$$

Preparing an equivalent list reversal in Curtains, and mindful of the lack of lambda metafunctions, we may consider class or alias templates. A *point-free* equivalent of the lambda function can instead be created, *(flip (.) . (:))*[13], and is found on line 4 of the complete Curtains *reverse* implementation below[14]:

```
1   template <class L>
2   using reverse_t = eval<
3                       foldr_q,
4                       eval<compose_q,eval<flip_q,compose_q>,cons_q>,
5                       id_q,
6                       L,
7                       list<>
8                   >;
9   using reverse_q = quote<reverse_t>;
```

Tools such as the Pointfree.io website can in fact produce an entirely point-free Haskell list reversal; see `reverse_pf_q` in Appendix A.6 for the code listing. In fact, preparing arbitrarily complicated fold operations by this approach becomes somewhat mechanical. Appendix A.9 includes a Curtains implementation of the Ackermann function, constructed using `foldr_q`.

5.3   The Strict Fixed-Point Combinator

A lazy language such as Haskell allows a concise definition of the fixed-point combinator:

---

[13] The Pointfree.io website is an excellent resource for producing such translations.

[14] A Curtains definition of the Haskell *flip* combinator is provided in Appendix A.4.

fix f = f (fix f)

However, as in traditional C++ template metaprogramming, expression evaluation in Curtains is *eager*. In eager functional languages, an η-expanded definition of the fixed-point combinator can be constructed, wherein the evaluation of *(fix f)* on the right-hand side is delayed when only a single argument is provided to the combinator. This strict form of the fixed-point combinator, sometimes referred to as the Z combinator, can be defined, say in OCaml, as follows:

let rec fix f x = f (fix f) x;;

Curtains adopts exactly the same approach. As usual, an alias template name cannot appear on the right-hand side of its definition; and only a class template can have a forward declaration; which explains the formulation shown below:

```
template <class,class> struct fix_c;

using fix = quote_c<fix_c>;

template <class F, class X>
struct fix_c : id<eval<F,eval<fix,F>,X>> {};
```

Curry's Y combinator defines a fixed point combinator without recursion. This too can be constructed as an η-expanded version of its symmetric form where $\lambda f.(\lambda x.f(xx))(\lambda x.f(xx))$, becomes $\lambda f.\lambda g.(\lambda x.\lambda a.f(xx)a)$ $(\lambda x.\lambda a.f(xx)a)g$. The Curtains version is shown below. The non-recursive factorial function from Appendix A.10 means `eval<fix,fix_fact,ic<3>>` $\equiv$ `eval<y,fix_fact,ic<3>>` $\equiv$ `ic<6>`.

```
template <class F, class X, class A>
using y_helper_t = eval<F,eval<X,X>,A>;
using y_helper   = quote<y_helper_t>;

template <class F, class G>
using y_t = eval<eval<y_helper,F>,eval<y_helper,F>,G>;
using y   = quote<y_t>;
```

6   Related Work

The use of C++ templates and macros for metaprogramming started with Unruh's code that emits some prime numbers as warning messages [35]. Veldhuizen introduced expression templates to the world of C++ metaprogramming [38]. Austern [6] exemplified some commonalities between the STL (the generic programming part of the C++98 [1] and C++11 [2] standard libraries) and functional programming. Alexandrescu [5] presented a *tour de force* of C++ metaprogramming and was the first to identify similarities between that and functional programming. Abrahams and Gurtovoy devoted their book [4] to the metaprogramming libraries of the Boost C++ library.

Golodotz [13] offers a tour on the functional programming nature of C++ metaprogramming by showing how to implement certain metaprograms by mimicking the respective Haskell programs. Sipos et al. [34] informally describe a method for systematically producing metafunctions out of functions written in the pure functional programming language CLEAN [36]. They advertise that their Eval metafunction evaluates the produced metaprograms according to the operational semantics of CLEAN. As detailed in [15], whilst they do not formally present their operational semantics, their informal explanation suggests remarkable differences between the operational semantics of CLEAN and that of theirs.

Sinkovics [30] offers certain solutions for improving the functional programming support in Boost.MPL and discusses why they are needed. Sinkovics and Porkoláb [32] advertise implementation of a λ-library on top of the operational semantics of Sipos et al. for embedded functional programming in C++. They also later advertise [28] extension of their λ-library to full support for Haskell. Sinkovics [30,31] offers a restricted solution for emulating let-bindings and explicit currying in template metaprogramming.

Haeri and Schupp [15] demonstrate a real-world exemplification of C++ metaprogramming being functional in nature; exploring impediments against fully automatic cross-lingual development between C++ metaprogramming and Haskell. Armed with that, they suggest further examination of semi-automatic cross-lingual development between C++ metaprogramming and hybrid functional programming languages. Haeri et al. [16] examine that suggestion for Scala and F$^\sharp$. Lincke et al. [19] discuss a real-world semi-automatic translation from Haskell specifications into efficient C++ metaprograms.

Milewski [26] has a number of posts on his personal blog that speak about Monads, their benefits for C++, and how to implement Monadic entities in C++. He also explains how Monads in Haskell can help the understanding of Boost.Proto – one of the most complicated C++ metaprogramming libraries. Moreover, he has a post on how template metaprogramming with variadic templates is similar to lazy list processing in Haskell. Finally, Sankel [29] shows how to implement algebraic datatypes in C++.

Developments in C++ since 2011 have revolutionised metaprogramming. Variadic templates; generalised constant expressions (`constexpr`); alias templates; and `constexpr-if` have made an especially notable impression. Louis Dionne's influential Hana library [9], now included with the C++ Boost libraries, exploits `constexpr`, with richly typed values allowing both runtime and compile-time overloading through a highly distinctive though traditional syntax. Eric Niebler exploits C++11 features in his 3500 line Meta library [27], which utilises variadic templates and demonstrates some support for explicit currying. Numerous other metaprogramming libraries focus on distinctive aspects, including performance [8]; or evaluation schemes, with Metal [10] originally using implicitly lazy evaluation; though now using eager evaluation. With subsets of these libraries now submitted regularly to Boost efforts have also been made [11] to include common patterns within the standard C++ runtime library.

7   Conclusion

C++ template metaprogramming is an expressive, Turing-complete language
which holds the potential to engineer libraries and embedded domain-specific
languages supported by compile-time formal verification. In this paper we have
introduced the Curtains API which provides a model of higher-order functional programming with implicit currying for C++ template metaprograms,
and which aligns with norms adopted by languages such as Haskell, OCaml
and F$^\sharp$.

Three distinct schemes are implemented and described in Sects. 3 and 4. The
first, and simplest, supports only fixed arity metafunctions; the second supports
variadic and nullary metafunctions; while the third can use variadic metafunctions, though only when each instance is annotated with an arity.

With the hope of wider uptake, and of further research, our implementation
has utilised structured recursion, permitting a concise, 30 line implementation
for the simplest of the three schemes described; and 50 lines for the most complex. The choice of the fold's binary combining operation alone accounts for the
difference in implementation between each of the three approaches.

A practical introduction to the API is included in Sect. 5, highlighting the
library's accommodation of a distinct equational definition syntax; as well as
demonstration of the potential for implicit currying to enable the use of structured recursion operators, such as *map* and *fold*; as opposed to the explicit
recursion more commonly employed.

In future we intend to prioritise C++ Concepts [3] integration. Concepts
allow a form of type checking for templates, and are implemented as an extension
within GCC since version 6.1. We believe Concepts can assist users of Curtains
with numerous concerns, including the typing of metafunction classes and their
parameters; and a consequential improvement to error messages. We expect this
should also support our aim to include support for Haskell-style type classes.
Future work will also introduce support for infix alphanumeric operators with
specified associativity and precedence.

A   Appendix A

A.1   Quotation for a Class Template Argument

```
template <template <class...> class M>
struct quote_c {
  template <class... Ts>
  using m_invoke = typename iv1430<void,M,Ts...>::type::type;
};
```

A.2   Curry-Invoke with Arity

```
template <class, class>
  struct curry_invoke_peekn;

template <class F, class T, auto N>
struct curry_invoke_peekn<bases<F,ic<N>>,T> :
id<bases<curry<F,T>,ic<N-1>>> {};

template <class F, class T>
struct curry_invoke_peekn<bases<F,ic<0>>,T>
    : curry_invoke_peekn<invoke<bases<F,ic<0>>>,T> {};

using curry_invoke_peekn_q = quote_c<curry_invoke_peekn>;
```

A.3   Conditional Invoke with Arity

```
template <class F>
struct invoke_ifn                  : id<F>                                {};

template <class F>
struct invoke_ifn<bases<F,ic<0>>> : invoke_ifn<invoke<bases<F,ic<0>>>> {};

template <class F>
using invoke_ifn_t = typename invoke_ifn<F>::type;

using invoke_ifn_q = quote<invoke_ifn_t>;
```

A.4   Additional Utility Metafunctions

```
template <class, class> struct cons;

template <class T, class... Ts>
struct cons<T,list<Ts...>> : id<list<T,Ts...>> {};

using cons_q = quote_c<cons>;

template <class F, class T, class U>
using flip_t = eval<F,U,T>;

using flip_q = quote<flip_t>;
```

A.5   A Sample Variadic Metafunction: `constv_q`

```
template <class T, class...> using constv_t = T;
                          using constv_q = quote<constv_t>;
```

A.6   Point-Free Reverse From a Right-Fold

```
using reverse_pf_q = eval<
                  flip_q,
                  eval<
                    foldr_q,
                    eval<compose_q,eval<flip_q,compose_q>,cons_q>,
                    id_q
                  >,
                  list<>
                >;
```

A.7   Point-Free Left-Fold From a Right-Fold

Implementation derived from Hutton [18]; with assistance from the Pointfree.io website; which provides: *(flip . flip foldr id . (flip (.) .) . flip)*.

```
using foldl_q = eval<
                  compose_q,
                  flip_q,
                  eval<
                    compose_q,
                    eval<flip_q,foldr_q,id_q>,
                    eval<
                      compose_q,
                      eval<compose_q,eval<flip_q,compose_q>>,
                      flip_q
                    >
                  >
                >;
```

A.8   The SKI Combinators

```
template <class X, class Y, class Z>
using S_t = eval<X,Z,eval<Y,Z>>;

using I = id_q;
using K = const_q;
using S = quote<S_t>;
```

A.9   Point-Free Ackermann Function from a Right-Fold

Here S and const_q are used in lieu of *(<*>)* and *pure*, for the Applicative instance of *((−>) r)*. The implementation is derived from Hutton [18]; with assistance from the Pointfree.io website.

```
using ack = eval<
                  foldr_q,
                  eval<
                    const_q,
```

```
        eval<
          S,
          eval<S,eval<const_q,foldr_q>,const_q>,
          eval<flip_q,dollar_q,list<void>>
          >
        >,
        eval<cons_q,void>
      >;
```

A.10   Non-recursive Factorial for Use with the Fixpoint Combinator

```
template <class, class>    struct mul_c;
template <auto M, auto N> struct mul_c<ic<M>, ic<N>> : id<ic<M*N>> {};
using mul = quote_c<mul_c>;

template <class F, class N>
struct fix_fact_c        : id<eval<mul,N,eval<F,eval<pred,N>>>> {};

template <class F>
struct fix_fact_c<F,ic<0>> : id<ic<1>> {};

using fix_fact = quote_c<fix_fact_c>;
```

A.11   Primitive Left-Fold from a C++17 Fold Expression

```
template <class T, class>
struct const_ { using type = T; };

template <class T, class U, class F>
auto operator+(const_<T,F>, const_<U,F>) {
  return const_<invoke<F,T,U>,F>{};
}

template <class F, class Z, class... Ts>
struct ifoldl {
  using type =
    typename decltype((const_<Z,F>{} + ... + const_<Ts,F>{}))::type;
};

using ifoldl_q = quote_c<ifoldl>;
```

A.12   Reduction Steps of a Sample Curtains Expression

```
eval<const_q,id_q,int,char>
   ≡ {eval alias template}
invoke<ifoldl_q,curry_invoke_q,id_q,const_q,id_q,int,char>
   ≡ {invoke alias template}
ifoldl_q::m_invoke<curry_invoke_q,id_q,const_q,id_q,int,char>
   ≡ {ifoldl_q alias template}
```

```
quote_c<ifoldl>::m_invoke<curry_invoke_q,id_q,const_q,id_q,int,char>
    ≡ {m_invoke alias template member of quote_c template}
iv1430<void,ifoldl,curry_invoke_q,id_q,const_q,id_q,int,char>::type::type
    ≡ {type member of iv1430 template specialisation}
ifoldl<curry_invoke_q,id_q,const_q,id_q,int,char>::type
    ≡ {type member of ifoldl specialisation}
ifoldl<curry_invoke_q,invoke<curry_invoke_q,id_q,const_q>,id_q,int,char>::type
    ≡ {invoke alias template}
ifoldl<curry_invoke_q,curry_invoke_q::m_invoke<id_q,const_q>,id_q,int,char>::type
    ≡ {curry_invoke_q alias template}
ifoldl<curry_invoke_q,quote_c<curry_invoke>::m_invoke<id_q,const_q>,id_q,int,char>::type
    ≡ {m_invoke alias template member of quote_c template}
ifoldl<curry_invoke_q,iv1430<void,curry_invoke,id_q,const_q>::type::type,id_q,int,char>::type
    ≡ {type member of iv1430 template specialisation}
ifoldl<curry_invoke_q,curry_invoke<id_q,const_q>::type,id_q,int,char>::type
    ≡ {type member of curry_invoke template specialisation}
ifoldl<curry_invoke_q,invoke<id_q,const_q>,id_q,int,char>::type
    ≡ {invoke alias template}
ifoldl<curry_invoke_q,id_q::m_invoke<const_q>,id_q,int,char>::type
    ≡ {id_q alias template}
ifoldl<curry_invoke_q,quote_c<id>::m_invoke<const_q>,id_q,int,char>::type
    ≡ {m_invoke alias template member of quote_c template}
ifoldl<curry_invoke_q,iv1430<void,id,const_q>::type::type,id_q,int,char>::type
    ≡ {type member of iv1430 template specialisation}
ifoldl<curry_invoke_q,id<const_q>::type,id_q,int,char>::type
    ≡ {type member of id template}
ifoldl<curry_invoke_q,const_q,id_q,int,char>::type
    ≡ {type member of ifoldl specialisation}
ifoldl<curry_invoke_q,invoke<curry_invoke_q,const_q,id_q>,int,char>::type
    ≡ {invoke alias template}
ifoldl<curry_invoke_q,curry_invoke_q::m_invoke<const_q,id_q>,int,char>::type
    ≡ {curry_invoke_q alias template}
ifoldl<curry_invoke_q,quote_c<curry_invoke>::m_invoke<const_q,id_q>,int,char>::type
    ≡ {m_invoke alias template member of quote_c template}
ifoldl<curry_invoke_q,iv1430<void,curry_invoke,const_q,id_q>::type::type,int,char>::type
    ≡ {type member of iv1430 template specialisation}
ifoldl<curry_invoke_q,curry_invoke<const_q,id_q>::type,int,char>::type
    ≡ {type member of curry_invoke primary template}
ifoldl<curry_invoke_q,curry<const_q,id_q>,int,char>::type
    ≡ {type member of ifoldl specialisation}
ifoldl<curry_invoke_q,invoke<curry_invoke_q,curry<const_q,id_q>,int>,char>::type
    ≡ {invoke alias template}
ifoldl<curry_invoke_q,curry_invoke_q::m_invoke<curry<const_q,id_q>,int>,char>::type
    ≡ {curry_invoke_q alias template}
ifoldl<curry_invoke_q,quote_c<curry_invoke>::m_invoke<curry<const_q,id_q>,int>,char>::type
    ≡ {m_invoke alias template member of quote_c template}
ifoldl<curry_invoke_q,iv1430<void,curry_invoke,curry<const_q,id_q>,int>::type::type
,char>::type
    ≡ {type member of iv1430 template specialisation}
ifoldl<curry_invoke_q,curry_invoke<curry<const_q,id_q>,int>::type,char>::type
    ≡ {type member of curry_invoke template specialisation}
ifoldl<curry_invoke_q,invoke<curry<const_q,id_q>,int>,char>::type
    ≡ {invoke alias template}
ifoldl<curry_invoke_q,curry<const_q,id_q>::m_invoke<int>,char>::type
```

```
 ≡ {m_invoke alias template member of curry template}
ifoldl<curry_invoke_q,invoke<const_q,id_q,int>,char>::type
 ≡ {invoke alias template}
ifoldl<curry_invoke_q,const_q::m_invoke<id_q,int>,char>::type
 ≡ {const_q alias template}
ifoldl<curry_invoke_q,quote<const_t>::m_invoke<id_q,int>,char>::type
 ≡ {m_invoke alias template member of quote template}
ifoldl<curry_invoke_q,iv1430<void,const_t,id_q,int>::type,char>::type
 ≡ {type member of iv1430 template specialisation}
ifoldl<curry_invoke_q,const_t<id_q,int>,char>::type
 ≡ {const_t alias template}
ifoldl<curry_invoke_q,id_q,char>::type
 ≡ {type member of ifoldl specialisation}
ifoldl<curry_invoke_q,invoke<curry_invoke_q,id_q,char>>::type
 ≡ {invoke alias template}
ifoldl<curry_invoke_q,curry_invoke_q::m_invoke<id_q,char>>::type
 ≡ {curry_invoke_q alias template}
ifoldl<curry_invoke_q,quote_c<curry_invoke>::m_invoke<id_q,char>>::type
 ≡ {m_invoke alias template member of quote_c template}
ifoldl<curry_invoke_q,iv1430<void,curry_invoke,id_q,char>::type::type>::type
 ≡ {type member of iv1430 template specialisation}
ifoldl<curry_invoke_q,curry_invoke<id_q,char>::type>::type
 ≡ {type member of curry_invoke specialisation}
ifoldl<curry_invoke_q,invoke<id_q,char>>::type
 ≡ {invoke alias template}
ifoldl<curry_invoke_q,id_q::m_invoke<char>>::type
 ≡ {id_q alias template}
ifoldl<curry_invoke_q,quote_c<id>::m_invoke<char>>::type
 ≡ {m_invoke alias template member of quote_c template}
ifoldl<curry_invoke_q,iv1430<void,id,char>::type::type>::type
 ≡ {type member of iv1430 template specialisation}
ifoldl<curry_invoke_q,id<char>::type>::type
 ≡ {type member of id template}
ifoldl<curry_invoke_q,char>::type
 ≡ {type member of ifoldl primary template}
char
```

References

1. International Standard ISO/IEC 14882:1998(E): Programming Languages – C++ (1998)
2. International Standard ISO/IEC 14882:2011: Information Technology - Programming Languages - C++ (2011)
3. International Standard ISO/IEC 19217:2015: Information Technology - Programming Languages - C++ Extensions for Concepts (2015)
4. Abrahams, D., Gurtovoy, A.: C++ Template Metaprogramming: Concepts, Tools, and Techniques from Boost and Beyond. AW Prof., Boston (2004)
5. Alexandrescu, A.: Modern C++ Design: Generic Programming and Design Patterns Applied. Addison-Wesley Longman Publishing, Boston (2001)
6. Austern, M.H.: Generic Programming and the STL: Using and Extending the C++ Standard Template Library. AW Prof. Comp. Series. AW Longman Publ. Co., Boston (1998)

7. Brown, W.E.: Proposing standard library support for the C++ detection idiom. Technical report, ISO WG21 C++ Working Group, April 2015. http://www.open-std.org/jtc1/sc22/wg21/docs/papers/2015/n4436.pdf
8. Deppe, N., Douwes, C., Fresk, E., Holmes, O., Poelen, J.: Kvasir::mpl (2017). https://github.com/kvasir-io/mpl
9. Dionne, L.: Hana (2013). https://github.com/boostorg/hana
10. Dutra, B.: Metal (2018). https://github.com/brunocodutra/metal
11. Escribá, V.J.B.: P0343R1: Meta-programming high-order functions. Technical report, ISO WG21 C++ Library Evolution Working Group (2016)
12. Gil, J., Gutterman, Z.: Compile time symbolic derivation with C++ templates. In: Proceedings of the 4th Conference on USENIX Conference on Object-Oriented Technologies and Systems - COOTS 1998, vol. 4, pp. 18–18. USENIX Association, Berkeley (1998). http://dl.acm.org/citation.cfm?id=1268009.1268027
13. Golodotz, S.: Functional Programming Using C++ Templates (Part 1), October 2007. http://accu.org/index.php/journals/1422
14. Guennebaud, G., Jacob, B., et al.: Eigen v3 (2010). http://eigen.tuxfamily.org
15. Haeri, S.H., Schupp, S.: Functional Metaprogramming in C++ and cross-lingual development with Haskell. Technical report, Uni. Kansas, October 2011. Draft Proceeding of 23rd Symposium on Implementation and Application of Functional Languages, ITTC-FY2012-TR-29952012-01
16. Haeri, S.H., Schupp, S., Hüser, J.: Using functional languages to facilitate C++ Metaprogramming. In: Proceedings of the 8th ACM SIGPLAN Workshop on Generic Programming, WGP 2012, pp. 33–44. ACM (2012)
17. Holmes, O., Kurdej, M., Poelen, J.: Brigand Meta-programming Library (2015). https://github.com/edouarda/brigand
18. Hutton, G.: A tutorial on the universality and expressiveness of fold. J. Funct. Program. 9(4), 355–372 (1999)
19. Lincke, D., Schupp, S., Ionescu, C.: Functional prototypes for generic C++ libraries: a transformational approach based on higher-order, typed signatures. Int. J. Soft. Tools Tech. Transf. 17(1), 91–105 (2015). https://doi.org/10.1007/s10009-014-0299-0
20. Lumsdaine, A., Siek, J., Lee, L.Q.: The Boost Graph Library: User Guide and Reference Manual. Addison-Wesley Longman Publishing Co., Inc, Boston (2002)
21. Mach, S.: Metatrace (2010). https://github.com/phresnel/metatrace
22. Marlow, S.: Haskell 2010 Language Report (2010)
23. McBride, C.: Faking it: simulating dependent types in Haskell. J. Funct. Program. 12(5), 375–392 (2002)
24. Meijer, E., Fokkinga, M., Paterson, R.: Functional programming with bananas, lenses, envelopes and barbed wire. In: Hughes, J. (ed.) FPCA 1991. LNCS, vol. 523, pp. 124–144. Springer, Heidelberg (1991). https://doi.org/10.1007/3540543961_7
25. Merrill, J.: C++ Core Issue 1430 (2011). http://www.open-std.org/jtc1/sc22/wg21/docs/cwg_active.html#1430
26. Milewski, B.: Bartosz Milewski's Programming Cafe. http://bartoszmilewski.wordpress.com
27. Niebler, E.: Meta: A Tiny Metaprogramming Library (2014). https://ericniebler.github.io/meta/index.html
28. Porkoláb, Z., Sinkovics, Á.: C++ template metaprogramming with embedded Haskell. In: Proceedings of 8th International Conference on Generative Programming & Component Engineering (GPCE 2009), pp. 99–108. ACM, New York (2009)
29. Sankel, D.: Algebraic Data Types Series, C++ Next: The Next Generation of C++. http://cpp-next.com/archive/2010/07/algebraic-data-types/

30. Sinkovics, Á.: Functional extensions to the boost metaprogram library. Electron. Notes Theor. Comput. Sci. **264**(5), 85–101 (2011). Proceedings of 2nd Workshop on Generative Technologies. https://doi.org/10.1016/j.entcs.2011.06.006
31. Sinkovics, Á.: Nested lamda expressions with let expressions in C++ template metaprograms, pp. 63–76 (2011)
32. Sinkovics, Á., Porkoláb, Z.: Expressing C++ template metaprograms as lambda expressions. In: TFP, pp. 1–15 (2009)
33. Sinkovics, Á., Porkoláb, Z.: Metaparse: Compile-Time Parsing with Template Metaprogramming. Aspen, USA (2012). https://github.com/boostcon/cppnow_presentations_2012/blob/master/papers/metaparse_paper.pdf
34. Sipos, Á., Porkoláb, Z., Pataki, N., Zsók, V.: Meta<Fun>: towards a functional-style interface for C++ template metaprograms. Technical report, Eötvös Loránd Uni, Fac. of Inf., Dept. Prog. Langs., Pázmány Péter sétány 1/C H-1117 Budapest, Hungary (2007)
35. Unruh, E.: Prime Number Computation (1994). ANSI X3J16-94-0075/ISO WG21-462
36. van Eekelen, M., de Mol, M.J.: Mixed lazy/strict graph semantics. In: Grelck, C., Huch, F. (eds.) 16th International Workshop on Implementation of Applied Functional Languages, IFL 2004, pp. 245–260. Technical report 0408, Christian-Albrechts-Universität zu Kiel, Lüebeck, Germany, September 2004
37. Vandevoorde, D., Josuttis, N.M., Gregor, D.: C++ Templates: The Complete Guide, 2nd edn. AW Prof., Boston (2018)
38. Veldhuizen, T.L.: Expression templates. C++ Rep. **7**(5), 26–31 (1995)
39. Veldhuizen, T.L.: Scientific computing: C++ versus Fortran: C++ has more than caught up. Dr. Dobb's J. Softw. Tools **22**(11), 34, 36–38, 91 (1997)

Towards Optic-Based Algebraic Theories: The Case of Lenses

J. López-González[1,2]([⊠]) [ID] and Juan M. Serrano[1,2]

[1] Habla Computing, S.L., Leganés, Spain
j.lopezgo@alumnos.urjc.es
[2] Universidad Rey Juan Carlos, Móstoles, Spain
juanmanuel.serrano@urjc.es

Abstract. Optics provide rich abstractions and composition patterns to access and manipulate immutable data structures. However, the state of real applications is mostly handled through databases, caches, web services, etc. In this effectful setting, the usefulness of optics is severely limited, whereas algebraic theories, thanks to their potential to abstract away from particular infrastructures, shine. Unfortunately, there is a severe lack of standard algebraic theories, e.g. like MonadState, that programmers can reuse to avoid writing their domain repositories from scratch. This paper argues that optics can serve as a fruitful metaphor to design a rich catalogue of state-based algebraic theories, and focuses on the paradigmatic case of lenses. It shows how lenses can be generalised into an algebraic theory; how compositionality of these algebraic theories can be founded on lens composition; and how to exploit the resulting abstractions in the modular design of data layers. The paper systematically uses Coq for all its definitions and proofs.

Keywords: Lens · Optic · Algebraic theory · Monad · State · Repository · Coq

1 Introduction

Optics provide rich abstractions and patterns to access and manipulate immutable data structures. They are also known as *functional references*, since they point at *parts* which are contained or determined by a *whole*. For instance, a *lens* [1] is an optic that points at a single value which is always available from the context; an *affine traversal* points at a single value that is not necessarily available; a *traversal* [2] points at a sequence of values; and so on. Each optic comes equipped with an interface which is specialized in evolving the whole data structure by evolving the parts it is pointing at. It is very common to find lenses pointing at particular fields of a record. We will use the following records to illustrate the idea, where the details about person are irrelevant[1]:

---

[1] Coq will be used throughout the paper.

Research Article. Main author is a research student.

M. Pałka and M. Myreen (Eds.): TFP 2018, LNCS 11457, pp. 74–93, 2019.
https://doi.org/10.1007/978-3-030-18506-0_4

```
Record department := mkDepartment
{ budget : nat
; lecturers : list person }.

Record university := mkUniversity
{ name : string
; departments : list department
; students : list person }.
```

For instance, we could define budgetLn, a lens that points at the budget field of department[2]. Among other methods, lenses supply a modifying operator ($\sim_{ln}$), which takes a function over the part and an original whole as arguments, and produces a new version of the whole as a result, where the part has been updated by applying the input function over it. We could exploit this operator to double the budget of the department as follows:

```
Definition doubleDepBudget : department → department :=
    budgetLn ∼ₗₙ (λ b ⇒ b * 2).
```

We may also define a lens for fields that refer to a sequence of values such as lecturers or departments. For instance, a lens departmentsLn would allow us to access and modify the whole list of departments of a given university. But traversals offer a much better interface in this case. For instance, they provide a modifying operator $\sim_{tr}$ which applies the same modifying function over all the foci that the traversal is pointing at, so you do not need to manipulate the list manually. Thus, we could use this operator to double the budget of every single department in the university:

```
Definition doubleUnivBudgets : university → university :=
    departmentsTr ∼ₜᵣ doubleDepBudget.
```

One of the most attractive features of optics is that they compose heterogeneously, e.g. it is possible to combine lenses with traversals. As an example, consider the following definition, where we emphasize this aspect:

```
Definition doubleUnivBudgets' : university → university :=
    (departmentsLn ▷ each ▷ budgetLn) ∼ₜᵣ (λb ⇒ b * 2).
```

Although you might ignore certain details from the previous definition, it is not difficult to infer that it is building a traversal that points at the budget of each department in a modular way, and invoking to its modifying operator. In fact, as the name suggests, this is just an alternative way of implementing the very same logic.

In summary, we can appreciate two major benefits from optics, namely the diversity of abstractions and their compositional capabilities. However, optics are restricted to work with immutable data structures, whereas the state of real applications, like university information systems, is mostly handled through databases, web services, caches and so forth. In this setting, the optic approach to handle state is not useless, but severely limited. Instead, one of the most prominent techniques in the realm of effectful systems are algebraic theories [3].

---

[2] For the moment, we will ignore the details about lens representations.

Basically, these theories allow us to strive for generality and define a *data layer* that abstracts away from the particular infrastructures that actually handle state (caches, databases, immutable state transformers, etc.). For instance, we could build an *ad hoc* repository to deal with university state in a general way. We encode it as a typeclass [4]:

```
Class UniversityAlg (p : Type → Type) :=
{ getName : p string
; modName (f : string → string) : p unit
; getDepartments : p (list department)
; modDepartments (f : department → department) : p unit }.
```

This algebraic theory defines the class of computational effects p that we may use to get or modify the name and departments of a given university[3]. Building our business logic upon algebraic repositories of this kind enables us to remain unaware of particular infrastructure details. Unfortunately, this approach has several difficulties, that we show in the next paragraphs.

Firstly, despite the fact that UniversityAlg hides the state of the university behind p, some of their methods are exposing the immutable department structure in their signatures. The information associated to a department could be large enough to make it non-optimal or even impractical to instantiate such a value. In these circumstances, the obvious choice is describing the data layer of a department in a separate algebraic theory, which would describe the accessors to the department fields and would have its own computational effect q. The problem with this arrangement is that it actually becomes cumbersome to compose the heterogeneous programs p, q, etc., generated by the different theories, specially when a large number of them are involved.

Secondly, we are not using standard abstractions to describe the university data layer, and therefore UniversityAlg contains very fine-grained methods. This contrasts with the optic approach, where lens or traversal provide standarized methods to get or modify fields of domain entities. In this regard, we could replace both getName and modName with a MonadState evidence with focus on the name. This standard algebraic theory fits perfectly to view and update this field in a general way. However, it does not provide specialized methods to handle sequences of values. Unluckily, we do not know of any other standard theory, analogous to traversal, to deal with multiple values at this abstract level. Even if we had them available, it would not be easy to determine a notion of composition for them.

In this paper, we argue that optics can serve as a fruitful metaphor to design a rich catalogue of state-based algebras, that serve as an *embedded domain specific language* (EDSL) [5] for the implementation of data layers, aimed at the software industry. This EDSL would allow programmers to write code at an algebraic level of abstraction while using a rich catalogue of standard and composable abstractions, analogous to that supplied by optics.

---

[3] We could also have defined accessors to *update* the name or departments with a new value passed as parameter, but they are not used in the upcoming examples.

More specifically, this paper sets out to establish the essential pillars in pursuit of this golden inventory of so-called optic algebras. In particular, it focuses on lenses and MonadState as the playing field to identify the first member of such a catalogue. These are the main contributions of the paper:

- We show that MonadState strictly generalises lenses. Particularly, we show that lenses can be represented as the state monad instance of this algebraic theory. Since MonadState distills the algebraic essence of a lens, we will refer to it as *lens algebra* (Sect. 3).
- We show how to generalise the state monad morphism representation of lenses [6] into *lens algebra homomorphisms* (Sect. 4). This abstraction enables composition between lens algebras.
- We provide a design pattern to implement the data layer and the business logic of applications, using lens algebras (Sect. 3.1) and lens algebra homomorphisms (Sect. 4.1) as building blocks. We use the university example as a guide for this task.

As mentioned in the previous paragraphs, Sects. 3 and 4 contain the bulk of this paper. Section 5 reviews related work in the context of our goals, particularly monadic lenses [7], entangled state monads [6,8] and profunctor optics [9]. Section 6 concludes by outlining a methodology to generalize other optics into their optic algebra counterparts, and points to *Stateless*, a work-in-progress EDSL implemented in Scala that aims to bring optic algebras to the software industry. All definitions, examples and propositions in this paper have been formalized using Coq and are supplied as complementary material in Sect. A. Before going into further detail, we will provide a brief background in Sect. 2.

2   Background

For the sake of brevity, we will illustrate the background definitions with an idealized version of Coq, where we adopt a notation closer to math. For instance, *fun* is replaced by λ, *forall* is replaced by $\forall$, and so on. In addition, we deliberately ignore *level* and *associativity* from Notation for simplicity. Additional adjustments will be mentioned as they arise.

2.1   Natural Transformations

Definition 1 (natural transformation). *Given functors f and g, a natural transformation is a family of morphisms that turns objects on f into objects on g. We can represent it as a polymorphic function.*

```
Class natTrans f g '{Functor f, Functor g} := mkNatTrans
{ runNatTrans : ∀ X, f X → g X }.
Notation "f ⤳ g" := natTrans f g.
```

The transformation must preserve the following commuting property.

```
Class natTransLaws f g '{Functor f, Functor g} (φ : f ↝ g) :=
{ natTrans_comm : ∀ A B (fa : f A) (g : A → B),
                  φ (fmap g fa) = fmap g (φ fa) }.
```

Note that we replaced runNatTrans φfx by φ fx to improve the readability of
definitions. Moving forward, natural transformations are composable.

```
Definition composeNT {f g h} '{Functor f, Functor g, Functor h}
                     (φ : g ↝ h) (ψ : f ↝ g) : f ↝ h :=
  mkNatTrans (λ _ fx ⇒ φ (ψ fx)).
Notation "φ · ψ" := composeNT φ ψ
```

The following definition arises naturally when we pay attention to monadic[4]
functors.

Definition 2 (monad morphism). *A monad morphism is a natural transformation between monadic type constructors that also satisfies these laws.*

```
Record monad_morphism {f g} '{Monad f, Monad g} (φ : f ↝ g) :=
{ returnMap : ∀ X (x : X),
              φ (ret x) = ret x
; distrBind : ∀ A B (fa : f A) (f : A → f B),
              φ (fa ≫= f) = φ fa ≫= (λ a ⇒ φ (f a)) }.
```

Broadly speaking, these laws are telling us that a monad morphism should distribute over ≫= and that mapping ret from the original monad should produce
ret in the destination monad. In effect, a monad morphism allows us to *push*
whole computations down into f and afterwards lifts the result back to g.

2.2   State

We recall the state monad [10]:

Definition 3 (state monad). *State is a data type that transforms a value
into a new version of it, while providing an additional output along with the
transformed value.*

```
Record state (S Out : Type) := mkState
{ runState : S → Out * S }.
```

State transformations can be composed using Monad *combinators:*

```
Instance Monad_state {S : Type} : Monad (state S) :=
{ ret  := λ A o ⇒ mkState (λ s ⇒ (o, s))
; bind := λ A B m f ⇒ mkState (λ s ⇒ let (o, s') := runState m s
                                      in runState (f o) s') }.
```

---

[4] We assume familiarity with monads. You can find the particular Coq encoding that
we use for Monad in the supplementary material (Sect. A).

The output provided by a state transformation can be used to include additional information about the transformation which has taken place.

We also provide a pair of convenience methods which will be helpful later on:

```
Definition evalState {S Out} (st : state S Out) (s : S) : Out :=
  fst (runState st s).
```

```
Definition execState {S Out} (st : state S Out) (s : S) : S :=
  snd (runState st s).
```

2.3   Lens

As stated in [1], lenses approach the view update problem for tree-structured data.

Definition 4 (asymmetric monomorphic lens). *An asymmetric lens consists of a pair of functions, one of them* views *the part from the whole and the other one* updates *the part from an old whole, returning a new whole. This is the concrete monomorphic[5] lens representation:*

```
Record lens (S A : Type) := mkLens
{ view : S → A
; update : S → A → S
; modify (f : A → A) : S → S :=λ s ⇒ update s (f (view s)) }.
Notation "ln ~ln f" :=modify ln f.
```

The type parameters S and A serve as the whole and the part, respectively. Lens operations must obey certain laws [11] to be considered very well-behaved [6]:

```
Record very_well-behaved {S A} (ln : lens S A) :=
{ view_update :    ∀ s,         update ln s (view ln s) = s
; update_view :    ∀ s a,       view ln (update ln s a) = a
; update_update : ∀ s a1 a2, update ln (update ln s a1) a2 =
                                update ln s a2 }.
```

From now on, we will assume asymmetric very well-behaved monomorphic lenses when we refer to *lens*, unless otherwise specified.

The very well-behaved class of lenses forms a category, where lenses position themselves as morphisms. The identity lens is the one where part and whole correspond to the same value:

```
Definition identityLn {A} : lens A A :=
  mkLens id (λ _ ⇒ id).
```

The composition of concrete lenses is clumsily achieved by the following function:

---

[5] There exists a polymorphic lens version which is more general, where update declares a different type for the part, leading to a different type for the resulting whole.

[6] If we discard update_update, we can talk about well-behaved lenses.

```
Definition composeLn {S A B}
    (ln1 : lens S A) (ln2 : lens A B) : lens S B :=
  mkLens (view ln2 · view ln1)
         (λ s a' ⇒ update ln1 s (update ln2 (view ln1 s) a')).
Notation "ln1 ▷ ln2" := composeLn ln1 ln2.
```

There are other lens representations that improve composability, the most popular ones being *van Laarhoven* [2] and *profunctor* [9] approaches. In this paper, however, our preferred choice is a representation based on monad morphisms [12], that also enjoys similar benefits with respect to compositionality:

Lemma 1. *A monad morphism* state A ⤳state S *is isomorphic to a very well-behaved* lens S A.

```
Definition lens' (S A : Type) := state A ⤳ state S.
```

Informally, the state monad morphism representation can be seen as a morphism from a program that evolves the part into a program that evolves the whole.

2.4   MonadState

We introduce now the MonadState typeclass [3], as an algebraic theory to manipulate state in a general way:

Definition 5 (MonadState typeclass). *MonadState classifies all those effects which are able to access and manipulate an inner state. It supplies a couple of methods, the first of them* gets *the current state and the second one* puts *a new state, by replacing the existing one.*

```
Class MonadState (A : Type) (m : Type → Type) '{Monad m} :=
{ get : m A
; put : A → m unit }.
```

These are the properties that should be held by MonadState *instances to be considered lawful:*

```
Record MonadState_Laws {A m} '{MonadState A m} :=
{ get_get : get ≫= (λ s1 ⇒ get ≫= (λ s2 ⇒ ret (s1, s2))) =
            get ≫= (λ s ⇒ ret (s, s))
; get_put : get ≫= put = ret tt
; put_get : ∀ s, put s ≫ get = put s ≫ ret s
; put_put : ∀ s1 s2, put s1 ≫ put s2 = put s2 }.
```

Among the effects that are able to instantiate this typeclass, state is probably the most widespread one:

```
Instance MonadState_state {S} : MonadState S (state S) :=
{ get := mkState (λ s ⇒ (s, s))
; put := λ s ⇒ mkState (λ _ ⇒ (tt, s)) }.
```

Note how the state hidden by state S matches with the focus S we are providing access to via the MonadState interface.

3   The Algebraic Theory for Lenses

There is a degree of overlap and a number of similarities between lens S A and
MonadState A m. Firstly, they provide analogous methods: both view and get
share the notion of reading a value from the current state; analogously, both
update and put share the notion of writing or replacing the state with a new
version of it. Secondly, both abstractions declare a set of properties that must
be held by their instances to be considered lawful. Letting aside get_get from
MonadState, it is easy to observe a strong correspondence among the rest of
them. Thirdly, the university example from Sect. 1 enabled us to appreciate that
both lens and MonadState are suited for accessing and manipulating a single
state which is always available from the context. Throughout this section, we will
show the precise connections between them, starting with an informal derivation
to pave the way.

If we pay attention to view : S → A and update : S → A → S from
lens, we can see that both methods contain an origin source S as first parameter.
However, the rest of the signature does not look homogeneous. In fact, view is
producing an output A and update requires an additional input A and produces
a new version of the state S as a result. Now, we will try to homogenise both
methods, so they both contemplate the notion of input, output and resulting
state, aiming at abstracting away the common parts. We show the process with
the following informal derivation[7]:

```
( view    : S        → A
, update : S → A →         S)
≃ [functional extensionality]
( λ s   ⇒ view s     : S        → A
, λ s a ⇒ update s a : S → A →         S)
≃ [add contrived input to view]
( λ s _ ⇒ view s     : S → 1 → A
, λ s a ⇒ update s a : S → A →         S)
≃ [add contrived resulting state to view]
( λ s _ ⇒ (view s, s) : S → 1 → A * S
, λ s a ⇒ update s a  : S → A →         S)
≃ [add contrived output to update]
( λ s _ ⇒ (view s, s)        : S → 1 → A * S
, λ s a ⇒ (tt, update s a) : S → A → 1 * S)
≃ [flip parameters]
( λ _ s ⇒ (view s, s)        : 1 → S → A * S
, λ a s ⇒ (tt, update s a) : A → S → 1 * S)
≃ [abstract with state monad]
( λ _ ⇒ mkState (λ s ⇒ (view s, s))       : 1 → state S A
, λ a ⇒ mkState (λ s ⇒ (tt, update s a)) : A → state S 1)
```

As can be seen, this normalisation process leads us to a pair of kleisli arrows
for the state monad with S as inner value. Having detected this common structure, we could abstract away state S from their signatures, which would result

---

[7] We represent unit as 1 to simplify signatures.

in 1 → m A for the derived view and A → m 1 for the derived update. These are exactly the signatures of the methods get and put supplied by MonadState. So, thinking of lens as an instance of MonadState – where A is the focus and state S is the monadic effect – seems plausible. Notice that this instance is not the same as MonadState_state (Sect. 2.4), where the focus type does match with the one that accompanies state. Now, converting concrete lenses into MonadState instances, and vice versa, turns out to be straightforward.

```
Instance lens_2_ms {S A} (ln : lens S A)
    : MonadState A (state S) :=
{ get   := mkState (λ s ⇒ (view ln s, s))
; put a := mkState (λ s ⇒ (tt, update ln s a)) }.
```

```
Definition ms_2_lens {S A} (ms : MonadState A (state S))
    : lens S A :=
{| view s     := evalState get s
;  update s a := execState (put a) s |}.
```

These methods evidence the following statement.

Proposition 1. *There is an isomorphism between any lawful instance of* MonadState A (state S) *and a very well-behaved* lens S A.

We claim therefore that MonadState is a generalisation of lens. Broadly speaking, MonadState captures the algebra to view and update a single state which is always available, but at a higher level of abstraction. This is the reason why we will refer to MonadState as *lens algebraic theory*, or just *lens algebra* for short.

Definition 6. *Lens algebra is an alternative way of referring to* MonadState, *emphasizing the fact that it generalizes a* lens *by distilling its algebraic essence.*

```
Record lensAlg (p : Type → Type) (A : Type) '{M : Monad p} :=
{ view : p A
; update : A → p unit
; modify (f : A → A) : p unit := view >>= (update · f) }.
Notation "ln ~ln f" := modify ln f.
```

Very well-behaved lens algebra laws are exactly MonadState *laws.*

```
Record lensAlgLaws {p A} '{Monad p} (ln : lensAlg p A) :=
{ view_view :
    view ln >>= (λ s1 ⇒ view ln >>= (λ s2 ⇒ ret (s1, s2))) =
    view ln >>= (λ s ⇒ ret (s, s))
; view_update : view ln >>= update ln = ret tt
; update_view : ∀ s, update ln s >> view ln = update ln s >> ret
    s
; update_update : ∀ s1 s2, update ln s1 >> update ln s2 =
                           update ln s2 }.
```

If we discard update_update *from the set we get well-behaved lens algebras.*

Remark 1. Normally, instances of `MonadState` where the focus and the state hidden by the effect differ are unusual in the functional programming community. This is probably a consequence of the functional dependency between the effect and the focus that some languages impose to this typeclass in order to avoid ambiguity while resolving instances [13]. We are not interested in resolving lens algebras implicitly, that is the reason why we use a `Record` to represent them.

Section 2.4 showed `MonadState_state` as the most widespread instance of `MonadState`. Its type is `MonadState S (state S)`, where the types of focus and inner value of `state` match. In fact, this instance corresponds to a well-known lens.

Corollary 1. `MonadState_state` *(Sect. 2.4) is isomorphic to* `identityLn` *(Sect. 2.3).*

Once we have positioned lens algebra, or `MonadState`, as a standard abstraction, analogous to lens, but at a more general setting, we will use it to implement the data layer of the university example.

3.1 Data Layer Design with Lens Algebras

Since this paper puts focus on lenses, we will simplify the original example, ignoring traversable structures. Thereby, instead of having a list of departments hanging from the university, we will assume a unique math department in the university repository:

```
Record UniversityAlg (p : Type → Type) :=
{ getName : p string
; modName (f : string → string) : p unit
; getMathDep : p department
; modMathDep (f : department → department) : p unit }.
```

As can be seen, we use a record instead of a class, for analogous reasons to the ones mentioned in Remark 1. Lens algebras encapsulate the functionality that we need to get, update or even modify (which we defined as a derived method) a particular field. Thereby, we could replace the corresponding fine-grained accessors from the university repository with this abstraction.

```
Record UniversityAlg p `{Monad p} :=
{ nameLn : lensAlg p string
; mathDepLn : lensAlg p department }.
```

The replacement requires the introduction of a `Monad` evidence to satisfy lens algebra dependencies.

As introduced in Sect. 1, it is not recommended to expose the immutable structure `department` in the data layer. To avoid that, we should segregate department into a new repository, and provide an evidence to it from the university algebraic theory. It would result in the following data layer:

```
Record DepartmentAlg p Dep '{Monad p} :=
{ budgetLn : lensAlg p nat }.

Record UniversityAlg p '{Monad p} :=
{ nameLn : lensAlg p string
; q : Type → Type
; Dep : Type
; ev : '{DepartmentAlg q Dep}
; mathDepLn : lensAlg p Dep }.
```

As a result, we get a new theory DepartmentAlg parameterized with its own effect p and a concrete type Dep. For its part, UniversityAlg has been extended to establish the link to the new algebraic theory[8]. Note that Dep does not necessarily correspond to the data structure department. Instead, it determines the minimal information that we need to know in order to interoperate with the particular infrastructure. For instance, it could be an *url*, the primary key in a database table, or any other kind of index.

Given this implementation of the data layer, we should be able to program the business logic that doubles the budget of a department.

```
Definition doubleDepBudget p Dep
  '{Monad p}
  (data : DepartmentAlg p Dep) : p unit :=
  budgetLn data ~ₗₙ (λ b ⇒ b * 2).
```

It is easy to see that we have to supply the department repository as an additional parameter. Then, we simply extract the lens algebra from it and invoke its modifying operator. The result type of this function is p unit, a program that achieves a modification over the department and outputs nothing.

We could also be interested in implementing the logic to double the university budgets[9]. To do so, we should be able to compose mathDepLn with budgetLn somehow. However, we do not have the means to adapt q programs, the ones that evolve a department, into p programs, the ones that evolve the whole university. We need new abstractions, close to natural transformations, to enable this kind of composability, which will be introduced in the next section.

4   Composable Lens Algebras

So far, we have taken concrete lenses to a more general setting by abstracting away state S from them, resulting in lens algebras. This abstraction provides an analogous interface to the one we find in lenses, but it does not contemplate the notion of composition. On the other hand, Sect. 1 introduced an alternative lens representation with better composition guarantees, encoded as a state monad morphism. In this section, we will achieve an analogous abstraction over this representation, aiming at enabling composition between lens algebras at this

---

[8] Here, we assume that ev also collects a Monad evidence.

[9] Note that this would only involve the math department in the new configuration.

general algebraic setting. Equipped with the new abstractions, we will evolve the university data layer to its final version, which will allow us to implement the logic to double the university budgets.

Fortunately, the alternative lens representation contains an explicit mention to state S, so we do not need additional derivations to be able to abstract this structure away. As a result, we get a new definition.

Definition 7. *lensAlg′ is a monad morphism* state A ⤳p *that adapts* state A *programs – which evolve the focus – into* p *programs – that contextualize and evolve the whole.*

```
Definition lensAlg′ (p : Type → Type) (A : Type) '{Monad p} :=
  state A ⤳ p.
```

As the name suggests, this abstraction is directly connected with the original lens algebra, and hence MonadState. Indeed, we could recover view and update methods by turning the new representation into the original one:

```
Definition lensAlg′_2_lensAlg {p A} '{Monad p}
  (φ : lensAlg′ p A) : lensAlg p A :=
{| view       := φ (mkState (λ a ⇒ (a, a)))
;  update a′ := φ (mkState (λ a ⇒ (tt, a′))) |}.
```

The connection also holds in the opposite direction.

Lemma 2. *There is an isomorphism between a lawful* lensAlg p A *and a monad morphism* lensAlg′p A.

Despite having defined an alternative representation for lens algebra which consists of a unique morphism, we face severe limitations when we try to compose a pair of them. Particularly, we need to fix the type of program for the second lens algebra to state X, where X corresponds to the type of focus for the first lens algebra. By doing so, the only program that we are able to generalize is the one which corresponds to the leftmost lens algebra in the composition chain. We need to overcome this strong limitation.

We have abstracted away state S from the alternative lens definition, but there remains an additional reference to state A in the resulting abstraction. Is it feasible to abstract it away as well? Interestingly, the state programs that are passed through the monad morphism in lensAlg′_2_lensAlg are exactly the ones that we defined in MonadState_state for get and put. Given this situation, we could abstract the reference to state A away while retaining the lens algebra interface, as long as we supply a MonadState evidence in exchange for it.

Definition 8. *Lens algebra homomorphisms abstract away any reference to* state A *from* lensAlg′p A, *resulting in a new higher kinded type parameter* q *which must be an instance of* MonadState A q.

```
Definition lensAlgHom p q A '{Monad p} '{MonadState A q} :=
  q ⤳ p.
```

The new definition does not contain explicit mentions to state any more, providing a general q instead. The MonadState evidence is all that we need to recover the interface of lens algebras.

```
Definition lensAlgHom_2_lensAlg {p q A}
  `{Monad p} `{MonadState A q}
   (φ : lensAlgHom p q A) : lensAlg p A :=
{| view       := φ get
;  update a' := φ (put a') |}.
```

Proposition 2. *A lens algebra homomorphism* lensAlgHom p q A *induces a lawful lens algebra* lensAlg p A.

As we can see, φ maps get into view and put into update. If we take Definition 6 into account, by doing so, we are actually mapping a lens algebra into another one. That is the reason why we refer to the new abstraction as *lens algebra homomorphism*. Particularly, we are turning an instance of lensAlg q A —or MonadState A q— into an instance of lensAlg p A, where the type of programs differ, but the focus A is exactly the same. In fact, the homomorphism is turning q programs that evolve the focus from certain context into p programs that evolve the very same focus from a broader one. This idea reassembles the notion of whole and part from ordinary lenses.

Remark 2. If lens algebra is an alternative way of representing MonadState, why do not we use the former in the definition of lens algebra homomorphisms? As we said in Remark 1, and contrary to lens algebras, MonadState usually declares a functional dependency that evidences that the type of program determines the type of focus. This is exactly the behaviour that we are interested in for the homomorphism constraint, since we want to keep the inner q program as close to the focus as possible. In this context, it is fine to exploit the mechanism for implicit typeclass resolution provided by the language.

Having abstracted state A from the new definition, composition becomes trivial. In fact, it is basically natural transformation composition:

```
Definition composeLnAlgHom {p q r A B}
   `{MonadState B r} `{MonadState A q} `{Monad p}
    (φ : lensAlgHom p q A)
    (ψ : lensAlgHom q r B) : lensAlgHom p r B :=
  φ · ψ.
Notation "hom1 ▷ hom2" := composeLnAlgHom hom1 hom2
```

The composition function is closed under composition and preserves identity and associativity laws, which leads us to the following lemma.

Corollary 2. *Lens algebra homomorphisms conform a category.*

All in all, a lens algebra homomorphism is a composable abstraction that supplies the interface of lens algebras. This abstraction is more general than lens algebras, but we can overwrite their alternative representation when we instantiate q to a state program on the focus:

```
Definition lensAlg' p A := lensAlgHom p (state A) A
```

Now, we will exploit lens algebra homomorphisms to evolve the university data layer to its final version.

4.1   Extending Data Layer Design with Homomorphisms

In Sect. 3.1 we faced some limitations to compose lens algebras, aggravated by the separation of algebraic theories for university and department. Here, we will overcome those limitations using the new definitions. Firstly, we will encode nameLn and budgetLn as lensAlg' structures. Secondly, we will replace mathDepLn with a lens algebra homomorphism, acting as the nexus between university and department. The resulting data layer is represented as follows:

```
Record DepartmentAlg p Dep '{MonadState Dep p} :=
{ budgetLn : lensAlg' p nat }.

Record UniversityAlg p '{Monad p} :=
{ nameLn : lensAlg' p string
; q : Type → Type
; Dep : Type
; ev : '{DepartmentAlg q Dep}
; mathDepLn : lensAlgHom p q Dep }.
```

Also notice how we extended the evidence in DepartmentAlg to be MonadState instead of simply Monad, since we need it to enable composition. Now, we have all the ingredients to implement the business logic to double university budgets.

```
Definition doubleMathBudget p
    '{Monad p}
    (data : UniversityAlg p): p unit :=
(mathDepLn data ▷ budgetLn (ev data)) ~ₗₙ (λ b ⇒ b * 2).
```

The implementation of this method reflects the same elegance which is customary in optic-based designs. First of all, the data accessors are composable, so we can combine the lens algebra that focuses on the university math department with the lens algebra that focuses on the department budget. Second of all, the resulting lens algebra can invoke the modifying operator ($\sim_{ln}$), passing the function that doubles the budget as argument. In contrast with common optic-based designs, however, this business logic is implemented once and for all, not only for immutable data structures, but for alternative state-based infrastructures (e.g. a relational database) as well.

Now imagine we are interested in knowing the resulting budget after doubling it. There is an obvious implementation for that logic: first we modify the value and then we consult it. Lens algebras provide such operations, and the monadic effect allows us to compose their results:

```
Definition doubleMathBudgetR p '{Monad p}
    (data : UniversityAlg p) : p nat :=
let ln := mathDepLn data ▷ budgetLn (ev data)
in ln ~ₗₙ (λ b ⇒ b * 2) ≫ view ln.
```

However, if we take into account the complexity of the potential underlying infrastructures, this implementation would not be optimal, since it requires accessing to the department twice. We could solve this situation by exploiting the distributive property over bind provided by lens algebra homomorphisms:

```
Definition doubleMathBudgetR' p '{Monad p}
    (data : UniversityAlg p) : p nat :=
  let bLn := budgetLn (ev data)
  in (mathDepLn data) (bLn ~ₗₙ (λ b ⇒ b * 2) ≫ view bLn).
```

Instead of performing two small operations – involving a particular field – over the whole state, this version performs a unique larger operation over the inner focus, and then lifts the result. This way of programming is essentially enabled by adopting natural transformations, and it turns out to be extremely handy for many situations, even when different fields are involved. Moreover, it may lead to significant optimizations in performance, since this strategy allows us in principle to push down whole programs to the underlying infrastructure of particular repositories, and reduce the number of interactions between them.

5   Related Work

5.1   Profunctor Lenses

There is a lens representation based on the notion of *profunctors*, which can be seen as a generalisation of functions, that has acquired major significance recently [9]. It is encoded as follows.

```
Definition pLens S T A B := ∀ p '{Cartesian p}, p A B → p S T.
```

Note that this representation corresponds with a polymorphic lens, hence the four type parameters. To recover the monomorphic version, we should restrict instances to pLens S S A A. If we ignore the Cartesian constraint, which is just a member of the profunctor hierarchy, we appreciate that this definition consists of a pure function that turns p A B, a generalized function on the part, into p S T, a generalized function on the whole.

Despite the generality provided by profunctors, we cannot use this lens representation to replace lens algebras. For instance, let us assume a profunctor lens focusing on the budget of a department, whose type is pLens Dep Dep nat nat, where Dep corresponds to an index, as introduced in Sect. 3.1. As any other profunctor lens, it works for all Cartesian instances. Pickering *et al.* illustrate that *UpStar* is an instance of that typeclass. If we combine it with the *Constant* functor, we recover the view method from the lens. In this context, we obtain a pure function from Dep to nat. This stands in conflict with Dep being an index, which imposes an effectful computation as the only way to retrieve the budget.

All in all, profunctor lens is yet another lens representation, and despite its great composition capabilities, it is also generalized by lens algebras (provided that we constraint ourselves to the monomorphic version of lenses). If we want to relate lens algebras with other abstractions, they must contemplate computational effects in their definition somehow.

5.2   Monadic Lenses

Monadic lenses are a novel approach to combine lenses with monadic effects [7]. Its definition is very similar to `lens`, though the updating method is effectful.

```
Record mLens S A m `{Monad m} := mkMLens
{ mview   : S → A
; mupdate : S → A → m S }.
```

Note that `mview` is lacking an effect in its result deliberately, since including it would lead to severe composition problems. The following laws hold for a well-behaved monadic lens:

```
Record mLensLaws {S A m} `{Monad m}
    (mln : mLens S A m) := mkMLensLaws
{ mview_mupdate : ∀ s, mupdate mln s (mview mln s) = ret s
; mupdate_mview : ∀ B (k : S → A → m B) s a,
    mupdate mln s a ≫= (λ s' ⇒ k s' (mview mln s')) =
    mupdate mln s a ≫= (λ s' ⇒ k s' a) }.
```

These laws establish that no effect should be produced when updating the whole with the current part, and that viewing the part should be consistent with the last update. If we set `m` to `Id` we recover an ordinary well-behaved lens.

Monadic lenses do not accommodate the stateful infrastructures that we are interested in. In this sense, the absence of effects in `mview` is probably the main evidence of it, in line with the discussion in Sect. 5.1. Broadly speaking, lens algebras and monadic lenses pursue different goals. On one hand, lens algebras abstracts away from immutable data structures by parameterizing the computational effect to access and manipulate state. On the other hand, monadic lenses aim at enriching plain lenses with all kind of effects, such as partiality or logging, but they target immutable data structures. We discuss whether lens algebras support such computational effects in Sect. 5.3.

That said, there are interesting observations from the discussion presented by Abou-Saleh *et al.* around effectful `mview`, that are relevant in our case. In particular, there is a question that arises naturally: is it safe to define an effectful `view` for lens algebra as we do? To answer this question, note that lens algebra laws (or `MonadState` laws) impose a strong condition over `view`, which is described as follows:

Lemma 3. *Consider a (very) well-behaved lens algebra* `ln` *with type* `lensAlg` `p A`. *The following property is derived from its laws:*

∀ (X : Type) (px : p X), view ln ≫ px = px.

This lemma tells us that an invocation to `view` where its result is ignored is redundant. However, if `view` produces an effect, it seems hard to reconcile this property. Strictly speaking, a program that executes a query in a database and then ignores its result, is not the same as a program that does not invoke such a query. For that reason, we need to relax the notion of equality for the laws, considering equivalence up to resulting state instead. In this sense, we can safely remove the ignored query from the program, since it will not affect the final state after executing the program. We can find a slight variation of this lemma for the state monad transformer in [6, Lemma 2.7].

5.3 Entangled State Monads

Entangled state monads [6] emerged in the context of bidirectional transformations as the initial model of the following definition:

```
Record BX (p : Type → Type) (A B : Type) : Type :=
{ getL : p A
; getR : p B
; putL : A → p unit
; putR : B → p unit }.
```

We can appreciate that BX p A B is MonadState p A with an additional focus B, and corresponding methods to access and manipulate it. Its associated laws duplicate MonadState laws for each focus and append a new law to state that getL and getR can be commuted. In this regard, the definition does not contemplate commutativity of putL and putR, since it would break up the entanglement among the states.

There are strong similarities between entangled state monads and our work. Firstly, Abou-Saleh *et al.* recovers a very well-behaved asymmetric lens S A as an instance BX (state S) S A, which provides methods to deal with both whole S and part A. This is basically the same approach that we follow in Proposition 1, where we also employ the state monad to recover lens. Secondly, BX is closely related to the way we encode data layers. In particular, the constraint id that we provide along with the repositories corresponds to the methods getL and putL, although we ignore them, since we are not interested in evolving the whole directly (at least, in the examples shown in this paper). For its part, getR and putR corresponds to a lens algebra hosted by the data layer, such as budgetLn.

Therefore, why do we not use BX to program data layers? First of all, composition is defined for well-behaved stateful BX [6, Definition 3.8]. A crucial feature of this class of instances is that getL and getR operations are essentially pure. Unfortunately, this does not hold in our most relevant use cases. For instance, if we need to instantiate DepartmentAlg with a state monad transformer to access the information from a relational database, the getR operation would not be pure. Second of all, we are interested in deploying different computational effects for the nested repositories, while BX composition requires a fixed one. Lens algebra homomorphisms support them, while preserving the look and feel of classic lenses in the implementation of business logic.

There is a relevant takeaway from entangled state monads, involving *overwritability*, that will allow us to answer the question whether lens algebras support additional effects, such as partiality or logging. Overwritability corresponds with the controversial [14] update_update law in the context of lens algebras. In this sense, very well-behaved lens algebras inherit the same limitations. In fact, if we aim at enriching instances with additional computational, we should embrace the notion of well-behaved lens algebras, where update_update is discarded.

6   Conclusions

Figure 1 summarizes the relationships established in this paper between optics (first row) and algebraic theories (second row), as far as lenses are concerned. All the relationships in this diagram were formalised as propositions in Coq.

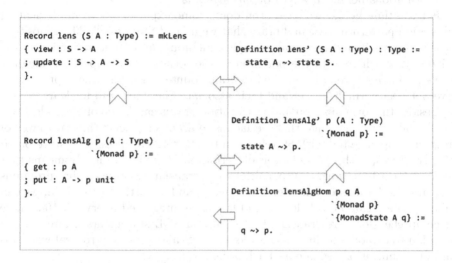

Fig. 1. Taking lenses to a higher level of abstraction

The left column of this diagram relates the concrete representation of very well-behaved lenses with the algebraic theory of MonadState. This relationship was shown to be a correct generalisation, insofar lens S A can be defined as MonadState A (state S). This justifies the alias of lensAlg for MonadState. The right column essentially deals with compositional issues. There, we start from an alternative representation of lenses with better compositional properties, state A ⤳ state S, and proceed towards lens algebra homomorphism, a strict generalisation that enjoys full compositional properties with respect to lensAlgs. This direct support for composability at the algebraic level is the major point of departure with respect to BX, the closest approach in the literature to our work. Crucially, we showed how this algebraic notion of compositionality can be founded on a strict generalisation of composable lens representations.

Current work focuses on applying the aforementioned approach that allowed us to turn lenses into algebraic theories, to other members of the optics catalogue. To this extent, in order to identify the algebraic counterparts of affines, traversals, getters, etc., the existence of alternative optic representations based on natural transformations, like the state monad morphism lens representation, becomes essential. Unfortunately, we have not found previous work describing such abstractions for other optics, so we are responsible for building them up.

This paper also provided a design pattern to implement the data layer of applications with better modularity guarantees. Particularly, instead of defining *ad hoc* repositories with get/set functions to manipulate particular fields, we promote lens algebras as a standard reusable abstraction that fulfills that objective. In addition, we have shown how lens algebra homomorphisms provide the glue to relate the different algebras that make up the whole data layer. By defining the data layer using this pattern, we hide the complexity details of natural transformations behind the API of lens algebras.

For the time being, we have been doing some experiments in implementing this design pattern in a Scala library that we named Stateless[10]. The repository for this project includes several examples, including an extended version of the university, which reflects the potential of the ideas in this paper. Although it shows preliminary versions of the algebraic counterparts for other optics, they have not been formalized yet and their associated laws are still unclear.

Besides the formalization and justification of this catalogue of optic algebras, the second great challenge that we face is guaranteeing that the data layer of programs implemented with Stateless can be interpreted in common state-based infrastructures, with *optimal* levels of performance. This essentially means that we don't incur in performance penalties when translating optic algebra programs to relational databases, microservices, caches, and so forth. In this vein, we can build upon existing knowledge around language-integrated query [15, 16], where for-comprehensions are translated into optimal SQL statements. Moreover, we also plan to exploit specific frameworks in the Scala ecosystem to deal with this kind of optimization techniques for EDSLs [17, 18].

Acknowledgments. We want to thank the anonymous reviewers for their helpful comments to a previous version of this paper. This work is partially supported by a Doctorate Industry Program grant to Habla Computing SL, from the Spanish Ministry of Economy, Industry and Competitiveness.

A   Definitions and Proofs

All definitions, examples and proofs have been formalized with Coq 8.7.1 (January 2018) and collected in a GitHub repository[11]. Source files have a direct correspondence with the different sections along the paper. We detected that many of the definitions and theorems appearing in the aforementioned repository could be reused for formalizing other functional programming research projects. Thereby, we decided to create *Koky*[12], an open-sourced typeclass library where we have been collecting them all, which is publicly accessible as well.

References

1. Foster, J.N., Greenwald, M.B., Moore, J.T., Pierce, B.C., Schmitt, A.: Combinators for bi-directional tree transformations: a linguistic approach to the view update problem. ACM SIGPLAN Not. **40**(1), 233–246 (2005)

---

[10] https://github.com/hablapps/stateless.
[11] https://github.com/hablapps/lensalgebra.
[12] https://github.com/hablapps/koky.

2. O'Connor, R.: Functor is to lens as applicative is to biplate: introducing multiplate. In: 7th ACM SIGPLAN Workshop on Generic Programming. ACM (2011)
3. Gibbons, J.: Unifying theories of programming with monads. In: Wolff, B., Gaudel, M.-C., Feliachi, A. (eds.) UTP 2012. LNCS, vol. 7681, pp. 23–67. Springer, Heidelberg (2013). https://doi.org/10.1007/978-3-642-35705-3_2
4. Wadler, P., Blott, S.: How to make ad-hoc polymorphism less ad hoc. In: Proceedings of the 16th ACM SIGPLAN-SIGACT Symposium on Principles of Programming Languages, pp. 60–76. ACM (1989)
5. Van Deursen, A., Klint, P., Visser, J.: Domain-specific languages: an annotated bibliography. ACM SIGPLAN Not. **35**(6), 26–36 (2000)
6. Abou-Saleh, F., Cheney, J., Gibbons, J., McKinna, J., Stevens, P.: Notions of bidirectional computation and entangled state monads. In: Hinze, R., Voigtländer, J. (eds.) MPC 2015. LNCS, vol. 9129, pp. 187–214. Springer, Cham (2015). https://doi.org/10.1007/978-3-319-19797-5_9
7. Abou-Saleh, F., Cheney, J., Gibbons, J., McKinna, J., Stevens, P.: Reflections on monadic lenses. In: Lindley, S., McBride, C., Trinder, P., Sannella, D. (eds.) A List of Successes That Can Change the World. LNCS, vol. 9600, pp. 1–31. Springer, Cham (2016). https://doi.org/10.1007/978-3-319-30936-1_1
8. Cheney, J., McKinna, J., Stevens, P., Gibbons, J., Abou, F., et al.: Entangled state monads. In: BX Workshop (2014)
9. Pickering, M., Wu, N., Gibbons, J.: Profunctor optics: modular data accessors. Art Sci. Eng. Program. **1**(2) (2017)
10. Wadler, P.: Monads for functional programming. In: Jeuring, J., Meijer, E. (eds.) AFP 1995. LNCS, vol. 925, pp. 24–52. Springer, Heidelberg (1995). https://doi.org/10.1007/3-540-59451-5_2
11. Fischer, S., Hu, Z., Pacheco, H.: A clear picture of lens laws. In: Hinze, R., Voigtländer, J. (eds.) MPC 2015. LNCS, vol. 9129, pp. 215–223. Springer, Cham (2015). https://doi.org/10.1007/978-3-319-19797-5_10
12. Shkaravska, O.: Side-effect monad, its equational theory and applications. Arvutiteaduse teooriaseminar (2005)
13. Jones, M.P.: Type classes with functional dependencies. In: Smolka, G. (ed.) ESOP 2000. LNCS, vol. 1782, pp. 230–244. Springer, Heidelberg (2000). https://doi.org/10.1007/3-540-46425-5_15
14. Johnson, M., Rosebrugh, R.: Lens put-put laws: monotonic and mixed. Electr. Commun. EASST **49** (2012)
15. Cheney, J., Lindley, S., Wadler, P.: A practical theory of language-integrated query. In: Proceedings of the 18th ACM SIGPLAN International Conference on Functional Programming, ICFP 2013, New York, NY, USA, pp. 403–416. ACM (2013)
16. Suzuki, K., Kiselyov, O., Kameyama, Y.: Finally, safely-extensible and efficient language-integrated query. In: Proceedings of the 2016 ACM SIGPLAN Workshop on Partial Evaluation and Program Manipulation, PEPM 2016, New York, NY, USA, pp. 37–48. ACM (2016)
17. Rompf, T., Odersky, M.: Lightweight modular staging: a pragmatic approach to runtime code generation and compiled DSLs. ACM SIGPLAN Not. **46**, 127–136 (2010)
18. Moors, A., Rompf, T., Haller, P., Odersky, M.: Scala-virtualized. In: Proceedings of the ACM SIGPLAN 2012 Workshop on Partial Evaluation and Program Manipulation, pp. 117–120. ACM (2012)

Saint: An API-Generic Type-Safe Interpreter

Maximilian Algehed[1] , Patrik Jansson[1(✉)] , Sólrún Halla Einarsdóttir[1] ,
and Alex Gerdes[1,2]

[1] Chalmers University of Technology, Gothenburg, Sweden
{algehed,patrikj,slrn}@chalmers.se
[2] University of Gothenburg, Gothenburg, Sweden
alex.gerdes@cse.gu.se

Abstract. Typed functional programming allows us to write interesting programs without sacrificing type safety. Programs that expose their API to an open world, however, are faced with the problem of dynamic type checking. In Haskell, existing techniques that address this problem, such as `Typeable` and `Dynamic`, are often closed and difficult to extend. We have constructed an extensible Haskell library for describing APIs using *annotated* type representations. As a result, API calls can be interpreted in a type-safe manner without extra programming effort. In addition, the user has full control over the universe of allowed types, which helps to catch misconceptions in an early stage. We have applied our technique to connect a real-world DSL (GRACe) to a JavaScript GUI.

Keywords: Domain Specific Language · Interpreter · Lambda calculus

1 Introduction

A large number of so-called Embedded Domain Specific Languages (EDSLs) have been implemented in Haskell for various purposes [1,7,11,16]. Embedding DSLs in a typed language like Haskell has many advantages, one of the major ones being that it removes the need for the implementation of tools like parsers and type-checkers. However, embedded languages require a full Haskell environment in order to be compiled and executed.

A Haskell EDSL may be used as part of a larger toolchain, in combination with other programs that may not be written in Haskell and may even be written in an untyped language. This necessitates communication between the Haskell EDSL and the untyped world. For instance, we may want to expose functions from an EDSL as an API to an untyped frontend, accessible through a web interface, and allow users to write programs using those functions which can be sent to our Haskell backend for execution.

For example, consider a small Haskell EDSL to build pictures using a set of functional geometry (FunGeo) combinators, as described by Henderson in [8,9]. An overview of the system can be seen in Fig. 1. The FunGeo EDSL consists of

© Springer Nature Switzerland AG 2019
M. Pałka and M. Myreen (Eds.): TFP 2018, LNCS 11457, pp. 94–113, 2019.
https://doi.org/10.1007/978-3-030-18506-0_5

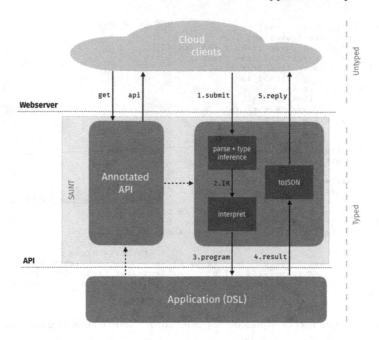

Fig. 1. A high-level overview of the system

a datatype for images and some image combinators. We have added *natrec* to make it a bit more powerful and to make sure more than one type is involved.

$$beside :: Image \rightarrow Image \rightarrow Image$$
$$above :: Image \rightarrow Image \rightarrow Image$$

$over \quad :: Image \rightarrow Image \rightarrow Image$	-- overlay
$rot \quad :: Image \rightarrow Image$	-- 90 degrees
$fish \quad :: Image$	-- a simple fish to start from
data *Image*	-- implemented as just a list of splines
$natrec :: Image \rightarrow$	-- base case
$\qquad (Int \rightarrow Image \rightarrow Image) \rightarrow$	-- step function
$\qquad Int \rightarrow Image$	-- main input and output

We would like to expose the ability to program safely in FunGeo where "safe" means "type correct"; we want to rule out raw expressions like *beside* 3 *fish* or *fish fish*. We do this in the following manner:

1. Parse the user-written program into an untyped expression (and find syntax errors).
2. Infer the types of the expression (find type errors).
3. Interpret the typed expression as a DSL value.
4. Send the result of the DSL computation back.

$$String$$
$$\downarrow parse$$
$$untyped\ Expr$$
$$\downarrow typeInference$$
$$typed\ Expr$$
$$\downarrow interpret$$
$$DSL\ value\ (Image)$$

An example program and its output is shown in Fig. 2.

```
let fish2 = flip (rot45 fish) in
let fish3 = rot (rot (rot fish2)) in
let t     = over fish (over fish2 fish3) in
let u     = over (over fish2 (rot fish2))
                 (over (rot (rot fish2))
                 fish3) in
let qrt   = \p.\q. \r.\s.
            above  (beside p q)
                   (beside r s) in
let cyc   = \p. qrt p (rot p)
                (rot (rot p))
                (rot (rot (rot p))) in
let side  = natrec blank (\n.\img.
            qrt img         img
            (rot t)   t)  in
let corn  = natrec blank (\n.\img.
            qrt img            (side n)
            (rot (side n)) u ) in
let bes3  = \a.\b.\c. besideS 1 2 a (beside b c) in
let abo3  = \a.\b.\c. aboveS  1 2 a (above  b c) in
let nnet  = \p.\q.\r. \s.\t.\u. \v.\w.\x. abo3 (bes3 p q r)
                                              (bes3 s t u)
                                              (bes3 v w x) in
let sqrl  = \n. nnet (corn n)      (side n) (rot (rot (rot (corn n))))
                (rot (side n)) u        (rot (rot (rot (side n))))
                (rot (corn n)) (rot (rot (side n))) (rot (rot (corn n))) in
scale 1000 (sqrl 3)
```

Fig. 2. The Escher Woodcut—Square Limit—source code and output.

1.1 APIs as Values

In order to expose our API of DSL functions to users, we describe it as a value of the type *Library*, which is a type-annotated lookup table containing an *Item* describing each function. An *Item* contains a function's name, its semantics, and a representation of its type. The name can be used for parsing, the semantics for interpretation, and the type representation for type checking. Our running example, the FunGeo EDSL, is easily described as a *Library* value.

data *Library* = *Library String* [*Item*]
data *Item*   = *Item String TypedValue*

funGeoLib :: *Library*
funGeoLib = *Library* "funGeo" (*funGeoCore* ++ *funGeoMore*)
funGeoCore, *funGeoMore* :: [*Item*]
funGeoCore =
    [*Item* "beside" $ *beside* ::: *image* --→ *image* --→ *image*
    , *Item* "above" $ *above* ::: *image* --→ *image* --→ *image*
    , *Item* "over" $ *over* ::: *image* --→ *image* --→ *image*
    , *Item* "rot" $ *rot* ::: *image* --→ *image*]

Here, triple colon (:::) is used to pair a semantic value with a representation of its type. The type representations are built from the base type representations (*image*, *int*), the function type combinator (--→), and *Tag* = (#) :: *String* → *TypeRep* → *TypeRep*. Our *TypeRep* is explained, and extended, in Sect. 2.

We use tags to annotate parts of the API with appropriate metadata, which can be used to display the API in the frontend.

$funGeoMore = [\,Item\,$ `"natrec"` $\$$
$\qquad\qquad natrec ::: $ `"Recursion over Nat"` $\#$
$\qquad\qquad\quad image \dashrightarrow$
$\qquad\qquad\quad$ `"Step function"` $\# (int \dashrightarrow image \dashrightarrow image) \dashrightarrow$
$\qquad\qquad\quad int \dashrightarrow image$
$\qquad\qquad , Item\,$ `"fish"` $\quad\$\, fish ::: $ `"Base case"` $\# image\,]$

1.2   Type Representations

At the core of the *Library* datatype is the type *TypedValue* which stores a value and a representation of its type. A first implementation version could be this:

$\quad$ **data** *TypedValue* **where** $(:::) :: a \rightarrow TypeRep\ a \rightarrow TypedValue$

Note that the type a is existentially quantified, which means that we can store values of different types in, say, a list of typed values, $ex1 :: [\,TypedValue\,]$:

$$ex1 = [((1+) :: Int \rightarrow Int) ::: int \dashrightarrow int, (3 :: Int) ::: int\,]$$

The representation of types, *TypeRep* is also parameterised by an a, the role of this parameter is to "keep track" of the type a *TypeRep* represents:

$\quad$ **data** *TypeRep* a **where**
$\qquad TRImage :: TypeRep\ Image$
$\qquad TRInt \quad :: TypeRep\ Int$
$\qquad TRFun \quad :: TypeRep\ a \rightarrow TypeRep\ b \rightarrow TypeRep\ (a \rightarrow b)$
$\qquad TRList \quad :: TypeRep\ a \rightarrow TypeRep\ [\,a\,]$
$\quad image = TRImage; int = TRInt; (\dashrightarrow) = TRFun$
$\quad$ **infixr** $1 \dashrightarrow$

The presented type representation and typed values are closely related to the Haskell library *Dynamic* together with its *TypeRep* type family [17]. We found that *Dynamic* and *TypeRep* almost, but not quite, provide the functionality we need. Their *TypeRep* is "deep" in that it represents the full type, and support for it is also built-in to GHC. However, their technique is rigid: *TypeRep* cannot be extended with extra constructs. We extend it to store tags *in the type (representation) tree* by introducing a variant with the *Tag* constructor.

$\quad$ **data** *TypeRep* t **where**
$\qquad TInt \quad :: TypeRep\ Int$
$\qquad TFun :: TypeRep\ a \rightarrow TypeRep\ b \rightarrow TypeRep\ (a \rightarrow b)$
$\qquad Tag \quad :: String \rightarrow TypeRep\ a \rightarrow TypeRep\ a$
$\quad int = TInt; (\dashrightarrow) = TFun; (\#) = Tag$

Usually this kind of type family is used to represent singleton types, where each (type) family member *TypeRep* t contains just one proper value $tr :: TypeRep\ t$

which is the representation of t. In our case, due to the *Tags*, there are more variants possible. It would be possible to represent these tags at the type level, but we wanted to keep the library reasonably simple.

1.3   Towards a Type-Safe Interpreter

We can define a generic parser to a "raw" syntax tree (using a datatype for untyped expressions). Using our *Library* as a parameter we then infer types and annotate the syntax tree provided to us by the parser to make typed expressions. In both of these two phases we discard "bad" inputs to make sure the interpreter only receives well-typed expressions to evaluate.

The combination of these phases is what we call a "type-safe interpreter": you can throw any input term at it but only the (syntax- and) type-correct inputs are run. The interpreter function itself still uses an *Either* type to report errors (in case of the *Env* does not cover all variables used, for example) but this should always succeed when called in combination with the type checker.

```
parse       :: String → Maybe UExpr
typeCheck :: Library → UExpr → Maybe Expr
interpret  :: Env → Expr → Maybe TypedValue
libToEnv  :: Library → Env
run         :: Library → String → Maybe TypedValue
```

This simplified view is expanded and details are explained in following sections.

1.4   Contributions

In this paper we make the following contributions:

- We construct a framework (called Saint) for exposing a typed API to untyped world (including a parser, type checker, and an interpreter).
- We provide a version of *Typeable* supporting tags (annotations in the *TypeRep*).
- We implement a method of evaluating programs in our framework in a type-safe way as internal Haskell values.
- We present case studies which show the application of our techniques to DSLs used in real-world applications.

All the code for our framework, Saint, and the FunGeo case study can be found online[1]. The Saint framework satisfies the following criteria:

- It is lightweight: we do not need an entire Haskell compiler to interpret code.
- It is reusable: new functionality can easily be added to a DSL.
- Interpretation of programs is type-safe.
- The results of interpreting client programs are available to the server as Haskell values, even when the denotation is a function.
- Type information and annotations are correctly exposed to the DSL user.

---

[1] The Saint library: https://github.com/GRACeFUL-project/Saint, and the case study: https://github.com/GRACeFUL-project/SaintCaseStudy.

2 Typed Values

Using our framework we can expose the API of an EDSL to external clients and can safely evaluate programs, expressed in terms of the exported API, to Haskell values. The two main components in our framework are: type reflection (representing types as values) and type-safe dynamic typing. This section shows how we have developed our type reflection implementation. The implementation is inspired by Typeable [14] but our approach has some advantages: it is extensible, general, and remains under the control of the programmer rather than being built in to the compiler.

We continue from the *TypeRep* GADT presented in the introduction, but call it *TRep* for brevity. The basic idea behind this encoding is not new, and variants of it appear for example in Eisenberg and Weirich [6]. We will now set up some infrastructure needed for the "type-safe interpreter": type equality, type representation equality, coercion, and computation with "typed values". The infrastructure consists of the following datatype and functions:

> **data** $a \equiv b$
> $(?=)$ :: $TRep\ a \rightarrow TRep\ b \rightarrow Maybe\ (a \equiv b)$
> $coerce$ :: $TypedValue \rightarrow TRep\ a \rightarrow Maybe\ a$
> app :: $TypedValue \rightarrow TypedValue \rightarrow Maybe\ TypedValue$

At first we define these functions using the basic *TRep* type representation from Sect. 1 but we will later base them on refined and generalised *TypeReps*.

An important feature of Typeable [14] is that we can determine equality between types at runtime, based on type reflection. Like Typeable, we represent equality between types by a GADT—the single constructor *Refl* supplies the evidence that two types are equal. Pattern-matching on *Refl* convinces the compiler that two types are in fact the same as shown in the example *foo* below.

> **data** $a \equiv b$ **where** $Refl :: a \equiv a$
> $foo :: (a \equiv Int) \rightarrow a \rightarrow Int$
> $foo\ Refl\ x = x$

Having defined a notion of equality between types, we can now implement equality checks between type representations:

> $(?=) :: TRep\ a \rightarrow TRep\ b \rightarrow Maybe\ (a \equiv b)$
> $TInt$ $?= TInt$ $= return\ Refl$
> $Tag \_ t$ $?= t'$ $= t\ ?=\ t'$
> t $?= Tag \_ t'$ $= t\ ?=\ t'$
> $TFun\ t0\ t1\ ?= TFun\ t0'\ t1' =$ **do**
> $Refl \leftarrow t0\ ?=\ t0'$
> $Refl \leftarrow t1\ ?=\ t1'$
> $return\ Refl$
> $\_ ?= \_ = Nothing$

We can construct a *TypedValue*, as we did before, to hide the type of an expression using existential quantification.

data *TypedValue* **where** (:::) :: $a \rightarrow$ *TRep a* $\rightarrow$ *TypedValue*

We combine a value of type *a* with its type representation *TRep a* and can subsequently treat that combination as an untyped value. For example, we can store values of different types in a single list. The type representation in a *TypedValue* can be used to 'escape' from the existential quantification and allows us to retrieve the original (typed) value. The function *coerce* retrieves the value from a *TypedValue* if it matches the given expected type representation.

```
coerce :: TypedValue → TRep a → Maybe a
coerce (a ::: t0) t1 = do
    Refl ← t0 ?= t1
    return a
```

This approach gives us a type-safe version of dynamic typing. In our interpreter we use the type information in a *TypedValue* to apply one *TypedValue* to another, because we can check if the actual values have matching types.

```
app :: TypedValue → TypedValue → Maybe TypedValue
app (f ::: TFun a b) (x ::: a') = do
    Refl ← a ?= a'
    return (f x ::: b)
app _ _ = Nothing
```

2.1 Generalising Type Representations

A downside of our type representation is that the universe of types, that is the set of types we can represent, is hard-coded in the *TRep* datatype. We suffer from the so-called expression problem [19]: adding more base types (or type constructors) requires changing both the implementation of *TRep* as well as functions working on it, such as (?=). A solution to this problem is to use the 'datatypes à la carte'-method, which represents a datatype as a co-product of its constructors [18].

data *CoProduct f g a* = *InL* (*f a*) | *InR* (*g a*)

The idea is that *f* and *g* are type constructors which each represent an individual constructor in the type *TRep* seen previously. For example, we could construct type representations for *Int* and *Bool* as the following datatypes *IntT* and *BoolT*:

data *IntT a*   **where** *IntT*   :: *IntT Int*
data *BoolT a* **where** *BoolT* :: *BoolT Bool*

Using these two base type representations we can construct the universe of type representations that can be either *Int* or *Bool* using *CoProduct*:

type *MyTRep a* = *CoProduct IntT BoolT a*

However, constructing values of type *TRep Int* and *TRep Bool* is quite cumbersome, requiring us to make use of the *InL* and *InR* constructors as well as *BoolT* and *IntT*. Datatypes à la carte solves this problem by allowing us to construct a subtyping typeclass which we can use with *CoProduct*, as shown below:

class $f :< g$ **where**
$\quad$ *inject* :: $f\ a \to g\ a$
$\quad$ *eject* :: $g\ a \to$ *Maybe* $(f\ a)$

The code for the simple instances for (:<) is elided:

instance $f :< f$ **where**$\quad$-- ...
instance $f :< $ *CoProduct* $f\ r$ **where**
instance {-# OVERLAPPABLE #-} $f :< r \Rightarrow f :< $ *CoProduct* $l\ r$ **where**

This formulation of (:<) requires the construction of *CoProducts* to be right-associated to work correctly, because $f :< $ *CoProduct* (*CoProduct* $g\ f$) h can not be made to hold by the instances above. It is also not possible to add another instance $f :< l \Rightarrow f :< $ (*CoProduct* $l\ r$) as this would overlap with the last instance above. Ideally, we would have a disjunctive instance $f :< l\ |\ f :< r \Rightarrow f :< $ (*CoProduct* $l\ r$), but these are not allowed in GHC (and it is not clear how to resolve such instances). We therefore present the user with a "smart constructor" for *CoProduct* in the form of a type family (:+:).

type *family* $f :+: g$ **where**
$\quad$ (*CoProduct* $f\ g$) :+: $h = $ *CoProduct* $f\ (g :+: h)$
$\quad$ $f :+: $ *CoProduct* $g\ h\quad = $ *CoProduct* $f\ (g :+: h)$
$\quad$ $f :+: g\qquad\qquad\quad = $ *CoProduct* $f\ g$

Using this smart constructor we can write generic representations, like *int* and *bool* below, to allow us to construct typed values conveniently.

int :: *IntT* :< $tr \Rightarrow tr$ *Int*
int = *inject IntT*

bool :: *BoolT* :< $tr \Rightarrow tr$ *Bool*
bool = *inject BoolT*

In order to make use of our new open type universe in *TypedValue* we need to alter the type slightly to move from a fixed family *TRep* (of codes for types) to a type parameter:

data *TypedValue tr* **where** (:::) :: $a \to tr\ a \to$ *TypedValue tr*

We can now use construct typed values in an open manner:

exI :: *IntT* :< $tr \Rightarrow$ *TypedValue tr*
exI = 42 ::: *int*

We can also use our approach to construct representations for types built from type constructors like *Maybe* and $(\to)$.

data *MaybeT tr a* **where**
   MaybeT :: *tr a* → *MaybeT tr* (*Maybe a*)

maybe :: *MaybeT tr* :< *tr* ⇒ *tr a* → *tr* (*Maybe a*)
maybe = *inject* ∘ *MaybeT*

data *FunT tr a* **where**
   FunT :: *tr a* → *tr b* → *FunT tr* (*a* → *b*)

(--→) :: *FunT tr* :< *tr* ⇒ *tr a* → *tr b* → *tr* (*a* → *b*)
a --→ *b* = *inject* (*FunT a b*)

We can use these representations to construct more interesting *TypedValues*:

exMI :: (*IntT* :< *tr*, *MaybeT tr* :< *tr*) ⇒ *TypedValue tr*
exMI = *Just* 42 ::: *maybe int*

exFI :: (*IntT* :< *tr*, *FunT tr* :< *tr*) ⇒ *TypedValue tr*
exFI = (λx → x + 1) ::: *int* --→ *int*

Note that each of these examples (*exI*, *exMI*, *exFI*) encodes in its type constraint the "minimum requirements" of a universe for them to fit into.

2.2   Type Equality for Generalised *TypedValues*

Deciding equality between types is an important part of what makes our *TypedValues* useful, so we need a way to do so in this generalised setting. What we would prefer, following our previous discussion (in Sect. 2), is a function *coerce* :: *TypedValue tr* → *tr a* → *Maybe a*. Recall that the implementation of the coercion function *coerce* shown previously relied on computing a value *Refl* of type $a \equiv a$ by comparing the type representation in the *TypedValue* with the coerced-to type. In *coerce* we did this using a function (?=) :: *TRep a* → *TRep b* → *Maybe* ($a \equiv b$). We now need to generalise over our type representation, and the natural way to do this is by using a type class:

class *TypeEquality tr* **where**
   (?=) :: *tr a* → *tr b* → *Maybe* ($a \equiv b$)

Next we need to make sure that instances of *TypeEquality* are modular in the same way that the construction of type universes is modular. The type equality should be extensible in the same way the type representation is. The first step to achieving this is to make sure that *CoProduct*s can be tested for type equality.

instance (*TypeEquality f*, *TypeEquality g*) ⇒
        TypeEquality (*CoProduct f g*) **where**
  InL a ?= *InL b* = *a* ?= *b*
  InR a ?= *InR b* = *a* ?= *b*
   _   ?= _   = *Nothing*

We also show how to construct the instances for *IntT* and *MaybeT*:

instance *TypeEquality IntT* **where**
   IntT ?= *IntT* = *Just Refl*

instance *TypeEquality tr* ⇒ *TypeEquality* (*MaybeT tr*) **where**
   MaybeT a ?= *MaybeT b* = **do**
      Refl ← *a* ?= *b*
      return Refl

Now we can finally define our new and improved version of *coerce*:

   coerce :: *TypeEquality tr* ⇒ *TypedValue tr* → *tr a* → *Maybe a*
   coerce (*v* ::: *a*) *a'* = **do**
      Refl ← *a* ?= *a'*
      return v

2.3   Constructing Universes

What we need next is the ability to construct a value *t a* to pass to (:::)
and *coerce*. We might be tempted to define a type like **type** *TypeUniverse* =
IntT :+: *MaybeT   TypeUniverse* in order that we may create types
TypeUniverse (*Maybe Int*) and *TypeUniverse* (*Maybe* (*Maybe Int*)) to serve
as type representations. However, we can't do that as GHC disallows cyclic type
synonyms, so instead we create a datatype:

   newtype *Close a* = *Close* ((*MaybeT Close* :+: *IntT*) *a*)

The choice of the name *Close* is not an accident as the type represents the
closure of the *IntT* and *MaybeT* operations for constructing a type universe.
Type equality is easily implemented for *Close*:

   instance *TypeEquality Close* **where**
      Close a ?= *Close b* = *a* ?= *b*

In order to use our "type formers" *int*, *maybe*, etc to construct values of type
Close we need instances of :< for each type of interest.

         instance *IntT* :< *Close* **where**
            inject = *Close* ∘ *inject*
            eject (*Close t*) = *eject t*

         instance *MaybeT Close* :< *Close* **where**
            inject = *Close* ∘ *inject*
            eject (*Close t*) = *eject t*

Defining instances like these for every universe we may want to construct can
become quite cumbersome. Based on the fact that *Close* looks a lot like the fix
point of a type-level function, it's tempting to write something along the lines of
the following (assuming a slightly more advanced type system than Haskell's):

```
data Close f a = Close (f (Close f) a)
instance t :< f (Close f) ⇒ t :< Close f where
  inject = Close ∘ inject
  eject (Close t) = eject t
```

```
type MyUniverse = Close (λc → MaybeT c :+: IntT)   -- not Haskell
```

This fails because GHC does not allow lambda abstraction on the type level. We may then be tempted to use a type synonym instead:

```
type MakeUniverse u = MaybeT u :+: IntT
type MyBadUniverse = Close MakeUniverse
```

However, this fails because *MakeUniverse* is partially applied in the definition of *MyBadUniverse*. It would appear there is no good way out of this mess!

But there is: by adding an extra type parameter like the one to *MaybeT* to all type representations including *CoProduct* we can generalise the definition, and type equality for *IntT tr* is constructed the same way as before.

```
data IntT (tr :: * → *) a where
  IntT :: IntT tr Int
data CoProduct f g (tr :: * → *) a = InL (f tr a) | InR (g tr a)
instance TypeEquality (IntT tr) where
  IntT ?= IntT = Just Refl
```

Now we can use our definition of *Close* to define universes without the recursive occurrence of *Close*:

```
type MyUniverse = Close (IntT :+: MaybeT)
int :: forall tr. IntT tr :< tr ⇒ tr Int
int = inject (IntT :: IntT tr Int)   -- a generic type code for Int
value :: Maybe Int
value = coerce (42 ::: int) (int :: MyUniverse Int)
```

Note that the use of *coerce* in *value* requires an instance of *TypeEquality* for *MyUniverse* in order to type check. The core to this instance is the instance of *TypeEquality* for our new *CoProduct* type:

```
instance ( TypeEquality (f tr), TypeEquality (g tr))
       ⇒ TypeEquality (CoProduct f g tr) where
```

Because *tr* is used both in the premise and the conclusion of the instance (much like in the instance for *Close* above) we are forced to use the GHC language extension `UndecidableInstances`. However, this does not cause any issue as the search for an instance will terminate when it hits *IntT tr* or similar instances which do not need to make use of type equality at *tr* in order to work.

It is possible to generalise the type formers from the previous section even further than we have done so far. Namely, it is possible to abstract the definition of any *n*-ary type representation. For nullary type formers this is straightforward:

```
data A0 typ (univ :: * → *) a where
  A0 :: A0 typ univ typ
instance TypeEquality (A0 typ univ) where
  A0 ?= A0 = Just Refl
int :: forall u. A0 Int u :< u ⇒ u Int
int = inject (A0 :: A0 Int u Int)
```

Unary and binary type formers can be constructed in the same way: here we show the unary case:

```
data A1 f univ a where
  A1 :: univ a → A1 f univ (f a)
instance TypeEquality univ ⇒ TypeEquality (A1 f univ) where
  A1 t ?= A1 t' = do
    Refl ← t ?= t'
    return Refl
maybe :: A1 Maybe u :< u ⇒ u a → u (Maybe a)
maybe = inject ∘ A1
```

And analogously for the binary case:

```
data A2 f univ a where
  A2 :: univ a → univ b → A2 f univ (f a b)
instance TypeEquality univ ⇒ TypeEquality (A2 f univ) where    -- ...
```

What we have obtained, then, is a general framework in which we can represent any type, and we have done it all without needing to change the GHC compiler.

2.4   Implementing Tags

As previously discussed, we use *Tags* to annotate our EDSL types with metadata. To implement tags for our generalised *TypedValues*, we want a function like:

```
(#) :: String → Close u a → Close u a
```

How would we implement (#)? One option is to add an external type former:

```
data TagT u a where
  TagT :: String → u a → TagT u a
(#) :: TagT u :< u ⇒ String → u a → u a
t # s = inject (TagT t s)
```

But what instance of *TypeEquality* should we give for *TagT*? That depends on what kind of equality we want to consider. If we want it to be the case that two types are not considered equal unless their tags are equal, we can use:

```
TagT s a ?= TagT s' b = if s ≢ s' then Nothing else a ?= b
```

However, if we wish for our tags to be transparent so that *TypeEquality* is independent of tags, that is, $(s \# t) ?= t = Just\ Refl$, this is not sufficient. To achieve that we need be able to compare a *Tag* to a constructor which is not a *Tag*. The simplest way of doing so is to not consider *Tag* as a separate type former, but rather introduce a separate notion of metadata, which we achieve by making *Tag* part of *Close*:

```
data Close f a = Tag String (Close f a)
               | Close (f (Close f) a)
```

instance *TypeEquality* (*t* (*Close t*)) ⇒ *TypeEquality* (*Close t*) **where**
```
Tag _ t ?= t'        = t ?= t'
t          ?= Tag _ t' = t ?= t'
Close t ?= Close t' = t ?= t'
```

(#) :: *String* → *Close t a* → *Close t a*
(#) = *Tag*

This tagging infrastructure allows us to attach arbitrary information anywhere in a type representation in the form of a *String*. Naturally, this could be generalised to any type of metadata with more structure than a simple type:

```
data Close f ann a = Tag ann (Close f ann a)
                   | Close (f (Close f ann) a)
```

Alongside the appropriate instance of *TypeEquality* and definition of (#).

This concludes our implementation of type representations. The system is extensible, yet allows for fine grained control over the type universe in question. Types can also be annotated with arbitrary information, this feature is particularly useful when exposing EDSLs to the outside world, where different types of metadata may need to be associated to functions in the EDSL.

2.5   The Saint API

We have presented a number of different encodings of type universes and typed values. It is time we took a step back and review the final API of Saint. First we review the generic constructs which form type representations:

```
data A0 :: (t :: *)              (univ :: * → *) a
data A1 :: (t :: * → *)         (univ :: * → *) a
   ...
data An :: (t :: * → ... → *) (univ :: * → *) a

A0 ::           A0 t u t
A1 :: u a →   A1 t u (t a)
   ...
An :: u a → u b → ... → u x → An t u (t a b ... x)
```

These type formers assume they are given a universe *u*. To construct a representation of a concrete universe we give a way to tie the knot:

```
data Close (f :: (* → *) → * → * → *) a
type (f :: (* → *) → * → * → *) ∺ (g :: (* → *) → * → * → *) :: (* → *) → * → * → *
```

Using which we can construct a concrete universe:

type *MyUniverse = Close (A0 Int :+: A1 Maybe :+: A2 Either)*

Elements of the universe can be constructed using smart constructors:

$$
\begin{aligned}
int &:: A0\ Int\ u :< u &&\Rightarrow u\ Int \\
maybe &:: A1\ Maybe\ u :< u &&\Rightarrow u\ a \to u\ (Maybe\ a) \\
(\dashrightarrow) &:: A2\ (\to)\ u :< u &&\Rightarrow u\ a \to u\ b \to u\ (a \to b)
\end{aligned}
$$
...

In order to add a new smart constructor we need only use the injection from the :< type class.

$$
\begin{aligned}
int &= inject\ A0 \\
maybe\ a &= inject\ (A1\ a) \\
a \dashrightarrow b &= inject\ (A2\ a\ b)
\end{aligned}
$$
...

Finally, a library can be created which is polymorphic in the representation of types:

data *Item = Item String (TypedValue u)*
data *Library u = Library String [Item u]*

We can now put everything together to create an example of a very simple library, containing only addition on integers.

$$
\begin{aligned}
myLibrary &:: (A0\ Int\ u :< u, A2\ (\to)\ u :< u) \Rightarrow Library\ u \\
myLibrary &= Library\ \texttt{"My Library"}\ [Item\ \texttt{"+"}\ ((+) ::: int \dashrightarrow int \dashrightarrow int)]
\end{aligned}
$$

With the library in place we can move on to interpreting programs written in the DSL.

3   Type-Safe Interpretation

We use our *TypedValues* to expose EDSLs to the outside world in a type-safe and useful way. The previous section showed how we can gather a group of functions into a *Library*. In this section we construct a type-safe function (*interpret*), which interprets a string as a program written in a small functional language and defined in terms of the *Library* functions. We start with the definition of a datatype for expressions, which we limit to the essentials for discussion purposes. The type *UExpr* (U for "untyped") contains constructors for variables (*UVar*), application (*UApp*), and lambda-abstraction (*ULam*).

data *UExpr* **where**
$$
\begin{aligned}
UVar &:: String \to UExpr \\
UApp &:: UExpr \to UExpr \to UExpr \\
ULam &:: String \to UExpr \to UExpr
\end{aligned}
$$

If we attempt to write an interpreter for expressions of this type we quickly run into trouble, as it's unclear how we should interpret the lambda case (*ULam*):

```
interpret :: (TypeEquality tr, A2 (→) tr :< tr)
           ⇒ Env tr → UExpr → Maybe (TypedValue tr)
interpret en e = case e of
  UVar v    → en v
  UApp f x  → do
    f' ←   interpret en f
    x' ←   interpret en x
    app f' x'
  ULam v e →
    let a    = _  -- should be the type of v
        b    = _  -- should be the type of e
        fun x = fromJust (interpret (extend en v (x ::: a)) e)
    in return (fun ::: a --→ b)

type Env tr = String → Maybe (TypedValue tr)
```

The first case in the definition is self-explanatory. The second case uses the *app* function below to apply one *TypedValue* to another.

```
app :: forall u. (TypeEquality u, A2 (→) u :< u)
        ⇒ TypedValue u → TypedValue u → Maybe (TypedValue u)
app (f ::: funType) (x ::: arg) = do
  A2 from to :: A2 (→) u _f ← eject funType
  Refl ← from ?= arg
  return (f x ::: to)
```

The third case is where things get interesting. How do we interpret lambdas? Clearly, lambda expressions should be interpreted as functions from some type a to some type b, but how should we choose a and b? The problem is that we do not have access to the type of the result or the argument of the lambda. There is no fundamental reason why this has to be the case, type inference for the simply typed lambda calculus with monomorphic constants is known to be a solved problem! From an untyped expression and a library we can easily derive a typed expression. Below is an encoding of the typed expressions:

```
data Expr tr where
  Var :: String → Expr tr
  App :: Expr tr → Expr tr → Expr tr
  Lam :: String → tr a → Expr tr → tr b → Expr tr
```

A value *Lam x ra e rb* represents a lambda expression $(\lambda x \to e) :: a \to b$ where $ra :: tr\ a$ and $rb :: tr\ b$. Using a standard type inference algorithm, like algorithm W [5], it is possible to infer the type annotations in an *Expr tr* from just an untyped *UExpr* and a *Library tr*. With type annotations in place, we can fix our interpreter to act correctly in the case for *Lam*.

$$
\begin{aligned}
&interpret \; :: \quad (TypeEquality\; u, A2\; (\rightarrow)\; u :< u) \\
&\qquad\quad \Rightarrow \quad Env\; u \rightarrow Expr\; u \rightarrow Maybe\; (TypedValue\; u) \\
&interpret\; en\; e = \mathbf{case}\; e\; \mathbf{of} \\
&\quad Var\; v \qquad \rightarrow en\; v \\
&\quad App\; f\; x \qquad \rightarrow \mathbf{do} \\
&\qquad f' \leftarrow interpret\; en\; f \\
&\qquad x' \leftarrow interpret\; en\; x \\
&\qquad app\; f'\; x' \\
&\quad Lam\; v\; a\; e\; b \rightarrow \\
&\qquad \mathbf{let}\; fun\; x\; = \mathbf{let}\; en' = extend\; en\; v\; (x ::: a) \\
&\qquad\qquad\qquad\qquad\quad Just\; res = interpret\; en'\; e \\
&\qquad\qquad\qquad\quad \mathbf{in}\; fromJust\; (coerce\; res\; b) \\
&\qquad \mathbf{in}\; return\; (fun ::: a \dashrightarrow b)
\end{aligned}
$$

Note the use of *fromJust* in the last row of the definition of *fun*. This is an ostensibly partial operation, but we claimed to have provided a *type-safe* interpreter! Not to worry, the interpreter always returns a *Just v* given a correct environment and a well-typed expression *e*. This means that we can safely use *interpret* in a context where expressions are type-checked before we call it. This means that we can build a safe function *run :: Complete tr* $\Rightarrow$ *Library tr* $\rightarrow$ *String* $\rightarrow$ *Maybe (TypedValue tr)*, where we have:

$$
\mathbf{type}\; Complete\; tr = (TypeEquality\; tr, A2\; (\rightarrow)\; tr :< tr)
$$

We elide the functions for parsing and type checking but present *run*:

$$
\begin{aligned}
&parse \qquad :: String \rightarrow Maybe\; UExpr \\
&typeCheck :: Complete\; tr \Rightarrow Library\; tr \rightarrow UExpr \rightarrow Maybe\; (Expr\; tr) \\
&libToEnv \;\; :: Library\; tr \rightarrow Env\; tr \\
\\
&run \qquad\;\; :: Complete\; tr \Rightarrow Library\; tr \rightarrow String \rightarrow Maybe\; (TypedValue\; tr) \\
&run\; l\; s = parse\; s \ggg typeCheck\; l \ggg interpret\; (libToEnv\; l)
\end{aligned}
$$

It would be possible to take one further step towards manifest type-safety: we could add type-indices to *Expr* and *Env* to obtain an interpreter without *Maybe*. If we ignore variable binding this would result in an interpreter in the style of *eval1 :: E a* $\rightarrow$ *a* for a type indexed expression type *E*. With binding, we would also need a parameter for the environment: *eval2 :: env* $\rightarrow$ *E env a* $\rightarrow$ *a*. But in our full setting, with parameterisation also over the universe, we decided this would take us too far from the intended application and leave it as future work.

4   Case Study: GRACe

The GRACe language [11] is a Haskell EDSL for working with diagrammatic systems of components implemented by constraint logic programming. The GRACe DSL is used in the GRACeFUL RAT [15] (Rapid Assessment Tool), which is a tool for graphical composition of maps representing causal relationships between parts of complex systems, such as systems describing urban design and its sensitivity to weather. The rapid assessment tool consists of a Haskell backend connected to a constraint solver and a web-based visual editor frontend [13]. The tool exposes a library of functions written in the DSL to the user as graphical widgets (Fig. 3).

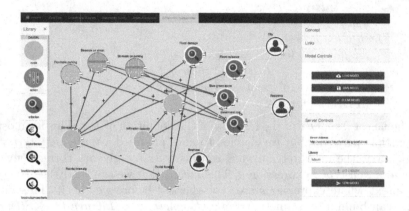

Fig. 3. A GRACe graph representation in the visual editor frontend.

The function widgets have parameter fields for the user to specify the function parameters, as well as input and output ports that can be connected to send the output of one function as the input to another. Using these widgets, the user constructs a program in the form of a graph. The graph is submitted to the Haskell backend using HTTP, at which point it is interpreted as a program in the GRACe EDSL.

The tool makes use of Typed Values to retain type information for the library functions exposed to the frontend which allows type-safe interpretation of the programs sent back from the frontend. The library contains a Typed Value representing each of the exposed functions, along with metadata concerning the visual presentation of the function on the frontend. When the program graph is submitted to the backend the appropriate library functions are applied to parameters provided by the user, which are communicated in a type-safe manner using Typed Values. The resulting value is sent back to the frontend to be displayed to the user.

Using Typed Values we can prevent users from causing type errors by making mistakes like giving function parameters of the wrong type or sending the output of one function as the input to a function with a different input type. We use the Typed Value tags to annotate the library of functions with metadata to specify how the functions should be presented on the frontend.

5   Related Work

In [17], Peyton Jones et al. present *Dynamic* and *TypeRep*, implemented with built-in support in GHC. We use a similar technique but can unfortunately not use their *TypeRep* directly because we want support for "labelling" of type representations to help communication with the external world. They support an open universe of all Haskell types rather than our "extensible but closed" universes.

In his lecture notes on "Typed Tagless Final Interpreters" [12], Kiselyov presents a technique (or design pattern) for representing typed higher-order languages (DSLs) in a typed metalanguage (Haskell), along with type-preserving interpretation. It is a powerful technique, but does not deal with connecting to the untyped world as we do.

Baars and Swierstra [2] present an approach for dynamic typing that is similar to the standard libraries *Dynamic* and *Typeable*, but they abstract over the actual type representation using an type class. Whereas they abstract over the type representation, we show how to control the range of type representation using an universe of types. We can extend an existing universe of types, instead of supplying a new instance for a type representation type class. The paper by Baars and Swierstra [2] also shows how to construct a typed evaluator that can interpret expressions using dynamic typing. The main difference is that the supported expressions need to be tagged with their types. We don't need to have such annotations since we infer the type of an expression.

Cheney and Hinze [4] use the same type representation encoding, but focus their library more on generic programming, rather than dynamic type checking. Similarly Bahr and Hvitved [3] present a compositional encoding of datatypes with an emphasis on recursion schemes. They do not focus their effort on encoding type representations, however.

6   Conclusions and Future Work

We have presented a framework for exposing Haskell EDSLs to the untyped world and interpreting the resulting EDSL programs in a type-safe manner. We have shown how this framework is useful in a small example (Henderson's functional geometry EDSL) as well as a larger real-world case study (GRACe). The mechanisms for achieving this have all been implemented in Haskell without special compiler support.

Future Work. Currently our technique only supports exposing monomorphic APIs; supporting polymorphic APIs is noted as future work. Achieving this would be both useful and technically interesting. To the best of our understanding, representing polymorphic types without special compiler support is a non-trivial task. Being able to expose polymorphic EDSLs using our technique would significantly increase the versatility of the language.

It would also be interesting to explore the extent to which our technique for adding annotations could be used to add semantically rich annotations. The tagging mechanism that allows us to attach additional documentation to a type in our *TypedValues* could be extended to express contracts in the style of Hinze et al. [10], stating properties that the attached value must satisfy. Adding contracts could potentially greatly increase the utility of the framework for the EDSL writer. Being able to specify pre- and post-conditions is useful both for the EDSL writer and the end user.

It would be interesting to evaluate the Saint library both in terms of usability (can new users easily apply it to their EDSLs) and efficiency (how much overhead, in memory and time, is used by Saint).

Finally it would be a natural direction to continue up the ladder of type safety to a type indexed expression datatype and a tag-less interpreter.

Acknowledgements. This work was partially supported by the projects GRACeFUL (grant #640954) and CoeGSS (grant #676547), which have received funding from the European Union's Horizon 2020 research and innovation programme. It was also partially supported by the Wallenberg Artificial Intelligence, Autonomous Systems and Software Program (WASP) funded by Knut and Alice Wallenberg Foundation.

References

1. Axelsson, E., et al.: Feldspar: a domain specific language for digital signal process-ing algorithms. In: 8th IEEE/ACM International Conference on Formal Methods and Models for Codesign (MEMOCODE 2010), pp. 169–178. IEEE (2010). https://doi.org/10.1109/MEMOCOD.2010.5558637
2. Baars, A.I., Swierstra, S.D.: Typing dynamic typing. In: Proceedings of the Seventh ACM SIGPLAN International Conference on Functional Programming, ICFP 2002, pp. 157–166. ACM, New York (2002). https://doi.org/10.1145/581478.581494
3. Bahr, P., Hvitved, T.: Compositional data types. In: Proceedings of the Seventh ACM SIGPLAN Workshop on Generic Programming, WGP 2011, pp. 83–94. ACM, New York (2011). https://doi.org/10.1145/2036918.2036930
4. Cheney, J., Hinze, R.: A lightweight implementation of generics and dynamics. In: Proceedings of the 2002 ACM SIGPLAN Workshop on Haskell, Haskell 2002, pp. 90–104. ACM, New York (2002). https://doi.org/10.1145/581690.581698
5. Damas, L., Milner, R.: Principal type-schemes for functional programs. In: Pro-ceedings of the 9th ACM SIGPLAN-SIGACT Symposium on Principles of Pro-gramming Languages, POPL 1982, pp. 207–212. ACM, New York (1982). https://doi.org/10.1145/582153.582176
6. Eisenberg, R.A., Weirich, S.: Dependently typed programming with singletons. In: Proceedings of the 2012 Haskell Symposium, Haskell 2012, pp. 117–130. ACM, New York (2012). https://doi.org/10.1145/2364506.2364522
7. Heeren, B., Jeuring, J., Gerdes, A.: Specifying rewrite strategies for interac-tive exercises. Math. Comput. Sci. **3**(3), 349–370 (2010). https://doi.org/10.1007/s11786-010-0027-4
8. Henderson, P.: Functional geometry. In: Proceedings of the 1982 ACM Symposium on LISP and Functional Programming, LFP 1982, pp. 179–187. ACM, New York (1982). https://doi.org/10.1145/800068.802148

9. Henderson, P.: Functional geometry. High.-Order Symbolic Comput. **15**(4), 349–365 (2002). https://doi.org/10.1023/A:1022986521797

10. Hinze, R., Jeuring, J., Löh, A.: Typed contracts for functional programming. In: Hagiya, M., Wadler, P. (eds.) FLOPS 2006. LNCS, vol. 3945, pp. 208–225. Springer, Heidelberg (2006). https://doi.org/10.1007/11737414_15

11. Jansson, P., et al.: D4.2: a domain specific language for GRACeFUL concept maps (2017). https://github.com/GRACeFUL-project/DSL-WP/raw/master/deliverables/d4.2.pdf, deliverable of the GRACeFUL project (640954)

12. Kiselyov, O.: Typed tagless final interpreters. In: Gibbons, J. (ed.) Generic and Indexed Programming. LNCS, vol. 7470, pp. 130–174. Springer, Heidelberg (2012). https://doi.org/10.1007/978-3-642-32202-0_3

13. Krishna Murthy, D.R., Wiens, V., Lohmann, S., Asmat, R.: D3.3: VA EDA tool prototype (2017). Deliverable of the GRACeFUL project. FETPROACT-1-2014 Grant No. 640954

14. Lämmel, R., Peyton Jones, S.: Scrap your boilerplate: a practical design pattern for generic programming. In: Proceedings of the 2003 ACM SIGPLAN International Workshop on Types in Languages Design and Implementation, TLDI 2003, pp. 26–37. ACM, New York (2003). https://doi.org/10.1145/604174.604179

15. Lohmann, S.: D2.5: CRUD RAT prototype (2017). Deliverable of the GRACeFUL project. FETPROACT-1-2014 Grant No. 640954

16. Mestanogullari, A., Hahn, S., Arni, J.K., Löh, A.: Type-level web APIs with servant: an exercise in domain-specific generic programming. In: Proceedings of the 11th ACM SIGPLAN Workshop on Generic Programming, pp. 1–12. ACM (2015). https://doi.org/10.1145/2808098.2808099

17. Peyton Jones, S., Weirich, S., Eisenberg, R.A., Vytiniotis, D.: A reflection on types. In: Lindley, S., McBride, C., Trinder, P., Sannella, D. (eds.) A List of Successes That Can Change the World. LNCS, vol. 9600, pp. 292–317. Springer, Cham (2016). https://doi.org/10.1007/978-3-319-30936-1_16

18. Swierstra, W.: Data types à la carte. J. Funct. Program. **18**(4), 423–436 (2008). https://doi.org/10.1017/S0956796808006758

19. Wadler, P.: The expression problem (1998). http://homepages.inf.ed.ac.uk/wadler/papers/expression/expression.txt, appeared on the Java-genericity mailing list

Improving Haskell

Martin A. T. Handley$^{(\boxtimes)}$ and Graham Hutton$^{(\boxtimes)}$

School of Computer Science, University of Nottingham, Nottingham, UK
{martin.handley,graham.hutton}@nottingham.ac.uk

Abstract. Lazy evaluation is a key feature of Haskell, but can make it difficult to reason about the efficiency of programs. Improvement theory addresses this problem by providing a foundation for proofs of program improvement in a call-by-need setting, and has recently been the subject of renewed interest. However, proofs of improvement are intricate and require an inequational style of reasoning that is unfamiliar to most Haskell programmers. In this article, we present the design and implementation of an inequational reasoning assistant that provides mechanical support for improvement proofs, and demonstrate its utility by verifying a range of improvement results from the literature.

1   Introduction

Reasoning about the efficiency of Haskell programs is notoriously difficult and counterintuitive. The source of the problem is Haskell's use of lazy evaluation, or more precisely, call-by-need semantics, which allows computations to be performed with terms that are not fully normalised. In practice, this means that the operational efficiency of a term does not necessarily follow from the number of steps it takes to evaluate to normal form, in contrast to a call-by-value setting where reasoning about efficiency is much simpler.

Moran and Sands' *improvement theory* [1] offers the following solution to this problem: rather than counting the steps required to normalise a term in isolation, we compare the number of steps required in all program contexts. This idea gives rise to a compositional approach to reasoning about efficiency in call-by-need languages that can be used to verify improvement results.

Improvement theory was originally developed in the 1990s, but has recently been the subject of renewed interest, with a number of general-purpose program optimisations being formally shown to be improvements [2–4]. In an effort to bridge the so-called correctness/efficiency 'reasoning gap' [5], these articles show that it is indeed possible to formally reason about the performance aspects of optimisation techniques in a call-by-need setting.

While improvement theory provides a suitable basis for reasoning about efficiency in Haskell, the resulting proofs are often rather intricate [2], and constructing them by hand is challenging. In particular, comparing the cost of evaluating terms in all program contexts requires a somewhat elaborate reasoning process, and the resulting *inequational* style of reasoning is inherently more demanding than the equational style that is familiar to most Haskell programmers.

© Springer Nature Switzerland AG 2019
M. Pałka and M. Myreen (Eds.): TFP 2018, LNCS 11457, pp. 114–135, 2019.
https://doi.org/10.1007/978-3-030-18506-0_6

```
  ≡ λxs.λys.✓(case xs of
      []      → ys
      (z:zs) → ((f zs) ++ [z]) ++ ys)
[18]> append-assoc-lr-i
  ⋧ λxs.λys.✓(case xs of
      []      → ys
      (z:zs) → (f zs) ++ ([z] ++ ys))
[19]> right
  ≡ λxs.λys.✓(case xs of
      []      → ys
      (z:zs) → (f zs) ++ ([z] ++ ys))
[20]> eval-i
  ⋧ λxs.λys.✓(case xs of
      []      → ys
      (z:zs) → (f zs) ++ (z:ys))
```

Fig. 1. An extract from a proof in our system

To support interactive *equational* reasoning about Haskell programs, the Hermit toolkit [6] was recently developed, and its utility has been demonstrated in a series of case studies [7–12]. Although inequational reasoning is more involved than its equational counterpart, both approaches share the same calculational style. In addition, the Hermit system and improvement theory are both based on the same underlying setting: the core language of the Glasgow Haskell Compiler. As such, a system developed in a similar manner to Hermit could prove to be effective in supporting inequational reasoning for proofs of program improvement, just as Hermit has proven to be effective in supporting equational reasoning for proofs of program correctness.

To the best of our knowledge, no such inequational reasoning system exists. To fill this gap, we developed the University of Nottingham Improvement Engine (Unie): an interactive, mechanised assistant for call-by-need improvement theory. More specifically, the article makes the following contributions:

- We show how the Kansas University Rewrite Engine (Kure), which forms the basis for equational reasoning in the Hermit system, can also form the basis for inequational reasoning in our system (Sect. 4);
- We implement Moran and Sands' tick algebra in our system, which is an inequational theory that allows evaluation costs to be moved around in terms, and verify a range of basic tick algebra results (Sects. 3.5 and 4);
- We explain how program contexts, a central aspect of improvement theory, are automatically managed by our system, and show how this simplifies reasoning steps in mechanised improvement proofs (Sect. 4.5);
- We demonstrate the practicality of our system by mechanically verifying all the improvement results in the article that renewed interest in improvement theory [2], and a number from the original article [1] (Sect. 6).

By way of example, an extract from an improvement proof in our system—concerning the *reverse* function on lists—is given in Fig. 1. In each step, the term highlighted in orange is being transformed. In the first step, the append operator $+\!\!\!+$ is reassociated to the right, which is an improvement, denoted using the $\gtrsim$ symbol. We then move to the right in the term, and evaluate the $+\!\!\!+$, which is also an improvement. The tick symbol $\checkmark$ in the proof represents a unit time cost. We will revisit this example in more detail throughout the article.

Our improvement assistant comprises approximately 13,000 lines of Haskell on top of the Kure framework, and is freely available online [13].

2   Example

To provide some intuition for improvement theory, and demonstrate how its technicalities can benefit from mechanical support, we begin with an example that underpins the proof in Fig. 1. Consider the following property, which formalises that Haskell's list append operator $+\!\!\!+$ is associative (for finite lists):

$$(xs +\!\!\!+ ys) +\!\!\!+ zs \ = \ xs +\!\!\!+ (ys +\!\!\!+ zs) \tag{1}$$

A common, informal argument about the above equation is that the left-hand side is less time efficient than the right-hand side, because the former traverses the list xs twice. This insight is often exploited when optimising functions defined in terms of append [14]. Optimisations of this kind typically demonstrate the correctness of (1), which can be verified by a simple inductive proof, but fail to make precise any efficiency claims about the equation. Can we do better?

Using improvement theory, we can formally verify which side of the equation is more efficient by comparing the evaluation costs of each term in all program contexts. That is, we can show that one side is 'improved by' the other, written:

$$(xs +\!\!\!+ ys) +\!\!\!+ zs \ \gtrsim \ xs +\!\!\!+ (ys +\!\!\!+ zs) \tag{2}$$

Before sketching how the above inequation can be proven, we introduce some necessary background material. As the focus here is on illustrating the basic ideas by means of an example, we simplify the theory where possible and will return to the precise details in the next section.

Contexts and Improvement. In the usual manner, contexts are 'terms with holes', denoted $[-]$, which can be substituted with other terms. Informally, a term M is *improved by* a term N, written $M \gtrsim N$, if in all contexts the evaluation of N requires no more function calls than the evaluation of M. If the evaluations of the terms require the same number of function calls in all contexts, then the terms are said to be *cost-equivalent*, written $M \lessgtr N$.

Ticks. While reasoning about improvement, it is necessary to keep track of evaluation cost explicitly within the syntax of the source language (see [1] for a detailed explanation). This is achieved by means of a tick annotation $\checkmark$ that represents a unit time cost, i.e. one function call. Denotationally, ticks have no effect on terms. Operationally, however, a tick represents a function call. Hence, a term M evaluates with n function calls iff $\checkmark M$ evaluates with $n+1$ function calls. Moreover, for any function definition $f\ x = M$, we have the cost-equivalence

$$f\ x \ \lessgtr \ \checkmark M \tag{3}$$

```
   (xs ++ ys) ++ zs
 ≡  { syntactic sugar }
    let ws = xs ++ ys in ws ++ zs
 ⟐  { unfold ++ }
    let ws = √case xs of
               []       → ys
               (u : us) → u : (us ++ ys)
    in ws ++ zs
 ⟐  { unfold ++ }
    let ws = √case xs of
               []       → ys
               (u : us) → u : (us ++ ys)
    in √case ws of
         []       → zs
         (v : vs) → v : (vs ++ zs)
 ⟐  { move tick inside D's hole, where
        D ≡ case [−] of
              []       → ys
              (u : us) → u : (us ++ ys) }
    let ws = case √xs of
               []       → ys
               (u : us) → u : (us ++ ys)
    in √case ws of
         []       → zs
         (v : vs) → v : (vs ++ zs)
 ⟐  { move D inside case, where
        D ≡ let ws = [−]
            in √case ws of
                 []       → zs
                 (v : vs) → v : (vs ++ zs) }
    case √xs of
      []       → let ws = ys in √case ws of
                   []       → zs
                   (v : vs) → v : (vs ++ zs)
      (u : us) → let ws = u : (us ++ ys) in √case ws of
                   []       → zs
                   (v : vs) → v : (vs ++ zs)
 ⟐  { move tick outside D's hole, where
        D ≡ case [−] of
              []       → ...
              (u : us) → ... }
    √case xs of
      []       → let ws = ys in √case ws of
                   []       → zs
                   (v : vs) → v : (vs ++ zs)
      (u : us) → let ws = u : (us ++ ys) in √case ws of
                   []       → zs
                   (v : vs) → v : (vs ++ zs)
 ⟐  { fold ++ }
    √case xs of
```

```
      []       → let ws = ys in ws ++ zs
      (u : us) → let ws = u : (us ++ ys) in √case ws of
                   []       → zs
                   (v : vs) → v : (vs ++ zs)
 ⟐  { inline ws and remove unused binding }
    √case xs of
      []       → √ys ++ zs
      (u : us) → let ws = u : (us ++ ys) in √case ws of
                   []       → zs
                   (v : vs) → v : (vs ++ zs)
 ⟐  { move tick outside D's hole, where
        D ≡ [−] ++ zs }
    √case xs of
      []       → √(ys ++ zs)
      (u : us) → let ws = u : (us ++ ys) in √case ws of
                   []       → zs
                   (v : vs) → v : (vs ++ zs)
 ⟐  { inline ws and remove unused binding }
    √case xs of
      []       → √(ys ++ zs)
      (u : us) → √case √(u : (us ++ ys)) of
                   []       → zs
                   (v : vs) → v : (vs ++ zs)
 ⟐  { move tick outside D's hole, where
        D ≡ case [−] of
              []       → zs
              (v : vs) → v : (vs ++ zs) }
    √case xs of
      []       → √(ys ++ zs)
      (u : us) → √√case u : (us ++ ys) of
                   []       → zs
                   (v : vs) → v : (vs ++ zs)
 ⟐  { evaluate case }
    √case xs of
      []       → √(ys ++ zs)
      (u : us) → √√(u : ((us ++ ys) ++ zs))
 ⪰  { remove ticks }
    √case xs of
      []       → √(ys ++ zs)
      (u : us) → u : ((us ++ ys) ++ zs)
 ≡  { renaming }
    √case xs of
      []       → √(ys ++ zs)
      (x : xs) → x : ((xs ++ ys) ++ zs)
 ≡  { define C, where
        C ≡ case xs of
              []       → √(ys ++ zs)
              (x : xs) → x : [−] }
    √C[(xs ++ ys) ++ zs]
```

Fig. 2. Proof of property (4)

because unfolding the definition eliminates the function call. Removing a tick improves a term, $\sqrt{M} \succsim M$, but the converse $M \succsim \sqrt{M}$ is not valid.

Improvement Induction. A difficulty with the definition of improvement is that it quantifies over all contexts, and hence proving (2) notionally requires considering all possible contexts. However, this is a standard issue with contextual definitions, and there are a number of methods for constructing proofs in a more tractable manner. We use improvement induction [1] for this purpose, presented here in a simplified form. For any context $\mathbb{C}$, we have:

$$\frac{M \succsim \sqrt{\mathbb{C}[M]} \qquad \sqrt{\mathbb{C}[N]} \succsim N}{M \succsim N}$$

Intuitively, this rule allows us to prove $M \succsim N$ by finding a single context $\mathbb{C}$ for which we can 'unfold' M to $\sqrt{\mathbb{C}[M]}$ and 'fold' $\sqrt{\mathbb{C}[N]}$ to N. For example, applying improvement induction to inequation (2) reduces the problem to finding a context $\mathbb{C}$ that satisfies the following two properties:

$$(xs ++ ys) ++ zs \quad \succsim \quad \sqrt{\mathbb{C}[(xs ++ ys) ++ zs]} \tag{4}$$

$$\sqrt{\mathbb{C}[xs \mathbin{+\mkern-8mu+} (ys \mathbin{+\mkern-8mu+} zs)]} \quad \stackrel{\scriptstyle\Leftrightarrow}{} \quad xs \mathbin{+\mkern-8mu+} (ys \mathbin{+\mkern-8mu+} zs) \tag{5}$$

Proof of Property (2). For the purposes of this example, we can assume that the source language is Haskell, with one small caveat: arguments to functions must be variables. Improvement theory requires this assumption and it is easy to achieve by introducing **let** bindings. For example, the term $(xs \mathbin{+\mkern-8mu+} ys) \mathbin{+\mkern-8mu+} zs$ can be viewed as syntactic sugar for **let** $ws = xs \mathbin{+\mkern-8mu+} ys$ **in** $ws \mathbin{+\mkern-8mu+} zs$.

Using improvement induction, we can prove (2) by finding a context $\mathbb{C}$ for which properties (4) and (5) hold. We prove the first of these properties in Fig. 2; the second proceeds similarly. As we have not yet presented the rules of the tick algebra (Sect. 3.5), the reader is encouraged to focus on the overall structure of the reasoning in Fig. 2, rather than the technicalities of each step. Our system is specifically designed to support and streamline such reasoning.

3   Improvement Theory

In this section, we return to the formalities of Moran and Sands' call-by-need improvement theory. While explaining the theory, we describe how our system supports, and in many cases simplifies, its resulting technicalities.

3.1   Syntax and Semantics

The operational model that forms the basis of call-by-need improvement theory is an untyped, higher-order language with mutually recursive let bindings. The call-by-need semantics is originally due to Sestoft [15] and reflects Haskell's use of lazy evaluation. Furthermore, the language is comparable to (a normalised version of) the core language of the Glasgow Haskell Compiler. We use these similarities to apply results from this theory directly to Haskell.

Terms of the language are defined by the following grammar, which also comprises the abstract syntax manipulated by our system:

$$M, N ::= x \mid \lambda x.M \mid M \; x \mid \textbf{let } \{ \boldsymbol{x} = \boldsymbol{M} \} \textbf{ in } N \mid c \; \boldsymbol{x} \mid \textbf{case } M \textbf{ of } \{ c_i \; \boldsymbol{x_i} \rightarrow N_i \}$$

We use the symbols x, y, z for variables, c for constructors, and write $\boldsymbol{x} = \boldsymbol{M}$ for a sequence of bindings of the form $x = M$. Similarly, we write $c_i \; \boldsymbol{x_i} \rightarrow N_i$ (or sometimes *alts*) for a sequence of **case** alternatives of the form $c \; \boldsymbol{x} \rightarrow N$. Literals are represented by constructors of arity 0, and all constructors are assumed to be fully applied. A term is a *value*, denoted V, if it is of the form $\lambda x.M$ or $c \; \boldsymbol{x}$, which corresponds to the usual notion of weak head normal form.

The abstract machine for evaluating terms maintains a state $\langle \Gamma, M, S \rangle$ consisting of a heap Γ given by a set of bindings from variables to terms, the term M currently being evaluated, and the evaluation stack S given by a list of tokens used by the abstract machine. The machine operates by evaluating the current term to a value, and then decides how to continue based on the top token on the stack. Bindings generated by **let**s are added to the heap, and only taken off when performing a **Lookup** operation. A **Lookup** executes by putting a token on top of the stack representing where the term was looked up, and then evaluating that term to a value before replacing it on the heap. This ensures that each binding is evaluated at most once: a key aspect of call-by-need semantics. Restricting function arguments to be variables means that all non-atomic arguments must be introduced via **let** statements and thus can be evaluated at most once.

The transitions of the machine are given in Fig. 3. The `Letrec` transition assumes that x is disjoint from (written here as $\natural$) the domain of Γ and S, which can always be achieved by alpha-renaming.

$$
\begin{array}{lll}
\langle \Gamma\{x = M\}, x, S \rangle & \longrightarrow \langle \Gamma, M, \#x : S \rangle & \{ \text{ Lookup } \} \\
\langle \Gamma, V, \#x : S \rangle & \longrightarrow \langle \Gamma\{x = V\}, V, S \rangle & \{ \text{ Update } \} \\
\langle \Gamma, M\ x, S \rangle & \longrightarrow \langle \Gamma, M, x : S \rangle & \{ \text{ Unwind } \} \\
\langle \Gamma, \lambda x.M, y : S \rangle & \longrightarrow \langle \Gamma, M[y/x], S \rangle & \{ \text{ Subst } \} \\
\langle \Gamma, \textbf{case } M \textbf{ of } alts, S \rangle & \longrightarrow \langle \Gamma, M, alts : S \rangle & \{ \text{ Case } \} \\
\langle \Gamma, c_j\ y, \{c_i\ x_i \longrightarrow N_i\} : S \rangle & \longrightarrow \langle \Gamma, N_j[y/x_j], S \rangle & \{ \text{ Branch } \} \\
\langle \Gamma, \textbf{let }\{x = M\} \textbf{ in } N, S \rangle & \longrightarrow \langle \Gamma\{x = M\}, N, S \rangle \quad x \natural \operatorname{dom}(\Gamma, S) & \{ \text{ Letrec } \}
\end{array}
$$

Fig. 3. Semantics of the call-by-need abstract machine

3.2   Contexts

Program contexts are defined by the following grammar:

$$\mathbb{C}, \mathbb{D} ::= [-] \mid x \mid \lambda x.\mathbb{C} \mid \mathbb{C}\ x \mid \textbf{let }\{x = \mathbb{C}\} \textbf{ in } \mathbb{D} \mid c\ x \mid \textbf{case } \mathbb{C} \textbf{ of } \{c_i\ x_i \to \mathbb{D}_i\}$$

Note that **let** and **case** statements admit contexts with multiple holes.

A *value context*, denoted $\mathbb{V}$, is a context that is in weak head normal form. There are also two other kinds of contexts, which can contain at most one hole that must appear as the target of evaluation: meaning evaluation cannot proceed until the hole is substituted. These are known as *evaluation contexts* and *applicative contexts*, and are defined by the following two grammars, respectively:

$$
\begin{aligned}
\mathbb{E} ::= &\ \mathbb{A} \\
\mid &\ \textbf{let }\{x = M\} \textbf{ in } \mathbb{A} \\
\mid &\ \textbf{let }\{\ y\ \ = M; \\
&\quad x_0\ = \mathbb{A}_0[x_1]; \\
&\quad x_1\ = \mathbb{A}_1[x_2]; \\
&\quad \cdots \\
&\quad x_n = \mathbb{A}_n\} \textbf{ in } \mathbb{A}[x_0]
\end{aligned}
\qquad
\begin{aligned}
\mathbb{A} ::= &\ [-] \\
\mid &\ \mathbb{A}\ x \\
\mid &\ \textbf{case } \mathbb{A} \textbf{ of } \{c_i\ x_i \to M_i\}
\end{aligned}
$$

As improvement is a contextual definition, intuitively, the transformation rules we apply when reasoning about improvement must also be defined contextually. In general, however, it is not the case that a given transformation rule is valid for *all* contexts. For example, a tick can be freely moved in and out of an evaluation context using the rule

$$\mathbb{E}[\checkmark M] \;\Lleftarrow\!\!\Rrightarrow\; \checkmark\mathbb{E}[M] \qquad\qquad (\checkmark\text{-}\mathbb{E})$$

but this is not the case for other kinds of contexts. Similarly, under certain conditions regarding free (FV) and bound (BV) variables, an evaluation context can be moved in and out of a **case** statement:

$$\mathbb{E}[\textbf{case } M \textbf{ of } \{pat_i \rightarrow N_i\}]$$
$$\leftrightsquigarrow \qquad FV(M) \not\fin BV(\mathbb{E}) \qquad FV(\mathbb{E}) \not\fin pat_i \qquad \text{(case-}\mathbb{E})$$
$$\textbf{case } M \textbf{ of } \{pat_i \rightarrow \mathbb{E}[N_i]\}$$

Consequently, when applying a transformation rule to a term, we must ensure that its syntactic form is compatible with the chosen rule. When conducted manually, the process of deconstructing a term $M \equiv \mathbb{C}[S]$ into a context $\mathbb{C}$ and substitution S becomes tedious, time consuming, and prone to error.

To address this problem, our system handles all aspects of context manipulation automatically. Each time a rule is applied, the system analyses the syntactic form of the term and ensures it is compatible with the rule's specification. If this is not the case, the system prevents the rule from being applied and reports an error. The same is also true if a rule's side conditions are not satisfied, such as those regarding free and bound variables for case-$\mathbb{E}$. Thus, with regards to contexts, not only does the Unie system make a correct transformation much easier to apply, it makes an incorrect transformation impossible to apply.

3.3   Improvement

Moran and Sands [1] showed that the total number of steps taken to evaluate any term is bounded by a function that is linear in the number of Lookup operations invoked during its evaluation. Therefore, evaluation cost can be measured *asymptotically* by just counting uses of Lookup. This is the notion of cost used in their work, and we also adopt it for our system.

Formally, we write $M\downarrow^n$ if the abstract machine proceeds from the initial state $\langle \emptyset, M, \epsilon \rangle$ to some final state $\langle \Gamma, V, \epsilon \rangle$ with n uses of Lookup. Similarly, we write $M\downarrow^{\leqslant n}$ to mean that $M\downarrow^m$ for some $m \leqslant n$. Using this cost model we can now formalise the notion of improvement: a term M is *improved by* a term N, written $M \gtrsim N$, if the following holds for all contexts $\mathbb{C}$:

$$\mathbb{C}[M]\downarrow^n \implies \mathbb{C}[N]\downarrow^{\leqslant n}$$

That is, one term is improved by another if the latter takes no more Lookup operations to evaluate than the former in all contexts. In turn, we say that two terms M and N are *cost-equivalent*, written $M \lessgtr N$, if for all contexts $\mathbb{C}$:

$$\mathbb{C}[M]\downarrow^n \iff \mathbb{C}[N]\downarrow^n$$

As before, we need to keep track of evaluation costs explicitly. Our informal introduction viewed the tick operator as a syntactic construct that represents a unit time cost. Here we follow [2] and define tick as a derived operation:

$$\checkmark M \equiv \textbf{let } \{x = M\} \textbf{ in } x \qquad \text{(x fresh)}$$

This definition takes precisely two steps to evaluate to M: one to add the binding to the heap, and the other to look it up. As one of these steps is a `Lookup` operation, the cost of evaluating M is increased by exactly one, as required. The following tick elimination rule still holds, but as before the reverse is not valid:

$$\checkmark M \mathbin{\gtrsim\kern-0.8em\raise0.4ex\hbox{$\scriptstyle\sim$}} M \qquad\qquad\qquad (\checkmark\text{-elim})$$

The relation $\gtrsim$ formalises when one term is at least as efficient as another in all contexts, but this is a strong requirement. We use the notion of *weak improvement* [2] when one term is at least as efficient as another within a constant factor. Formally, M is *weakly improved by* N, written $M \mathbin{\gtrsim\kern-0.8em\raise0.4ex\hbox{$\scriptstyle\sim$}} N$, if there exists a linear function $f(x) = kx + c$ (for $k, c \geqslant 0$) such that for all contexts $\mathbb{C}$:

$$\mathbb{C}[M]\!\downarrow^n \implies \mathbb{C}[N]\!\downarrow^{\leqslant f(n)}$$

This can be interpreted as "replacing M with N may make programs worse, but will not make them asymptotically worse" [2]. Analogous to cost-equivalence, we also have weak cost-equivalence, written $M \mathbin{\lessgtr\kern-0.8em\raise0.4ex\hbox{$\scriptstyle\sim$}} N$, which is defined in the obvious manner. As weak improvement ignores constant factors, we can introduce and eliminate ticks while preserving weak cost-equivalence:

$$M \mathbin{\lessgtr\kern-0.8em\raise0.4ex\hbox{$\scriptstyle\sim$}} \checkmark M \qquad\qquad\qquad (\checkmark\text{-intro})$$

3.4 Inequational Reasoning

When constructing improvement proofs, careful attention must be paid to their respective improvement relations. This is because the transformation rules we apply during reasoning steps are defined using the different notions of improvement ($\gtrsim, \mathbin{\gtrsim\kern-0.8em\raise0.4ex\hbox{$\scriptstyle\sim$}}, \lessgtr, \mathbin{\lessgtr\kern-0.8em\raise0.4ex\hbox{$\scriptstyle\sim$}}$), some of which may not entail the relation in question. For example, given that $\gtrsim \subseteq \mathbin{\gtrsim\kern-0.8em\raise0.4ex\hbox{$\scriptstyle\sim$}}$, any transformation defined using $\gtrsim$ automatically entails $\mathbin{\gtrsim\kern-0.8em\raise0.4ex\hbox{$\scriptstyle\sim$}}$, but the converse is not true. Similarly, removing a tick ($\checkmark$-elim) is an improvement, whereas unfolding a function's definition (3) is not.

In this instance, our system simplifies the necessary inequational reasoning by ensuring that each transformation rule applied by the user entails a particular improvement relation established prior to the start of the reasoning process. If the user attempts to apply a rule that does not entail this relation, the system will reject it and display an error message.

3.5 The Tick Algebra

We conclude this section by discussing the *tick algebra* [1], which is a collection of laws for propagating evaluation costs around terms while preserving or increasing efficiency. These laws make up a large proportion of the transformation rules that are provided by our system, and are a rich inequational theory that subsumes all axioms of the call-by-need calculus of Ariola et al. [16].

We refer the reader to [1] for the full tick algebra, but present two example laws below to illustrate their nature and complexity:

$$
\begin{array}{l}
\text{let } \{x = L\} \text{ in let } \{y = M\} \text{ in } N \\
\overset{\Leftrightarrow}{} \qquad x \notmid y \qquad y \notmid FV(L) \qquad\qquad\qquad \text{(let-flatten)} \\
\text{let } \{x = L, y = M\} \text{ in } N
\end{array}
$$

$$
\begin{array}{l}
\checkmark\text{let } \{x = z, y = M[z/w]\} \text{ in } N[z/w] \\
\gtrsim \qquad\qquad\qquad\qquad\qquad\qquad\qquad\qquad\qquad \text{(var-expand)} \\
\text{let } \{x = z, y = M[x/w]\} \text{ in } N[x/w]
\end{array}
$$

The (let-flatten) rule is a cost-equivalence, and allows us to merge the binders of two **let**s modulo binder collisions and variable capture. In turn, (var-expand) is an improvement that allows us to replace a binding with its binder provided there is a tick in front of the **let** to pay for this expansion. Also included in the tick algebra are ($\checkmark$-$\mathbb{E}$) and (case-$\mathbb{E}$) introduced previously.

The laws discussed above are only a small fragment of the tick algebra, however, it should be evident from these examples that applying such rules manually can be a difficult task. In particular, the use of different improvement relations, different kinds of contexts, and each rule having a unique syntactic form, makes it challenging to know when a rule can be applied correctly. Furthermore, many laws have side conditions, often concerning free and bound variables as with (case-$\mathbb{E}$) and (let-flatten), which must be checked every time they are applied.

A key strength of our system is that it provides mechanical support for all of these tasks, and moreover, it will automatically perform, for example, alpha-renaming to enable rules such as (let-flatten) to be applied correctly. Thus, the system allows the user to focus on the key aspects of their improvement calculations by handling tedious but important technical details on their behalf.

4   System Architecture

The main components of our system are illustrated in Fig. 4. The *read-evaluate-print-loop* (Repl) handles interaction with the user. The *inequational layer* checks that transformation rules invoked by the user are safe to apply in the current proof state. The *primitive rewrites* and *congruence combinators* are basic building blocks used to define transformation rules in a modular manner [12], and are implemented using the Kure rewrite engine [17]. The *history* records successful commands entered by the user, and the resultant proof state of each command. In turn, the *library* maintains a collection of term, context, and cost-equivalent context definitions for use during proofs, together with a collection of command scripts that can be used to define transformation *sequences*. Finally, the *context manipulation* component supports the automatic generation, matching, and checking of the different kinds of program contexts.

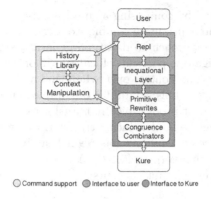

○ Command support   ◉ Interface to user   ◉ Interface to Kure

Fig. 4. Architecture of our system

4.1 Read-Eval-Print-Loop (Repl)

A necessary aspect of constructing interactive proofs is transforming sub-terms. We prioritise this requirement by maintaining a focus into the term being transformed, and providing navigation commands for changing the focus. Transformations are then applied to the sub-term currently in focus. By default, only the focused sub-term is displayed, which is updated each time a navigation command is executed. For situations when it may be beneficial to always display the whole term or some designated part, the system provides an option for the current focus to be highlighted. This feature is exhibited in Fig. 1.

4.2 Inequational Layer

Each time a transformation rule is invoked, the system checks that it is safe to apply in the current proof state. One aspect of this verification step is to ensure that the rule's corresponding operator entails the proof's improvement relation. If this is not the case, the transformation rule is rejected. Not only is this essential to ensuring well-formed calculations, it also permits users to safely experiment with improvement rules (for example, those from the tick algebra).

4.3 Primitive Rewrites, Congruence Combinators, and Kure

Similarly to the equational reasoning assistant Hermit [6], our system utilises the Kansas University Rewrite Engine (Kure) [17] for specifying and applying transformations to the abstract syntax of its operational model.

In brief, Kure is a strategic programming language [18] that provides a principled method for traversing and transforming data types. The fundamental idea behind Kure is to separate the implementations of traversals and the implementations of transformations. Traversal strategies and transformation rules can thus be reused and combined independently. For our system, this allows a sophisticated library of transformation rules, tailored to the needs of improvement theory, to be constructed by composing a small number of primitive operations using a selection of Kure's primitive combinators.

In addition, Kure's approach to datatype-generic programming [19] means that traversals can navigate to particular locations in order to apply type-specific transformations, giving fine control over when and where transformations are applied within a data type. This is vital for our implementation, as each reasoning step in an improvement proof typically transforms only a single sub-term.

Overall, our approach to implementing transformations rules using *primitive rewrites* and *congruence combinators* has been heavily inspired by the Hermit system, and builds on the work in [6,12]. We refer the reader to [6,17] for a detailed discussion of the relevant concepts.

4.4   Cost-Equivalent Contexts

The system maintains a library of *cost-equivalent contexts*. These are contexts whose syntactic forms do not satisfy the requirements for a particular kind of context (value, evaluation, applicative) but are nevertheless cost-equivalent to a context of this kind, and hence admit the same laws. Such contexts occur frequently in improvement proofs [1,2], as they lead to simplified reasoning steps. Once added by the user, cost-equivalent contexts are manipulated by the system in the same manner as other kinds of contexts (see Sect. 6 for an example).

4.5   Context Manipulation

Managing contexts is one of the primary intricacies in constructing improvement proofs. In this section, we explain how this is handled by our system.

Context Matching. In our system, a *context pattern* is simply a shorthand for a context, allowing sub-terms to be specified implicitly using wildcards and constructor patterns. For example, the context **let** $\{x = a; y = b\}$ **in** $[-]$ may be described by any of the following context patterns (among others):

$$\textbf{let } \{x = a; \_\} \textbf{ in } [-] \qquad \textbf{let } \{x = VAR; \_\} \textbf{ in } [-] \qquad \textbf{let } \_ \textbf{ in } [-]$$

The underscores above are wildcards that match with any term, while VAR is a constructor pattern that matches with any variable.

Context patterns do not represent unique contexts, but when used in conjunction with a specific transformation rule, are often sufficient to determine a unique context. In practice, they are used to simplify the amount of input required from a user interacting with the system. Recall the following rule, which allows ticks to be moved in and out of evaluation contexts:

$$\mathbb{E}[\checkmark M] \;\Leftrightarrow\; \checkmark\mathbb{E}[M] \tag{$\checkmark$-E}$$

Suppose we wish to apply this rule to the term $\checkmark(a\ b\ c)$. To do so, we must determine an evaluation context $\mathbb{E}$ and a term M for which $\checkmark\mathbb{E}[M] \equiv \checkmark(a\ b\ c)$. In this case it is simple, such as by taking $\mathbb{E} = [-]\ b\ c$ and $M = a$. Applying $\checkmark$-E (right to left) then allows us to move the tick inside the context:

$$\sqrt{(a\ b\ c)}$$
$$\Leftrightarrow \{\ \sqrt{\text{-}}\mathbb{E}\quad [-]\ b\ c\ \}$$
$$(\sqrt{a})\ b\ c$$

This transformation can be mirrored almost identically in our system:

```
unie> trans $`(a b c)$
√(a b c)
[1]> untick-eval $[-] b c$
⇗ √a b c
```

Here the system uses the specified context $[-]\ b\ c$ and the given term $\sqrt{(a\ b\ c)}$ to verify the preconditions necessary for $\sqrt{\text{-}}\mathbb{E}$'s safe application. That is, it checks $[-]\ b\ c$ is a valid evaluation context and, by calculating the substituted term $M = a$, ensures the initial term has the required form $\sqrt{\mathbb{E}[M]}$. If any of these preconditions were not met, the transformation step would be rejected.

Suppose now that the context $\mathbb{E}$ from the above example was more complex, such as a **let** statement with multiple bindings. In this case, it would be impractical to expect the user to manually enter its full definition. Context patterns address this problem by allowing users to specify contexts by shorthand representations. The system uses these representations to automatically calculate valid contexts on the user's behalf, by *matching* the specified pattern against the syntax of the term being transformed. For example, we can use wildcard patterns to apply the above transformation in a simplified manner:

```
unie> trans $`(a b c)$
√(a b c)
[1]> untick-eval $[-] _ _$
⇗ √a b c
```

Context Generation. If we apply the same transformation rule as above, but without specifying a context parameter, the system will respond as follows:

```
unie> trans $`(a b c)$
√(a b c)
[1]> untick-eval
Select a context/substitution option:
(1) E = [-],      M = a b c
(2) E = [-] c,    M = a b
(3) E = [-] b c,  M = a
```

That is, three possible context/substitution pairs have been automatically *generated* by the system, each allowing $\sqrt{\text{-}}\mathbb{E}$ to be correctly applied to the given term. Option three corresponds to our previous choice:

```
[1]> 3
⇗ √a b c
```

Context generation is available when applying any of the system's transformation rules. This feature has proven to be invaluable when validating proofs from the original improvement theory article [1], as the calculations in this article only specify the rules that are applied, and not how they are applied. Context generation often allows us to fill in these details automatically.

4.6 Inequational Reasoning

A central feature of our system is its support for inequational reasoning. The relationship between the different improvement relations that were introduced in Sect. 3 are summarised in the following lattice:

An improvement proof is initiated by the user entering a proof statement, such as $\sqrt{}x \gtrsim x$. The system uses this statement to establish a 'global' improvement relation, in this case $\gtrsim$. Each time a transformation is applied, the corresponding operator is checked to ensure that it entails this global relation in the above lattice. If this is not the case, the transformation is prevented from being applied and an error message is displayed. For example:

```
unie> trans $``x$ IMP $x$
Global relation set: ≳.
Transformation goal set: x.
√√x
[1]> tick-elim
≳ √x
[2]> untick-intro
Relation error: ⋦ ⇏ ≳.
```

5 Worker/Wrapper Transformation

During the development of the Unie system, we were guided by the desire to mechanically verify all the results from the paper that renewed interest in improvement theory [2]. In this section, we review the main result of this paper, which shows that the worker/wrapper transformation is an improvement, and an example application of this result, which shows how a naive reverse function on lists can be improved to a more efficient version. In the next section, we will show how the latter result can be mechanised in our system.

5.1 Correctness

The worker/wrapper transformation is a technique for improving the performance of recursive programs by changing their types [20]. Given a recursive program of some type, the basic idea is to factorise the program into a *worker* program of a different type, together with a *wrapper* program that acts as an interface between the original program and the new worker. The intention is that if the worker type supports more efficient operations than the original type, then this efficiency should result in a more efficient program overall.

More formally, suppose we are given a recursive program defined as the least fixed point *fix f* of a function *f* on some type *A*. Now consider a more efficient program that performs the same task, defined by first taking the least fixed point *fix g* of a function *g* on some other type *B*, and then migrating the resulting value back to the original type by applying a conversion function *abs*. The equivalence between the two programs is captured by the following equation:

$$\textit{fix } f = abs \ (\textit{fix } g)$$

This equation states that the original program *fix f* can be factorised into the application of a wrapper function *abs* to a worker program *fix g*. As one may expect, the validity of the equation depends on some properties of the functions *f*, *g*, and *abs*, together with a dual conversion function *rep*. These properties are summarised in the following worker/wrapper correctness theorem [21]: given functions $f : A \to A$, $g : B \to B$, $abs : B \to A$, and $rep : A \to B$ satisfying one of the assumptions (A–C) and one of the conditions (1–3),

(A)	$abs \circ rep$	$= id_A$		(1)	g	$= rep \circ f \circ abs$
(B)	$abs \circ rep \circ f$	$= f$		(2)	$g \circ rep$	$= rep \circ f$
(C)	$\textit{fix} \ (abs \circ rep \circ f)$	$= \textit{fix} f$		(3)	$f \circ abs$	$= abs \circ g$

then we have the correctness equation *fix f* = *abs* (*fix g*).

5.2   Improvement

The previous section formalised that the worker/wrapper transformation is correct, in the sense that the original and new programs have the same denotational meaning. We now formalise that the transformation improves efficiency, in the sense that the new program improves the runtime performance of the original.

To reformulate the correctness theorem as an improvement theorem, we must first make some changes to the basic setup to take account of the differences between the underlying denotational and operational theories. In particular, functions are replaced by contexts, i.e. the functions *f* and *g* become contexts $\mathbb{F}$ and $\mathbb{G}$; the use of a *fix* operator is replaced by recursive **let** bindings, i.e. *fix f* becomes **let** $x = \mathbb{F}[x]$ **in** x; and the use of equality is replaced by an appropriate improvement relation, i.e. = becomes $\gtrsim$, $\gtrsim$ or $\gtrsim\!\!\!\lessgtr$. Using these modifications, we have the following worker/wrapper improvement theorem [2]: given value contexts $\mathbb{F}$, $\mathbb{G}$, **Abs**, and **Rep** satisfying one of the assumptions (where x is free)

(A)	$\texttt{Abs}[\texttt{Rep}[x]]$	$\gtrsim\!\!\!\lessgtr$	x
(B)	$\texttt{Abs}[\texttt{Rep}[\mathbb{F}[x]]]$	$\gtrsim\!\!\!\lessgtr$	$\mathbb{F}[x]$
(C)	**let** $x = \texttt{Abs}[\texttt{Rep}[\mathbb{F}[x]]]$ **in** x	$\gtrsim\!\!\!\lessgtr$	**let** $x = \mathbb{F}[x]$ **in** x

and one of the conditions

$$
\begin{array}{lll}
(1) & \mathbb{G}[x] & \lesssim\gtrsim \quad \mathrm{Rep}[\mathbb{F}[\mathrm{Abs}[x]]] \\
(2) & \mathbb{G}[\checkmark\mathrm{Rep}[x]] & \lesssim \quad \mathrm{Rep}[\checkmark\mathbb{F}[x]] \\
(3) & \mathrm{Abs}[\checkmark\mathbb{G}[x]] & \lesssim\gtrsim \quad \mathbb{F}[\checkmark\mathrm{Abs}[x]]
\end{array}
$$

then we have the improvement inequality **let** $x = \mathbb{F}[x]$ **in** $x \gtrsim$ **let** $x = \mathbb{G}[x]$ **in** $\mathrm{Abs}[x]$. The assumptions and conditions above that ensure the original recursive program **let** $x = \mathbb{F}[x]$ **in** x is improved by **let** $x = \mathbb{G}[x]$ **in** $\mathrm{Abs}[x]$ are natural extensions of the corresponding properties for correctness. For example, correctness condition (1), $g = rep \circ f \circ abs$, is replaced by improvement condition (1), $\mathbb{G}[x] \lesssim\gtrsim \mathrm{Rep}[\mathbb{F}[\mathrm{Abs}[x]]]$. Note that because improvement theory is untyped, there are no typing requirements on the contexts.

The proof of the above theorem utilises two other results: a 'rolling' rule and a fusion rule. Both are central to the worker/wrapper transformation [20], and can be proven using tick algebra laws. Consequently, the worker/wrapper improvement theorem is itself a direct result of the tick algebra's inequational theory. All aforementioned results have been verified using our system [13].

5.3   Example

Consider the following naive definition for the *reverse* function on lists:

$$
\begin{array}{l}
reverse \;\; = \textbf{let } f = \mathrm{Revbody}[f] \textbf{ in } f \\
\mathrm{Revbody} = \lambda xs.\textbf{case } xs \textbf{ of} \\
\qquad\qquad\qquad [] \qquad \to [] \\
\qquad\qquad\qquad (y : ys) \to [-] \; ys \mathbin{+\!\!+} [y]
\end{array}
$$

Here the function is defined using a recursive **let** binding rather than explicit recursion, and the context Revbody captures the non-recursive part of the function's definition. This implementation is inefficient due to the use of the append operator $+\!\!+$, which takes linear time in the length of its first argument. We would like to use the worker/wrapper technique to improve it.

The first step is to select a new type to replace the original type $[a] \to [a]$, and define contexts to perform the conversions between the two types. In this case, we utilise the type $[a] \to [a] \to [a]$ that provides an additional argument that is used to accumulate the resulting list [14]. The contexts to convert between the original and new types are then defined as follows [2]:

$$
\mathrm{Abs} = \lambda xs.[-] \; xs \; [] \qquad\qquad \mathrm{Rep} = \lambda xs.\lambda ys.[-] \; xs \mathbin{+\!\!+} ys
$$

We must now verify that the conversion contexts Abs and Rep satisfy one of the worker/wrapper assumptions. We verify assumption (B) as follows:

$\mathrm{Abs}[\mathrm{Rep}[\mathrm{Revbody}[f]]]$
$\equiv$ { apply definitions of Abs and Rep }
$\lambda xs.(\lambda xs.\lambda ys.\mathrm{Revbody}[f]\ xs \mathbin{+\!\!+} ys)\ xs\ []$
$\overset{\curvearrowright}{\approx}$ { β-reduction }
$\lambda xs.\mathrm{Revbody}[f]\ xs \mathbin{+\!\!+} []$
$\equiv$ { apply definition of Revbody }
$\lambda xs.(\lambda xs.\mathbf{case}\ xs\ \mathbf{of}$
$\quad []\quad \rightarrow []$
$\quad (y:ys) \rightarrow f\ ys \mathbin{+\!\!+} [y])\ xs \mathbin{+\!\!+} []$
$\overset{\curvearrowright}{\approx}$ { β-reduction }
$\lambda xs.(\mathbf{case}\ xs\ \mathbf{of}$
$\quad []\quad \rightarrow []$
$\quad (y:ys) \rightarrow f\ ys \mathbin{+\!\!+} [y]) \mathbin{+\!\!+} []$

$\overset{\curvearrowright}{\approx}$ { case-$\mathbb{E}$ rule, where $\mathbb{E} \equiv [-] \mathbin{+\!\!+} []$ }
$\lambda xs.\mathbf{case}\ xs\ \mathbf{of}$
$\quad []\quad \rightarrow [] \mathbin{+\!\!+} []$
$\quad (y:ys) \rightarrow (f\ ys \mathbin{+\!\!+} [y]) \mathbin{+\!\!+} []$
$\overset{\curvearrowright}{\approx}$ { associativity of $\mathbin{+\!\!+}$ }
$\lambda xs.\mathbf{case}\ xs\ \mathbf{of}$
$\quad []\quad \rightarrow [] \mathbin{+\!\!+} []$
$\quad (y:ys) \rightarrow f\ ys \mathbin{+\!\!+} ([y] \mathbin{+\!\!+} [])$
$\overset{\curvearrowright}{\approx}$ { evaluate $[] \mathbin{+\!\!+} []$ and $[y] \mathbin{+\!\!+} []$ }
$\lambda xs.\mathbf{case}\ xs\ \mathbf{of}$
$\quad []\quad \rightarrow []$
$\quad (y:ys) \rightarrow f\ ys \mathbin{+\!\!+} [y]$
$\equiv$ { unapply definition of Revbody }
$\mathrm{Revbody}[f]$

Note that the above calculation uses the fact that $\mathbin{+\!\!+}$ is associative up to weak cost-equivalence, that is, $(xs \mathbin{+\!\!+} ys) \mathbin{+\!\!+} zs \overset{\curvearrowright}{\approx} xs \mathbin{+\!\!+} (ys \mathbin{+\!\!+} zs)$.

Next we must verify that one of the worker/wrapper conditions is satisfied. In this example, we can use condition (2) as a *specification* for the context $\mathbb{G}$, whose definition can then be calculated using laws from the tick algebra. We omit the details here for brevity, but they are included in the original paper [2], and result in the following context definition:

$\mathbb{G} = \lambda xs.\lambda ys.\mathbf{case}\ xs\ \mathbf{of}$
$\quad []\quad\quad \rightarrow ys$
$\quad (z:zs) \rightarrow \mathbf{let}\ ws = (z:ys)\ \mathbf{in}\ [-]\ zs\ ws$

The crucial step in the construction of $\mathbb{G}$ is applying property (2) from our example in Sect. 2, which expresses that reassociating append to the right is an improvement, i.e. $(xs \mathbin{+\!\!+} ys) \mathbin{+\!\!+} zs \gtrsim xs \mathbin{+\!\!+} (ys \mathbin{+\!\!+} zs)$.

Finally, if we define $fastrev = \mathbf{let}\ x = \mathbb{G}[x]\ \mathbf{in}\ \mathrm{Abs}[f]$, then by applying the worker/wrapper improvement theorem, we have shown that the original version of *reverse* is improved by the new version, i.e. $reverse \gtrsim fastrev$. Expanding out the definition of *fastrev* and renaming/simplifying the resulting **let** binding gives the familiar fast version of the original function:

$fastrev :: [a] \rightarrow [a]$
$fastrev\ xs = revcat\ xs\ []$

$revcat :: [a] \rightarrow [a] \rightarrow [a]$
$revcat\ []\ ys\quad\quad = ys$
$revcat\ (x:xs)\ ys = revcat\ xs\ (x:ys)$

6   Mechanising Fast Reverse

In this section, we demonstrate how to improve the naive reverse function mechanically using our system. In doing so, we illustrate a number of the system's key features, and show how it supports interactive reasoning using transformation and navigation rules. All of the interaction is taken directly from the system itself, with some minor reformatting for the paper-based medium.

As in the previous section, we focus on the proof of assumption (B). Prior to constructing the proof, we must ensure that the system has access to the definitions from Sect. 5, which are required at different stages throughout. For convenience we have stored them in a file, which is imported into the system's library using the `import-lib` command, and the names of the new definitions displayed using `show-lib defs`. We have also included the definition of ++, as this is required in a number of proof steps involving evaluation.

```
unie> import-lib ./libs/reverse
Info: library updated.

unie> show-lib defs
Terms:    (++), reverse
Contexts: Abs, Rep, Revbody
```

We instruct the system to enter its transformation mode using `trans`. The relevant proof statement Abs[Rep[Revbody[f]]] $\lessapprox$ Revbody[f] is supplied as a parameter, and determines the proof's global relation and goal. The global relation will prevent rules being applied whose operators do not entail weak cost-equivalence $\lessapprox$, and we will be notified when the goal Revbody[f] is reached. When entering terms into the system, the kinds of contexts must be specified. Abs, Rep, and Revbody are value contexts, so we use the V_ prefix.

```
unie> trans $V_Abs[V_Rep[V_Revbody[f]]]$ WCE $V_Revbody[f]$
Global relation set: ⪝.
Transformation goal set: V_Revbody[f].
```

As with the paper proof, we begin by applying the definitions of Abs and Rep, and beta-reducing inside the body of the outer lambda abstraction. In order to reduce the correct sub-terms, we must navigate using `left` and `right`, which move the focus to the current terms left and right child, respectively. The last step uses `top`, which restores focus to the full term.

```
V_Abs[V_Rep[V_Revbody[f]]]
  [1]> apply-def 'Abs ; apply-def 'Rep
  ≡ λxs.(λxs.λys.(V_Revbody[f] xs) ++ ys) xs []
  [3]> right
  ≡ (λxs.λys.(V_Revbody[f] xs) ++ ys) xs []
  [4]> left
  ≡ (λxs.λys.(V_Revbody[f] xs) ++ ys) xs
  [5]> beta
  ⪝ λys.(V_Revbody[f] xs) ++ ys
  [6]> up ; beta
  ⪝ (V_Revbody[f] xs) ++ []
  [8]> top
  ≡ λxs.(V_Revbody[f] xs) ++ []
```

Next we apply the definition of Revbody and beta-reduce the resulting redex. We then move up to focus on the application of append.

```
  [9]> apply-def 'Revbody
  ≡ λxs.((λxs.case xs of
      []     → []
      (y:ys) → (f ys) ++ [y]) xs) ++ []
  [10]> right ; left
  ≡ (++) ((λxs.case xs of
      []     → []
      (y:ys) → (f ys) ++ [y]) xs)
  [12]> right
  ≡ (λxs.case xs of
      []     → []
      (y:ys) → (f ys) ++ [y]) xs
```

```
[13]> beta
⟨⟩ case xs of
    []       →  []
    (y:ys)   →  (f ys) ++ [y]
[14]> up ; up
≡ (case xs of
    []       →  []
    (y:ys)   →  (f ys) ++ [y]) ++ []
```

Now recall the case-$\mathbb{E}$ rule, which allows an evaluation context to be moved inside a **case** statement (subject to certain conditions regarding free and bound variables, which are automatically checked by our system):

$$\mathbb{E}[\textbf{case } M \textbf{ of } \{pat_i \to N_i\}] \quad \langle\!\!\langle \quad \textbf{case } M \textbf{ of } \{pat_i \to \mathbb{E}[N_i]\}$$

Here we would like to use this rule to move $+\!\!\!+\ []$ inside the **case** statement. We know that the system can generate evaluation contexts, so we can attempt to apply the rule without specifying a parameter:

```
[16]> case-eval
Error: no valid evaluation contexts.
```

However, an error results because the context $[-] +\!\!\!+\ []$ we wish to use is not strictly speaking an evaluation context, but is only cost-equivalent to an evaluation context [2]. By default, only contexts of the correct syntactic form are accepted by the system, meaning that even if we manually specified the desired context as a parameter to `case-eval`, it would be rejected as invalid.

The solution is to add $[-] +\!\!\!+\ []$ to the library of cost-equivalent evaluation contexts, which allows the system to treat it as if it were strictly an evaluation context. This is done using the `add-lib` command. In fact, the proof in [2] is more general than this particular example, and shows that $[-] +\!\!\!+\ xs$ is cost-equivalent to an evaluation context for any list xs. This can be captured using the constructor pattern $LIST$ that matches with any list:

```
[16]> add-lib EVAL $[-] ++ LIST$
Info: library updated.
```

Cost-equivalent contexts are incorporated into the system's context generation and matching mechanisms, meaning that when we apply `case-eval` again without a parameter, the correct context is used automatically. Note that in this example, the context pattern $[-] +\!\!\!+\ LIST$ has been instantiated to $[-] +\!\!\!+\ []$ in order to apply the transformation rule correctly.

```
[16]> case-eval
⟨⟩ case xs of
    []       →  [] ++ []
    (y:ys)   →  ((f ys) ++ [y]) ++ []
```

We have almost completed the proof. All that is left to do is evaluate the applications of append that have resulted from $+\!\!\!+\ []$ being moved inside both alternatives in the **case** statement. Note that in the second alternative, we wish to evaluate $[y] +\!\!\!+\ []$. In order to do so we must first reassociate the term using the fact that append is associative up to weak cost-equivalence.

```
[17]> right ; rhs
≡ [] ++ []
[19]> eval-wce
⇗ []
[20]> up ; next ; rhs
≡ ((f ys) ++ [y]) ++ []
[23]> append-assoc-lr-wce
⇗ (f ys) ++ ([y] ++ [])
[24]> right ; eval-wce
⇗ [y]
[26]> top
≡ λxs.case xs of
     []      → []
     (y:ys)  → (f ys) ++ [y]
```

Finally, we unapply the definition of Revbody and are notified that we have reached our goal. The proof of the property is complete:

```
[27]> unapply-def 'Revbody
Info:  transformation goal reached!
≡ V_Revbody[f]
```

In conclusion, the above calculation demonstrates how improvement proofs can be constructed using our system. By following the same pattern as the original paper proof, with the addition of navigation steps to make the point of application of each rule clear, we were able to mechanise the calculation by simply entering the transformation rules as commands into the system. Behind the scenes, the technicalities of each proof step were administered automatically on our behalf to ensure the resulting proof is correct. Moreover, by entering commands without parameters, we allowed the system to simplify the development of proof steps by automatically generating the necessary contexts.

7   Related Work

Several tools have been developed to mechanise *equational* reasoning about Haskell programs [22–25]. Most relevant to our system is Hermit [6], which builds upon the Haskell Equational Reasoning Assistant (Hera) [26]. There appears to be no other systems in the literature that directly support *inequational* reasoning about Haskell programs, and to the best of our knowledge, our system is the first to provide mechanical support for improving Haskell programs.

In other languages, the Algebra of Programming in Agda (AoPA) library [27] is designed to encode relational program derivations, which supports a form of inequational reasoning. The Jape proof calculator [28,29] provides step-by-step interactive development of proofs in formal logics, and supports both equational and inequational reasoning. Improvement theory has not been explored within either of these settings, however. More generally, automated theorem provers [30, 31] can be used to provide formal, machine-checked proofs of program properties, but require expertise in dependently-typed programming.

Other methods for reasoning about time performance in a lazy setting include [32,33]. Most notably is the work of Okasaki [34], who used a notion of *time credits* to analyse the amortized performance of a range of purely functional data structures. This approach has recently been implemented in Agda [35]. Research has also been conducted on type-based methods for cost analysis, for example in [36,37], but in general these frameworks do not incorporate call-by-need semantics. GHC itself provides *cost centres*, which can be used to annotate source code so that the GHC profiler can indicate which parts of a program cost the most to execute. A formal cost semantics for GHC core programs based on the notion of cost centres is presented in [38].

8   Conclusion and Further Work

In this article, we have presented the design and implementation of an inequational reasoning assistant that provides mechanical support for proofs of program improvement. In doing so, we have highlighted a number of difficulties in manually constructing improvement proofs, and described how the system has been developed to address these challenges. We have illustrated the applicability of our system by verifying a range of improvement results from the literature. Specifically, we have mechanised all proofs in [2], including the proof of the worker/wrapper improvement theorem, which relates to a highly general optimisation technique. We have also mechanically verified a number of proofs in [1]. All of these proofs are freely available online as scripts that can be loaded into our system, along with the system itself [13].

We have three main avenues for further work. First of all, we would like to investigate higher-level support for navigating through terms during improvement proofs, for which we expect to be guided by our experience using the Hermit system [6]. Secondly, we would like to extend our system to produce proof objects that can be independently checked using an external proof assistant such as Coq or Agda, to provide a formal guarantee of their correctness. And finally, we are also interested in lightweight approaches to verifying improvement properties, for example, in a similar manner to which the QuickCheck [39] system supports lightweight verification of correctness properties.

Acknowledgements. We'd like to thank Jennifer Hackett and Neil Sculthorpe for many useful discussions, and the anonymous referees for their useful suggestions. This work was funded by EPSRC grant EP/P00587X/1, *Mind the Gap: Unified Reasoning About Program Correctness and Efficiency*.

References

1. Moran, A.K., Sands, D.: Improvement in a Lazy Context: An Operational Theory for Call-By-Need. Extended version of [40] (1999)
2. Hackett, J., Hutton, G.: Worker/wrapper/makes it/faster. In: ICFP (2014)
3. Schmidt-Schauß, M., Sabel, D.: Improvements in a functional core language with call-by-need operational semantics. In: PPDP (2015)
4. Hackett, J., Hutton, G.: Parametric polymorphism and operational improvement. University of Nottingham (2017, in preparation)

5. Harper, R.: The Structure and Efficiency of Computer Programs. Carnegie Mellon University (2014)
6. Farmer, A.: Hermit: Mechanized Reasoning During Compilation in the Glasgow Haskell Compiler. Ph.D. thesis, University of Kansas (2015)
7. Sculthorpe, N., Farmer, A., Gill, A.: The HERMIT in the tree: mechanizing program transformations in the GHC core language. In: Hinze, R. (ed.) IFL 2012. LNCS, vol. 8241, pp. 86–103. Springer, Heidelberg (2013). https://doi.org/10.1007/978-3-642-41582-1_6
8. Farmer, A., Höner zu Siederdissen, C., Gill, A.: The Hermit in the stream. In: PEMP (2014)
9. Farmer, A., Sculthorpe, N., Gill, A.: Reasoning with the Hermit: tool support for equational reasoning on GHC core programs. In: Haskell Symposium (2015)
10. Adams, M.D., Farmer, A., Magalhães, J.P.: Optimizing SYB Is easy! In: PEPM (2014)
11. Adams, M.D., Farmer, A., Magalhães, J.P.: Optimizing SYB traversals is easy!. Sci. Comput. Program. **112**, 170–193 (2015)
12. Farmer, A., Gill, A., Komp, E., Sculthorpe, N.: The Hermit in the machine: a plugin for the interactive transformation of GHC core language programs. In: Haskell Symposium (2012)
13. Handley, M.A.T.: GitHub Repository for the University of Nottingham Improvement Engine (Unie) (2017). https://github.com/mathandley/Unie
14. Wadler, P.: The Concatenate Vanishes. University of Glasgow (1987)
15. Sestoft, P.: Deriving a lazy abstract machine. JFP **7**(3), 231–264 (1997)
16. Ariola, Z.M., Maraist, J., Odersky, M., Felleisen, M., Wadler, P.: A call-by-need lambda calculus. In: POPL (1995)
17. Sculthorpe, N., Frisby, N., Gill, A.: The Kansas university rewrite engine. JFP **24**, 434–473 (2014)
18. Lämmel, R., Visser, E., Visser, J.: The Essence of Strategic Programming (2002)
19. Gibbons, J.: Datatype-generic programming. In: Backhouse, R., Gibbons, J., Hinze, R., Jeuring, J. (eds.) SSDGP 2006. LNCS, vol. 4719, pp. 1–71. Springer, Heidelberg (2007). https://doi.org/10.1007/978-3-540-76786-2_1
20. Gill, A., Hutton, G.: The worker/wrapper transformation. JFP **19**(2), 227–251 (2009)
21. Sculthorpe, N., Hutton, G.: Work it, wrap it, fix it, fold it. JFP **24**(1), 113–127 (2014)
22. Tullsen, M.A.: Path, A Program Transformation System for Haskell. Ph.D. thesis. Yale University (2002)
23. Guttmann, W., Partsch, H., Schulte, W., Vullinghs, T.: Tool support for the interactive derivation of formally correct functional programs. J. Univers. Comput. Sci. **9**, 173 (2003)
24. Thompson, S., Li, H.: Refactoring tools for functional languages. JFP **23**(3), 293–350 (2013)
25. Li, H., Reinke, C., Thompson, S.: Tool support for refactoring functional programs. In: Haskell Workshop (2003)
26. Gill, A.: Introducing the Haskell equational reasoning assistant. In: Haskell Workshop (2006)
27. Mu, S.C., Ko, H.S., Jansson, P.: Algebra of programming in Agda: dependent types for relational program derivation. JFP **19**(5), 545–579 (2009)
28. Bornat, R., Sufrin, B.: Jape: a calculator for animating proof-on-paper. In: McCune, W. (ed.) CADE 1997. LNCS, vol. 1249, pp. 412–415. Springer, Heidelberg (1997). https://doi.org/10.1007/3-540-63104-6_41

29. Bornat, R., Sufrin, B.: Animating formal proof at the surface: the jape proof calculator. Comput. J. **42**(3), 177–192 (1999)
30. Bertot, Y., Castéran, P.: Interactive Theorem Proving and Program Development: Coq'Art: The Calculus of Inductive Constructions. Springer, Heidelberg (2013). https://doi.org/10.1007/978-3-662-07964-5
31. Norell, U.: Towards a Practical Programming Language Based on Dependent Type Theory. Ph.D. thesis, Chalmers University of Technology (2007)
32. Wadler, P.: Strictness analysis aids time analysis. In: POPL (1988)
33. Bjerner, B., Holmström, S.: A composition approach to time analysis of first order lazy functional programs. In: FPCA (1989)
34. Okasaki, C.: Purely Functional Data Structures. Cambridge University Press, Cambridge (1999)
35. Danielsson, N.A.: Lightweight semiformal time complexity analysis for purely functional data structures. In: POPL (2008)
36. Brady, E., Hammond, K.: A dependently typed framework for static analysis of program execution costs. In: Butterfield, A., Grelck, C., Huch, F. (eds.) IFL 2005. LNCS, vol. 4015, pp. 74–90. Springer, Heidelberg (2006). https://doi.org/10.1007/11964681_5
37. Çiçek, E., Barthe, G., Gaboardi, M., Garg, D., Hoffmann, J.: Relational cost analysis. In: POPL (2017)
38. Sansom, P.M., Peyton Jones, S.L.: Formally based profiling for higher-order functional languages. TOPLAS (1997)
39. Claessen, K., Hughes, J.: QuickCheck: a lightweight tool for random testing of Haskell Programs. In: ICFP (2011)
40. Moran, A.K., Sands, D.: Improvement in a lazy context: an operational theory for call-by-need. In: POPL (1999)

High-Performance Defunctionalisation
in Futhark

Anders Kiel Hovgaard(iD), Troels Henriksen(iD), and Martin Elsman$^{(\boxtimes)}$(iD)

DIKU, University of Copenhagen, Copenhagen, Denmark
hzs554@alumni.ku.dk, {athas,mael}@di.ku.dk

Abstract. General-purpose massively parallel processors, such as
GPUs, have become common, but are difficult to program. Pure functional programming can be a solution, as it guarantees referential trans-
parency, and provides useful combinators for expressing data-parallel
computations. Unfortunately, higher-order functions cannot be efficiently
implemented on GPUs by the usual means. In this paper, we present a
defunctionalisation transformation that relies on type-based restrictions
on the use of expressions of functional type, such that we can completely
eliminate higher-order functions in all cases, without introducing any
branching. We prove the correctness of the transformation and discuss
its implementation in Futhark, a data-parallel functional language that
generates GPU code. The use of these restricted higher-order functions
has no impact on run-time performance, and we argue that we gain
many of the benefits of general higher-order functions, without in most
practical cases being hindered by the restrictions.

Keywords: Defunctionalisation · GPGPU · Compilers

1 Introduction

Higher-order functional languages enable programmers to write abstract, compositional, and modular programs [24], and are often considered well-suited for
parallel programming, due to the lack of shared state and side effects. The emer-
gence of commodity massively parallel processors, such as GPUs, has exacer-
bated the need for developing practical techniques for programming parallel
hardware. However, GPU programming is notoriously difficult, since GPUs offer
a significantly more restricted programming model than that of CPUs. For example, GPUs do not readily allow for higher-order functions to be implemented,
mainly because GPUs have only limited support for function pointers.

If higher-order functions cannot be implemented directly, we may opt to
remove them by means of a program transformation that replaces them by a
simpler language mechanism. The canonical such transformation is *defunctionalisation*, which was first described by Reynolds [31]. Reynolds' defunctionalisation
abstracts each functional value by a set of records representing each particular
instance of the function, and the functional values in a program are abstracted

© Springer Nature Switzerland AG 2019
M. Pałka and M. Myreen (Eds.): TFP 2018, LNCS 11457, pp. 136–156, 2019.
https://doi.org/10.1007/978-3-030-18506-0_7

```
                              let g' (env:{a:i32}) (y:i32) =
                                let a = env.a in y+a
let twice (g:i32->i32) =        let f' (env:{g:{a:i32}})
  \x -> g (g x)                   (x:i32) =
                                  let g = env.g
                                in g' g (g' g x)
let main =                      let main =
  let f =                         let f = let a = 5
    let a = 5                             in {g = {a = a}}
    in twice (\y -> y+a)         in f' f 1 + f' f 2
  in f 1 + f 2
```

(a) Source program   (b) Target program

Fig. 1. Example demonstrating the defunctionalisation transformation

by the disjoint union of these sets. Each application in a program is then replaced by a call to an *apply* function, which performs a case match on each of the functional forms and essentially serves as an interpreter for the functional values in the original program. The most basic form will add a case to the *apply* function for every function abstraction in the source program. This amount of branching is very problematic for GPUs because of the issue of *branch divergence*. Since threads in a GPU execute together in lockstep, in so called *warps* of usually 32 threads, a large amount of branching will cause many threads to be idle in the branches where they are not executing instructions.

By restricting the use of functions in programs, we are able to statically determine the form of the applied function at every application. Specifically, we disallow conditionals and loops from returning functional values, and we disallow arrays from containing functions. These restrictions allow defunctionalisation by specializing each application to the particular form of function that may occur at run time. The result is essentially equivalent to inlining completely the *apply* function in a program produced by Reynolds defunctionalisation. Notably, the transformation does not introduce any additional branching.

We have used the Futhark language [17–21] to demonstrate this idea. Futhark is a data-parallel, purely functional array language with the main goal of generating high-performance parallel code. Although the language itself is hardware-agnostic, the main focus is on the implementation of an aggressively optimizing compiler that generates efficient GPU code via OpenCL.

To illustrate the basic idea, we show a simple Futhark program in Fig. 1a and the resulting program after defunctionalisation in Fig. 1b (simplified slightly). The result is a first-order program that explicitly pass closure environments, in the form of records capturing the free variables, in place of first-class functions in the source program.

The principal contributions of this paper are:

- A defunctionalisation transformation expressed on a simple data-parallel functional array language, with type rules that restrict the use of higher-order functions to allow for the defunctionalisation to remove effectively higher-order functions in all cases, without introducing any branching.
- A correctness proof of the transformation: A well-typed program will translate to another well-typed program and the translated program will evaluate to a value, corresponding to the value of the original program, or fail with an error if the original program fails.
- A description and evaluation of the transformation as implemented in the compiler for a real high-performance functional language (Futhark).

In the following, we use the notation $(\mathcal{Z}_i)^{i \in 1..n}$ to denote a sequence of objects $\mathcal{Z}_1, \ldots, \mathcal{Z}_n$, where each $\mathcal{Z}_i$ may be a syntactic object, a derivation of a judgment, and so on. Further, we sometimes write $\mathcal{D} :: \mathcal{J}$ to give the name $\mathcal{D}$ to the derivation of the judgment $\mathcal{J}$ so that we can refer to it later.

2 Language

To be able to formally define and reason about the defunctionalisation transformation, to be presented in Sect. 3, we define a simple functional language on which the transformation will operate. Conceptually, the transformation goes from a source language to a target language, but since the target language will be a sublanguage of the source language, we shall generally treat them as one and the following definitions will apply to both languages, unless stated otherwise.

The language is a λ-calculus extended with various features to resemble the Futhark language, including records, arrays with in-place updates, a parallel map, and a sequential loop construct. In the following, we define its abstract syntax, operational semantics, and type system.

2.1 Syntax

The set of *types* of the source language is given by the following grammar. The meta-variable $\ell \in \textbf{Lab}$ ranges over record *labels*.

$$\tau ::= \textbf{int} \mid \textbf{bool} \mid \tau_1 \to \tau_2 \mid \{(\ell_i : \tau_i)^{i \in 1..n}\} \mid []\tau$$

Record types are considered identical up to permutation of fields.

The abstract syntax of *expressions* of the source language is given by the following grammar. The meta-variable $x \in \textbf{Var}$ ranges over *variables* of the source language. We assume an injective function $Lab : \textbf{Var} \to \textbf{Lab}$ that maps variables to labels. Additionally, we let $n \in \mathbb{Z}$.

$$e ::= x \mid \overline{n} \mid \textbf{true} \mid \textbf{false} \mid e_1 + e_2 \mid e_1 \leq e_2 \mid \textbf{if } e_1 \textbf{ then } e_2 \textbf{ else } e_3$$
$$\mid \lambda x : \tau. \, e_0 \mid e_1 \, e_2 \mid \textbf{let } x = e_1 \textbf{ in } e_2 \mid \{(\ell_i = e_i)^{i \in 1..n}\} \mid e_0.\ell$$
$$\mid [(e_i)^{i \in 1..n}] \mid e_1[e_2] \mid e_0 \textbf{ with } [e_1] \leftarrow e_2 \mid \textbf{length } e_0$$
$$\mid \textbf{map } (\lambda x. \, e_1) \, e_2 \mid \textbf{loop } x = e_1 \textbf{ for } y \textbf{ in } e_2 \textbf{ do } e_3$$

Expressions are considered identical up to renaming of bound variables. Array literals are required to be non-empty in order to simplify the rules and relations in the following and in the meta theory.

The syntax of expressions of the target language is identical to that of the source language except that it does not have λ-abstractions and application. Similarly, the types of the target language does not include function types.[1]

We define a judgment, τ orderZero, given by the following rules, which assert that a type τ does not contain any function type as a subterm:

$$\frac{}{\textbf{int}\,\text{orderZero}} \qquad \frac{}{\textbf{bool}\,\text{orderZero}} \qquad \frac{(\tau_i\,\text{orderZero})^{i \in 1..n}}{\{(\ell_i \colon \tau_i)^{i \in 1..n}\}\,\text{orderZero}} \qquad \frac{\tau\,\text{orderZero}}{[\,]\tau\,\text{orderZero}}$$

2.2 Typing Rules

The typing rules for the language are mostly standard except for restrictions on the use of functions in certain places. Specifically, a conditional may not return a function, arrays are not allowed to contain functions, and a loop may not produce a function. These restrictions are enforced by the added premise of the judgment τ orderZero in the rules for conditionals, array literals, parallel maps, and loops. Aside from these restrictions, the use of higher-order functions and functions as first-class values is not restricted and, in particular, records are allowed to contain functions of arbitrarily high order.

A *typing context* (or *type environment*) Γ is a finite sequence of variables associated with their types:

$$\Gamma ::= \cdot \mid \Gamma, x : \tau$$

The empty context is denoted by $\cdot$, but is often omitted from the actual judgments. The variables in a typing context are required to be distinct. This requirement can always be satisfied by renaming bound variables as necessary.

The set of variables bound by a typing context is denoted by dom Γ and the type of a variable x bound in Γ is denoted by $\Gamma(x)$ if it exists. We write Γ, Γ' to denote the typing context consisting of the mappings in Γ followed by the mappings in Γ'. Note that since the variables in a context are distinct, the ordering is insignificant. Additionally, we write $\Gamma \subseteq \Gamma'$ if $\Gamma'(x) = \Gamma(x)$ for all $x \in \text{dom}\,\Gamma$. The typing rules for the language are given in Fig. 2.

2.3 Semantics

For the sake of the meta theory presented later, we choose to define a big-step operational semantics with an evaluation environment and function closures.

Evaluation environments Σ and *values* v are defined mutually inductively:

$$\Sigma ::= \cdot \mid \Sigma, x \mapsto v$$

$$v ::= \overline{n} \mid \textbf{true} \mid \textbf{false} \mid clos(\lambda x \colon \tau. \, e_0, \Sigma) \mid \{(\ell_i = v_i)^{i \in 1..n}\} \mid [(v_i)^{i \in 1..n}]$$

---

[1] In the actual implementation, the target language does include application of first-order functions, but in our theoretical work we just inline the functions for simplicity.

$$\boxed{\Gamma \vdash e : \tau}$$

$$\text{T-VAR:} \quad \frac{}{\Gamma \vdash x : \tau} \; (\Gamma(x) = \tau) \qquad \text{T-NUM:} \quad \frac{}{\Gamma \vdash \overline{n} : \mathbf{int}}$$

$$\text{T-TRUE:} \quad \frac{}{\Gamma \vdash \mathbf{true} : \mathbf{bool}} \qquad \text{T-FALSE:} \quad \frac{}{\Gamma \vdash \mathbf{false} : \mathbf{bool}}$$

$$\text{T-PLUS:} \quad \frac{\Gamma \vdash e_1 : \mathbf{int} \qquad \Gamma \vdash e_2 : \mathbf{int}}{\Gamma \vdash e_1 + e_2 : \mathbf{int}} \qquad \text{T-LEQ:} \quad \frac{\Gamma \vdash e_1 : \mathbf{int} \qquad \Gamma \vdash e_2 : \mathbf{int}}{\Gamma \vdash e_1 \le e_2 : \mathbf{bool}}$$

$$\text{T-IF:} \quad \frac{\Gamma \vdash e_1 : \mathbf{bool} \qquad \Gamma \vdash e_2 : \tau \qquad \Gamma \vdash e_3 : \tau \qquad \tau \, \text{orderZero}}{\Gamma \vdash \mathbf{if} \; e_1 \; \mathbf{then} \; e_2 \; \mathbf{else} \; e_3 : \tau}$$

$$\text{T-LAM:} \quad \frac{\Gamma, x : \tau_1 \vdash e_0 : \tau_2}{\Gamma \vdash \lambda x : \tau_1. \, e_0 : \tau_1 \to \tau_2} \qquad \text{T-APP:} \quad \frac{\Gamma \vdash e_1 : \tau_2 \to \tau \qquad \Gamma \vdash e_2 : \tau_2}{\Gamma \vdash e_1 \, e_2 : \tau}$$

$$\text{T-LET:} \quad \frac{\Gamma \vdash e_1 : \tau_1 \qquad \Gamma, x : \tau_1 \vdash e_2 : \tau}{\Gamma \vdash \mathbf{let} \; x = e_1 \; \mathbf{in} \; e_2 : \tau} \qquad \text{T-RCD:} \quad \frac{(\Gamma \vdash e_i : \tau_i)^{i \in 1..n}}{\Gamma \vdash \{(\ell_i = e_i)^{i \in 1..n}\} : \{(\ell_i : \tau_i)^{i \in 1..n}\}}$$

$$\text{T-PROJ:} \quad \frac{\Gamma \vdash e_0 : \{(\ell_i : \tau_i)^{i \in 1..n}\}}{\Gamma \vdash e_0.\ell_k : \tau_k} \; (1 \le k \le n) \qquad \text{T-LENGTH:} \quad \frac{\Gamma \vdash e_0 : [\,]\tau}{\Gamma \vdash \mathbf{length} \; e_0 : \mathbf{int}}$$

$$\text{T-ARRAY:} \quad \frac{(\Gamma \vdash e_i : \tau)^{i \in 1..n} \qquad \tau \, \text{orderZero}}{\Gamma \vdash [e_1, \ldots, e_n] : [\,]\tau} \qquad \text{T-INDEX:} \quad \frac{\Gamma \vdash e_0 : [\,]\tau \qquad \Gamma \vdash e_1 : \mathbf{int}}{\Gamma \vdash e_0[e_1] : \tau}$$

$$\text{T-UPDATE:} \quad \frac{\Gamma \vdash e_0 : [\,]\tau \qquad \Gamma \vdash e_1 : \mathbf{int} \qquad \Gamma \vdash e_2 : \tau}{\Gamma \vdash e_0 \; \mathbf{with} \; [e_1] \leftarrow e_2 : [\,]\tau} \qquad \text{T-MAP:} \quad \frac{\tau \, \text{orderZero} \qquad \Gamma \vdash e_2 : [\,]\tau_2 \qquad \Gamma, x : \tau_2 \vdash e_1 : \tau}{\Gamma \vdash \mathbf{map} \; (\lambda x. \, e_1) \; e_2 : [\,]\tau}$$

$$\text{T-LOOP:} \quad \frac{\Gamma \vdash e_0 : \tau \qquad \Gamma \vdash e_1 : [\,]\tau' \qquad \Gamma, x : \tau, y : \tau' \vdash e_2 : \tau \qquad \tau \, \text{orderZero}}{\Gamma \vdash \mathbf{loop} \; x = e_0 \; \mathbf{for} \; y \; \mathbf{in} \; e_1 \; \mathbf{do} \; e_2 : \tau}$$

Fig. 2. Typing rules

Evaluation environments Σ map variables to values and have the same properties and notations as the typing context with regards to extension, variable lookup, and distinctness of variables. A function *closure*, denoted $clos(\lambda x : \tau. \, e_0, \Sigma)$, is a value that captures the environment in which a λ-abstraction was evaluated. The values of the target language are the same, but without function closures.

Because the language involves array indexing and updating that may fail, we introduce the special term **err** to denote an out-of-bounds error and we define a *result* r to be either a value or **err**.

The big-step operational semantics for the language is given by the derivation rules in Fig. 3. In case any subexpression evaluates to **err**, the entire expression should evaluate to **err**, so it is necessary to give derivation rules for propagating these error results. Unfortunately, this error propagation involves creating many extra derivation rules and duplicating many premises. We show the rules that introduce **err**; however, we choose to omit the ones that propagate errors and instead just note that for each of the non-axiom rules below, there are a number of additional rules for propagating errors. For instance, for the rule E-APP, there are additional rules E-APPERR$\{1, 2, 0\}$, which propagate errors in the applied expression, the argument, and the closure body, respectively. Techniques exist for limiting this duplication [6, 30], but, for simplicity, we have chosen a traditional style of presentation.

The rule E-LOOP refers to an auxiliary judgment form, defined in Fig. 4, which performs the iterations of the loop, given a starting value and a sequence of values to iterate over. Like the main evaluation judgment, this one also has rules for propagating **err** results, which are again omitted.

3   Defunctionalisation

We now define the defunctionalisation transformation which translates an expression in the source language to an equivalent expression in the target language that does not contain any higher-order subterms or use of first-class functions.

Translation environments (or *defunctionalisation environments*) E and *static values* sv are defined mutually inductively, as follows:

$$E ::= \cdot \mid E, x \mapsto sv$$
$$sv ::= Dyn\ \tau \mid Lam\ x\ e_0\ E \mid Rcd\ \{(\ell_i \mapsto sv_i)^{i \in 1..n}\} \mid Arr\ sv_0$$

Translation environments map variables to static values. We assume the same properties as we did for typing contexts and evaluation environments, and we use analogous notation. As the name suggests, a static value is essentially a static approximation of the value that an expression will eventually evaluate to. Static values resemble the role of types, which also approximate the values of expressions, but static values posses more information than types. As a result of the restrictions on the use of functions in the type system, the static value *Lam*, which approximates functional values, will contain the actual function parameter and body, along with a defunctionalisation environment containing static values approximating the values in the closed-over environment. The two other constructors *Rcd* and *Arr* complete the correspondence between types and static values.

The defunctionalisation translation takes place in a defunctionalisation environment, as defined above, which mirrors the evaluation environment by approximating the values by static values, and it translates a given expression e to a *residual expression* e' and its corresponding static value sv. The residual expression resembles the original expression, but λ-abstractions are translated into record expressions that capture the values in the environment at the time of evaluation. Applications are translated into **let**-bindings that bind the record expression, the closed-over variables, and the function parameter.

$$\boxed{\Sigma \vdash e \downarrow r}$$

E-VAR: $\dfrac{}{\Sigma \vdash x \downarrow v}\,(\Sigma(x) = v)$ E-NUM: $\dfrac{}{\Sigma \vdash \overline{n} \downarrow \overline{n}}$ E-TRUE: $\dfrac{}{\Sigma \vdash \mathbf{true} \downarrow \mathbf{true}}$

E-PLUS: $\dfrac{\Sigma \vdash e_1 \downarrow \overline{n_1} \qquad \Sigma \vdash e_2 \downarrow \overline{n_2}}{\Sigma \vdash e_1 + e_2 \downarrow \overline{n_1 + n_2}}$ E-FALSE: $\dfrac{}{\Sigma \vdash \mathbf{false} \downarrow \mathbf{false}}$

E-LEQT: $\dfrac{\begin{array}{c}\Sigma \vdash e_1 \downarrow \overline{n_1} \\ \Sigma \vdash e_2 \downarrow \overline{n_2}\end{array}}{\Sigma \vdash e_1 \leq e_2 \downarrow \mathbf{true}}\,(n_1 \leq n_2)$ E-LEQF: $\dfrac{\begin{array}{c}\Sigma \vdash e_1 \downarrow \overline{n_1} \\ \Sigma \vdash e_2 \downarrow \overline{n_2}\end{array}}{\Sigma \vdash e_1 \leq e_2 \downarrow \mathbf{false}}\,(n_1 > n_2)$

E-IFT: $\dfrac{\Sigma \vdash e_1 \downarrow \mathbf{true} \qquad \Sigma \vdash e_2 \downarrow v}{\Sigma \vdash \mathbf{if}\ e_1\ \mathbf{then}\ e_2\ \mathbf{else}\ e_3 \downarrow v}$ E-IFF: $\dfrac{\Sigma \vdash e_1 \downarrow \mathbf{false} \qquad \Sigma \vdash e_3 \downarrow v}{\Sigma \vdash \mathbf{if}\ e_1\ \mathbf{then}\ e_2\ \mathbf{else}\ e_3 \downarrow v}$

E-LAM: $\dfrac{}{\Sigma \vdash \lambda x\colon \tau.\,e_0 \downarrow clos(\lambda x\colon \tau.\,e_0, \Sigma)}$

E-APP: $\dfrac{\Sigma \vdash e_1 \downarrow clos(\lambda x\colon \tau.\,e_0, \Sigma_0) \qquad \Sigma \vdash e_2 \downarrow v_2 \quad \Sigma_0, x \mapsto v_2 \vdash e_0 \downarrow v}{\Sigma \vdash e_1\ e_2 \downarrow v}$ E-LET: $\dfrac{\Sigma \vdash e_1 \downarrow v_1 \qquad \Sigma, x \mapsto v_1 \vdash e_2 \downarrow v}{\Sigma \vdash \mathbf{let}\ x = e_1\ \mathbf{in}\ e_2 \downarrow v}$

E-RCD: $\dfrac{(\Sigma \vdash e_i \downarrow v_i)^{i \in 1..n}}{\Sigma \vdash \{(\ell_i = e_i)^{i \in 1..n}\} \downarrow \{(\ell_i = v_i)^{i \in 1..n}\}}$

E-PROJ: $\dfrac{\Sigma \vdash e_0 \downarrow \{(\ell_i = v_i)^{i \in 1..n}\}}{\Sigma \vdash e_0.\ell_k \downarrow v_k}\,(1 \leq k \leq n)$

E-ARRAY: $\dfrac{(\Sigma \vdash e_i \downarrow v_i)^{i \in 1..n}}{\Sigma \vdash [(e_i)^{i \in 1..n}] \downarrow [(v_i)^{i \in 1..n}]}$ E-INDEX: $\dfrac{\begin{array}{c}\Sigma \vdash e_0 \downarrow [(v_i)^{i \in 1..n}] \\ \Sigma \vdash e_1 \downarrow \overline{k}\end{array}}{\Sigma \vdash e_0[e_1] \downarrow v_k}\,(1 \leq k \leq n)$

E-INDEXERR: $\dfrac{\Sigma \vdash e_0 \downarrow [(v_i)^{i \in 1..n}] \qquad \Sigma \vdash e_1 \downarrow \overline{k}}{\Sigma \vdash e_0[e_1] \downarrow \mathbf{err}}\,(k < 1 \lor k > n)$

E-UPDATE: $\dfrac{\Sigma \vdash e_0 \downarrow [(v_i)^{i \in 1..n}] \qquad \Sigma \vdash e_1 \downarrow \overline{k} \qquad \Sigma \vdash e_2 \downarrow v'_k}{\Sigma \vdash e_0\ \mathbf{with}\ [e_1] \leftarrow e_2 \downarrow [(v_i)^{i \in 1..k-1}, v'_k, (v_i)^{i \in k+1..n}]}\,(1 \leq k \leq n)$

E-UPDATEERR: $\dfrac{\Sigma \vdash e_0 \downarrow [(v_i)^{i \in 1..n}] \qquad \Sigma \vdash e_1 \downarrow \overline{k}}{\Sigma \vdash e_0\ \mathbf{with}\ [e_1] \leftarrow e_2 \downarrow \mathbf{err}}\,(k < 1 \lor k > n)$

E-LENGTH: $\dfrac{\Sigma \vdash e_0 \downarrow [(v_i)^{i \in 1..n}]}{\Sigma \vdash \mathbf{length}\ e_0 \downarrow \overline{n}}$ E-MAP: $\dfrac{\begin{array}{c}\Sigma \vdash e_2 \downarrow [(v_i)^{i \in 1..n}] \\ (\Sigma, x \mapsto v_i \vdash e_1 \downarrow v'_i)^{i \in 1..n}\end{array}}{\Sigma \vdash \mathbf{map}\ (\lambda x.\,e_1)\ e_2 \downarrow [(v'_i)^{i \in 1..n}]}$

E-LOOP: $\dfrac{\Sigma \vdash e_0 \downarrow v_0 \qquad \Sigma \vdash e_1 \downarrow [(v_i)^{i \in 1..n}] \qquad \Sigma; x = v_0; y = (v_i)^{i \in 1..n} \vdash e_2 \downarrow v}{\Sigma \vdash \mathbf{loop}\ x = e_0\ \mathbf{for}\ y\ \mathbf{in}\ e_1\ \mathbf{do}\ e_2 \downarrow v}$

Fig. 3. Big-step operational semantics

As with record types, we consider *Rcd* static values to be identical up to reordering of the label-entries. Additionally, we consider *Lam* static values to be identical up to renaming of the parameter variable, as for λ-abstractions.

The transformation is defined by the derivation rules in Figs. 5 and 6.

$$\boxed{\Sigma; x = v_0; y = (v_i)^{i \in 1..n} \vdash e \downarrow r}$$

EL-NIL: $$\dfrac{}{\Sigma; x = v_0; y = \cdot \vdash e \downarrow v_0}$$

EL-CONS: $$\dfrac{\Sigma, x \mapsto v_0, y \mapsto v_1 \vdash e \downarrow v_0' \qquad \Sigma; x = v_0'; y = (v_i)^{i \in 2..n} \vdash e \downarrow v}{\Sigma; x = v_0; y = (v_i)^{i \in 1..n} \vdash e \downarrow v}$$

Fig. 4. Auxiliary judgment for the semantics of loops

$$\boxed{E \vdash e \rightsquigarrow \langle e', sv \rangle}$$

D-VAR: $$\dfrac{}{E \vdash x \rightsquigarrow \langle x, sv \rangle} \ (E(x) = sv) \qquad \text{D-NUM:} \ \dfrac{}{E \vdash \overline{n} \rightsquigarrow \langle \overline{n}, Dyn \ \mathbf{int} \rangle}$$

D-TRUE: $$\dfrac{}{E \vdash \mathbf{true} \rightsquigarrow \langle \mathbf{true}, Dyn \ \mathbf{bool} \rangle} \qquad \text{(equivalent rule D-FALSE)}$$

D-PLUS: $$\dfrac{E \vdash e_1 \rightsquigarrow \langle e_1', Dyn \ \mathbf{int} \rangle \qquad E \vdash e_2 \rightsquigarrow \langle e_2', Dyn \ \mathbf{int} \rangle}{E \vdash e_1 + e_2 \rightsquigarrow \langle e_1' + e_2', Dyn \ \mathbf{int} \rangle} \qquad \text{(rule D-LEQ)}$$

D-IF: $$\dfrac{E \vdash e_1 \rightsquigarrow \langle e_1', Dyn \ \mathbf{bool} \rangle \qquad E \vdash e_2 \rightsquigarrow \langle e_2', sv \rangle \qquad E \vdash e_3 \rightsquigarrow \langle e_3', sv \rangle}{E \vdash \mathbf{if} \ e_1 \ \mathbf{then} \ e_2 \ \mathbf{else} \ e_3 \rightsquigarrow \langle \mathbf{if} \ e_1' \ \mathbf{then} \ e_2' \ \mathbf{else} \ e_3', sv \rangle}$$

D-LAM: $$\dfrac{}{E \vdash \lambda x : \tau. \, e_0 \rightsquigarrow \langle \{(Lab(y) = y)^{y \in \mathrm{dom} \, E}\}, Lam \ x \ e_0 \ E \rangle}$$

D-APP: $$\dfrac{E \vdash e_1 \rightsquigarrow \langle e_1', Lam \ x \ e_0 \ E_0 \rangle \qquad E \vdash e_2 \rightsquigarrow \langle e_2', sv_2 \rangle \qquad E_0, x \mapsto sv_2 \vdash e_0 \rightsquigarrow \langle e_0', sv \rangle}{E \vdash e_1 \ e_2 \rightsquigarrow \langle e', sv \rangle}$$
$$\text{where } e' = \mathbf{let} \ env = e_1' \ \mathbf{in} \ (\mathbf{let} \ y = env.Lab(y) \ \mathbf{in})^{y \in \mathrm{dom} \, E_0}$$
$$\mathbf{let} \ x = e_2' \ \mathbf{in} \ e_0'$$

D-LET: $$\dfrac{E \vdash e_1 \rightsquigarrow \langle e_1', sv_1 \rangle \qquad E, x \mapsto sv_1 \vdash e_2 \rightsquigarrow \langle e_2', sv \rangle}{E \vdash \mathbf{let} \ x = e_1 \ \mathbf{in} \ e_2 \rightsquigarrow \langle \mathbf{let} \ x = e_1' \ \mathbf{in} \ e_2', sv \rangle}$$

Fig. 5. Derivation rules for the defunctionalisation transformation

In the implementation, the record in the residual expression of rule D-LAM captures only the free variables in the λ-abstraction. Likewise, the defunctionalisation environment embedded in the static value is restricted to the free variables. This refinement is not hard to formalise, but it does not add anything interesting to the development, so we have omitted it for simplicity.

Notice how the rules include aspects of both evaluation and type checking, in analogy to how static values are somewhere in-between values and types. For instance, the rules ensure that variables are in scope, and that a conditional has a *Dyn* boolean condition and the branches have the same static value. Interestingly, this constraint on the static values of branches allows for a conditional to

$$\boxed{E \vdash e \rightsquigarrow \langle e', sv \rangle}$$

D-RCD:
$$\frac{(E \vdash e_i \rightsquigarrow \langle e'_i, sv_i \rangle)^{i \in 1..n}}{E \vdash \{(\ell_i = e_i)^{i \in 1..n}\} \rightsquigarrow \langle \{(\ell_i = e'_i)^{i \in 1..n}\}, Rcd \{(\ell_i \mapsto sv_i)^{i \in 1..n}\} \rangle}$$

D-PROJ:
$$\frac{E \vdash e_0 \rightsquigarrow \langle e'_0, Rcd \{(\ell_i \mapsto sv_i)^{i \in 1..n}\} \rangle}{E \vdash e_0.\ell_k \rightsquigarrow \langle e'_0.\ell_k, sv_k \rangle} \quad (1 \le k \le n)$$

D-ARRAY:
$$\frac{(E \vdash e_i \rightsquigarrow \langle e'_i, sv \rangle)^{i \in 1..n}}{E \vdash [e_1, \dots, e_n] \rightsquigarrow \langle [e'_1, \dots, e'_n], Arr\ sv \rangle}$$

D-INDEX:
$$\frac{E \vdash e_1 \rightsquigarrow \langle e'_1, Arr\ sv \rangle \qquad E \vdash e_2 \rightsquigarrow \langle e'_2, Dyn\ \mathbf{int} \rangle}{E \vdash e_1[e_2] \rightsquigarrow \langle e'_1[e'_2], sv \rangle}$$

D-UPDATE:
$$\frac{E \vdash e_0 \rightsquigarrow \langle e'_0, Arr\ sv \rangle \qquad E \vdash e_1 \rightsquigarrow \langle e'_1, Dyn\ \mathbf{int} \rangle \qquad E \vdash e_2 \rightsquigarrow \langle e'_2, sv \rangle}{E \vdash e_0\ \mathbf{with}\ [e_1] \leftarrow e_2 \rightsquigarrow \langle e'_0\ \mathbf{with}\ [e'_1] \leftarrow e'_2, Arr\ sv \rangle}$$

D-LENGTH:
$$\frac{E \vdash e_0 \rightsquigarrow \langle e'_0, Arr\ sv \rangle}{E \vdash \mathbf{length}\ e_0 \rightsquigarrow \langle \mathbf{length}\ e'_0, Dyn\ \mathbf{int} \rangle}$$

D-MAP:
$$\frac{E \vdash e_2 \rightsquigarrow \langle e'_2, Arr\ sv_2 \rangle \qquad E, x \mapsto sv_2 \vdash e_1 \rightsquigarrow \langle e'_1, sv_1 \rangle}{E \vdash \mathbf{map}\ (\lambda x.\ e_1)\ e_2 \rightsquigarrow \langle \mathbf{map}\ (\lambda x.\ e'_1)\ e'_2, Arr\ sv_1 \rangle}$$

D-LOOP:
$$\frac{E \vdash e_1 \rightsquigarrow \langle e'_1, sv \rangle \qquad E \vdash e_2 \rightsquigarrow \langle e'_2, Arr\ sv_2 \rangle \qquad E, x \mapsto sv, y \mapsto sv_2 \vdash e_3 \rightsquigarrow \langle e'_3, sv \rangle}{\begin{array}{c} E \vdash \mathbf{loop}\ x = e_1\ \mathbf{for}\ y\ \mathbf{in}\ e_2\ \mathbf{do}\ e_3 \\ \rightsquigarrow \langle \mathbf{loop}\ x = e'_1\ \mathbf{for}\ y\ \mathbf{in}\ e'_2\ \mathbf{do}\ e'_3, sv \rangle \end{array}}$$

Fig. 6. Derivation rules for the defunctionalisation transformation (cont.)

return functions in its branches, as long as the functions are α-equivalent. The same is true for arrays and loops.

This transformation translates any order-zero expression into an equivalent expression that does not contain any higher-order functions. Any first-order expression can be translated by converting the types of its parameters (which are necessarily order zero) to static values, by mapping record types to Rcd static values and base types to Dyn static values, and including these as bindings for the parameter variables in an initial translation environment.

By a relatively simple extension to the system, we can support any number of top-level function definitions that take parameters of arbitrary type and can have any return type, as long as the designated *main* function is first-order.

4   Meta Theory

In this section, we show type soundness and argue for the correctness of the defunctionalisation transformation presented in Sect. 3. We show that the transformation of a well-typed expression always terminates and yields another well-typed expression. Finally, we show that the meaning of a defunctionalised expression is equivalent to the meaning of the original expression.

4.1 Type Soundness and Normalisation

We first show type soundness. Since we are using a big-step semantics, the situation is a bit different from the usual approach of showing progress and preservation for a small-step semantics. One of the usual advantages of using a small-step semantics is that it allows distinguishing between diverging and stuck terms, whereas for a big-step semantics, neither a diverging term nor a stuck term is related to any value. As we shall see, however, for the big-step semantics that we have presented, any well-typed expression will evaluate to a result that is either **err** or a value that is, semantically, of the same type. Thus, we also establish that the language is strongly normalizing, which comes as no surprise given the lack of recursion and bounded number of iterations of loops.

To this end, we first define a relation between values and types, given by derivation rules in Fig. 7, and extend it to relate evaluation environments and typing contexts.

$$\boxed{\vDash v : \tau}$$

$$\overline{\vDash \bar{n} : \mathbf{int}} \qquad \overline{\vDash \mathbf{true} : \mathbf{bool}} \qquad \overline{\vDash \mathbf{false} : \mathbf{bool}}$$

$$\frac{\forall v_1. \ \vDash v_1 : \tau_1 \implies \exists r. \ \Sigma, x \mapsto v_1 \vdash e_0 \downarrow r \land (r = \mathbf{err} \lor (r = v_2 \land \vDash v_2 : \tau_2))}{\vDash clos(\lambda x : \tau_1 . \, e_0, \Sigma) : \tau_1 \to \tau_2}$$

$$\frac{(\vDash v_i : \tau_i)^{i \in 1..n}}{\vDash \{(\ell_i = v_i)^{i \in 1..n}\} : \{(\ell_i : \tau_i)^{i \in 1..n}\}} \qquad \frac{(\vDash v_i : \tau)^{i \in 1..n}}{\vDash [(v_i)^{i \in 1..n}] : []\tau}$$

$$\boxed{\vDash \Sigma : \Gamma}$$

$$\overline{\vDash \cdot : \cdot} \qquad \frac{\vDash \Sigma : \Gamma \qquad \vDash v : \tau}{\vDash (\Sigma, x \mapsto v) : (\Gamma, x : \tau)}$$

Fig. 7. Relation between values and types, and evaluation environments and typing contexts, respectively

We then state and prove type soundness as follows. We do not go into the details of the proof and how the relation between values and types is used. The cases for T-LAM and T-APP are the most interesting in this regard, but we omit the details in favor of other results which more directly pertain to defunctionalisation. A similar relation and its role in the proof of termination and preservation of typing for the defunctionalisation transformation is described in more detail in Sect. 4.2.

Lemma 1 (Type Soundness). *If $\Gamma \vdash e : \tau$ (by $\mathcal{T}$) and $\vDash \Sigma : \Gamma$, for some Σ, then $\Sigma \vdash e \downarrow r$, for some r, and either $r = \mathbf{err}$ or $r = v$, for some v, and $\vDash v : \tau$.*

Proof. By induction on the typing derivation $\mathcal{T}$. In the case for T-LAM, we prove the implication in the premise of the rule relating closure values and function types. In the case for T-APP, we use this implication to obtain the needed derivations for the body of the closure. In the case for T-LOOP, in the subcase where the first two subexpressions evaluate to values, we proceed by an inner induction on the structure of the corresponding sequence of values for the loop iterations. □

4.2   Translation Termination and Preservation of Typing

In this section, we show that the translation of a well-typed expression always terminates and that the translated expression is also well-typed, with a typing context and type that can be obtained from the defunctionalisation environment and the static value, respectively.

We first define a mapping from static values to types, which shows how the type of a residual expression can be obtained from its static value:

$$\llbracket Dyn\ \tau \rrbracket_{\mathrm{tp}} = \tau$$

$$\llbracket Lam\ x\ e_0\ E \rrbracket_{\mathrm{tp}} = \{(Lab(y) : \llbracket sv_y \rrbracket_{\mathrm{tp}})^{(y \mapsto sv_y) \in E}\}$$

$$\llbracket Rcd\ \{(\ell_i \mapsto sv_i)^{i \in 1..n}\} \rrbracket_{\mathrm{tp}} = \{(\ell_i : \llbracket sv_i \rrbracket_{\mathrm{tp}})^{i \in 1..n}\}$$

$$\llbracket Arr\ sv \rrbracket_{\mathrm{tp}} = [\,](\llbracket sv \rrbracket_{\mathrm{tp}})$$

This mapping is extended to map defunctionalisation environments to typing contexts, by mapping each individual static value in an environment.

$$\llbracket \cdot \rrbracket_{\mathrm{tp}} = \cdot$$

$$\llbracket E, x \mapsto sv \rrbracket_{\mathrm{tp}} = \llbracket E \rrbracket_{\mathrm{tp}}, x : \llbracket sv \rrbracket_{\mathrm{tp}}$$

In order to be able to show termination and preservation of typing for defunctionalisation, we first define a relation, $\vDash sv : \tau$, between static values and types, similar to the previous relation between values and types, and further extend it to relate defunctionalisation environments and typing contexts. This relation is given by the rules in Fig. 8.

By assuming this relation between some defunctionalisation environment E and a typing context Γ for a given typing derivation, we can show that a well-typed expression will translate to some expression and additionally produce a static value that is related to the type of the original expression according to the above relation. Additionally, the translated expression is well-typed in the typing context obtained from E with a type determined by the static value. This strengthens the induction hypothesis to allow the case for application to go through, which would otherwise not be possible. This approach is quite similar to the previous proof of type soundness and normalisation of evaluation.

$\boxed{\vDash sv : \tau}$

$$\frac{}{\vDash Dyn \text{ int} : \text{int}} \qquad \frac{}{\vDash Dyn \text{ bool} : \text{bool}}$$

$$\frac{\forall sv_1. \ \vDash sv_1 : \tau_1 \implies \exists e_0', sv_2. \ E_0, x \mapsto sv_1 \vdash e_0 \rightsquigarrow \langle e_0', sv_2 \rangle}{\wedge \ \vDash sv_2 : \tau_2 \ \wedge \ [\![E_0, x \mapsto sv_1]\!]_{\mathrm{tp}} \vdash e_0' : [\![sv_2]\!]_{\mathrm{tp}}}{\vDash Lam \ x \ e_0 \ E_0 : \tau_1 \to \tau_2}$$

$$\frac{(\vDash sv_i : \tau_i)^{i \in 1..n}}{\vDash Rcd \ \{(\ell_i \mapsto sv_i)^{i \in 1..n}\} : \{(\ell_i : \tau_i)^{i \in 1..n}\}} \qquad \frac{\vDash sv : \tau \qquad \tau \, \mathrm{orderZero}}{\vDash Arr \ sv : [\,]\tau}$$

$\boxed{\vDash E : \Gamma}$

$$\frac{}{\vDash \cdot : \cdot} \qquad \frac{\vDash E : \Gamma \qquad \vDash sv : \tau}{\vDash (E, x \mapsto sv) : (\Gamma, x : \tau)}$$

Fig. 8. Relation between static values and types, and defunctionalisation environments and typing contexts, respectively

We first prove an auxiliary lemma about the above relation between static values and types, which states that for types of order zero, the related static value is uniquely determined. This property is crucial for the ability of defunctionalisation to determine uniquely the function at every application site, and it is used in the proof of Theorem 1 in the cases for conditionals, array literals, array updates, and loops.

Lemma 2. *If* $\vDash sv : \tau$, $\vDash sv' : \tau$, *and* $\tau \, \mathrm{orderZero}$, *then* $sv = sv'$.

Proof. By induction on the derivation of $\vDash sv : \tau$.   □

The following lemma states that if a static value is related to a type of order zero, then the static values maps to the same type. This property is used to establish that the types of order zero terms are unchanged by defunctionalisation. It is also used in the cases for conditionals, array literals, loops, and maps in the proof of Theorem 1.

Lemma 3. *For any* sv, *if* $\vDash sv : \tau$ *and* $\tau \, \mathrm{orderZero}$, *then* $[\![sv]\!]_{\mathrm{tp}} = \tau$.

Proof. By induction on the structure of sv.   □

Finally, we can state and prove termination and preservation of typing for the defunctionalisation translation as follows:

Theorem 1. *If* $\Gamma \vdash e : \tau$ *(by* $\mathcal{T}$*) and* $\vDash E : \Gamma$, *for some* E, *then* $E \vdash e \rightsquigarrow \langle e', sv \rangle$, $\vDash sv : \tau$, *and* $[\![E]\!]_{\mathrm{tp}} \vdash e' : [\![sv]\!]_{\mathrm{tp}}$, *for some* e' *and* sv.

Proof. By induction on the typing derivation $\mathcal{T}$. Most cases are straightforward applications of the induction hypothesis to the subderivations, often reasoning by inversion on the obtained relations between static values and types, and extending the assumed relation $\vDash E : \Gamma$ to allow for further applications of the induction hypothesis. Then the required derivations are subsequently constructed directly. For details, please consult [23].   □

4.3 Preservation of Meaning

In this section, we show that the defunctionalisation transformation preserves the meaning of expressions in the following sense: If an expression e evaluates to a value v in an environment Σ, then the translated expression e' will evaluate to a corresponding value v' in a corresponding environment Σ', and if e evaluates to **err**, then e' will evaluate to **err** in the context Σ' as well (the notion of correspondence will be made precise shortly).

We first define a simple relation between source language values and static values, given in Fig. 9, and extend it to relate evaluation environments and defunctionalisation environments in the usual way. Note that this relation actually defines a function from values to static values.

$$\boxed{\vDash v : sv}$$

$$\overline{\vDash \overline{n} : Dyn \; \mathbf{int}} \qquad \overline{\vDash \mathbf{true} : Dyn \; \mathbf{bool}} \qquad \overline{\vDash \mathbf{false} : Dyn \; \mathbf{bool}}$$

$$\frac{\vDash \Sigma : E}{\vDash clos(\lambda x : \tau . e_0, \Sigma) : Lam \; x \; e_0 \; E}$$

$$\frac{(\vDash v_i : sv_i)^{i \in 1..n}}{\vDash \{(\ell_i = v_i)^{i \in 1..n}\} : Rcd \; \{(\ell_i \mapsto sv_i)^{i \in 1..n}\}} \qquad \frac{(\vDash v_i : sv)^{i \in 1..n}}{\vDash [(v_i)^{i \in 1..n}] : Arr \; sv}$$

Fig. 9. Relation between values and static values

Next, we define a mapping from source language values to target language values, which simply converts each function closure to a corresponding record expression that contains the converted values from the closure environment:

$$[\![v]\!]_{\mathrm{val}} = v, \quad \text{for } v \in \{\overline{n}, \mathbf{true}, \mathbf{false}\}$$
$$[\![clos(\lambda x : \tau . e_0, \Sigma)]\!]_{\mathrm{val}} = \{(Lab(y) = [\![v_y]\!]_{\mathrm{val}})^{(y \mapsto v_y) \in \Sigma}\}$$
$$[\![\{(\ell_i = v_i)^{i \in 1..n}\}]\!]_{\mathrm{val}} = \{(\ell_i = [\![v_i]\!]_{\mathrm{val}})^{i \in 1..n}\}$$
$$[\![[(v_i)^{i \in 1..n}]]\!]_{\mathrm{val}} = [([\![v_i]\!]_{\mathrm{val}})^{i \in 1..n}]$$

We extend this mapping homomorphically to evaluation environments. The case for arrays is actually moot, since arrays will never contain function closures.

The following lemma states that if a value is related to a type of order zero, according to the previously defined relation between values and types used in the proof of type soundness, then the value maps to itself, that is, values that do not contain function closures are unaffected by defunctionalisation:

Lemma 4. *If $\vDash v : \tau$ and τ orderZero, then $[\![v]\!]_{\mathrm{val}} = v$.*

Proof. By induction on the derivation of $\vDash v : \tau$.   □

We now prove the following theorem, which states that the defunctionalisation transformation preserves the meaning of an expression that is known to evaluate to some result, where the value of the defunctionalised expression and the values in the environment are translated according to the translation from source language values to target language values given above.

Theorem 2 (Semantics Preservation). *If $\Sigma \vdash e \downarrow r$ (by $\mathcal{E}$), $\vDash \Sigma : E$ (by $\mathcal{R}$), and $E \vdash e \rightsquigarrow \langle e', sv \rangle$ (by $\mathcal{D}$), then if $r = \mathbf{err}$, then also $[\![\Sigma]\!]_{\mathrm{val}} \vdash e' \downarrow \mathbf{err}$ and if $r = v$, for some value v, then $\vDash v : sv$ and $[\![\Sigma]\!]_{\mathrm{val}} \vdash e' \downarrow [\![v]\!]_{\mathrm{val}}$.*

Proof. By structural induction on the big-step evaluation derivation $\mathcal{E}$. For details, please consult [23].   □

4.4 Correctness of Defunctionalisation

To summarize the previous properties and results relating to the correctness of the defunctionalisation transformation, we state the following corollary which follows by type soundness (Lemma 1), normalisation and preservation of typing for defunctionalisation (Theorem 1), and semantics preservation of defunctionalisation (Theorem 2), together with Lemmas 3 and 4.

Corollary 1 (Correctness). *If $\vdash e : \tau$ and τ orderZero, then $\vdash e \downarrow r$, for some r, $\vdash e \rightsquigarrow \langle e', sv \rangle$, for some e' and sv, and $\vdash e' : \tau$ and $\vdash e' \downarrow r$ as well.*

5 Implementation

The defunctionalisation transformation that was presented in Sect. 3 has been implemented in the Futhark compiler, which is developed in the open on GitHub and publicly available at https://github.com/diku-dk/futhark.

In this section, we discuss how our implementation diverges from the theoretical description. As Futhark is a real language with a fairly large number of syntactical constructs, as well as features such as uniqueness types for supporting in-place updates and size-dependent types for reasoning about the sizes of arrays, it would not be feasible to do a formal treatment of the entire language.

Futhark supports a small number of parallel higher-order functions, such as `map`, `reduce`, `scan`, and `filter`, which are specially recognized by the compiler, and exploited to perform optimisations and generate parallel code. User-defined parallel higher-order functions are ultimately defined in terms of these. As a result, the program produced by the defunctionaliser is not *exclusively* first-order, but may contain fully saturated applications of these built-in functions.

5.1 Polymorphism, Function Types, and Monomorphisation

Futhark supports parametric let-polymorphism. Defunctionalisation, however, works only on monomorphic programs and therefore, programs are *monomorphized* before being passed to the defunctionaliser.

Due to our restrictions on function types, it is necessary to distinguish between type variables which may be instantiated with any type, and type variables which may only take on types of order zero. Without such distinction, one could write an invalid program that we would not be able to defunctionalise, for example by instantiating the type a with a function type in the following:

```
let ite 'a (b: bool) (x: a) (y: a) : a =
    if b then x else y
```

To prevent this situation from happening, we have introduced the notion of *lifted type variables*, written '^a, which are unrestricted in the types that they may be instantiated to, while the regular type variables may only take on types of order zero. Consequently, a lifted type variable must be considered to be of order greater than zero and is thus restricted in the same way as function types.

The Futhark equality and inequality operators == and != are overloaded operators, which also work on structural types, such as arrays and tuples. However, Futhark does not support type classes [29] or equality types [11]. Allowing the equality and inequality operators to work on values of abstract types (i.e., on all non-lifted types) could potentially violate abstraction properties, which is the reason for the special treatment of equality types and equality type variables in the Standard ML programming language.

5.2   Array Shape Parameters

Futhark employs a system of runtime-checked size-dependent types, where the programmer may give shape declarations in function definitions to express shape invariants about parameter and result arrays. Shape parameters (listed before ordinary parameters and enclosed in brackets) are not explicitly passed on application. Instead, they are implicitly inferred from the arguments of the value parameters. Defunctionalisation could potentially destroy the shape invariants. For example, consider partially applying a function such as the following:

```
let f [n] (xs: [n]i32) (ys: [n]i32) = ...
```

In the implementation, we preserve the connection between the shapes of the two array parameters by capturing the shape parameter n along with the array parameter xs in the record for the closure environment. In the case of the function f, the defunctionalised program will look something like the following:

```
let f^ {n: i32, xs: []i32} (ys: [n]i32) = ...
let f [n] (xs: [n]i32) = {n=n, xs=xs}
```

The Futhark compiler will then insert a dynamic check to verify that the size of array ys is equal to the value of argument n.

Of course, built-in operations that truly rely on these invariants, such as zip, will perform this shape check regardless, but by maintaining these invariants in general, we prevent code from silently breaching the contract that was specified by the programmer through the shape annotations in the types.

Having extended Futhark with higher-order functions, it is useful to be able to specify shape invariants on expressions of function type in general. This feature can be implemented by eta-expanding the function expression and inserting type ascriptions with shape annotations on the order-zero parameters and bodies. For instance, the type ascription

```
e : ([n]i32 -> [m]i32) -> [m]i32
```

would be translated into the expression

```
\x -> (e (\(y:[n]i32) -> x y : [m]i32)) : [m]i32
```

This feature has not yet been implemented in Futhark.

5.3 Optimisations

When the defunctionalisation algorithm processes an application, the D-APP rule will replicate the lambda body (e_0) at the point of application. This implicit copying is equivalent to fully inlining all functions, which will produce very large programs if the same function is called in many locations. In our implementation, we instead perform lambda lifting [25] to move the definition of the lambda to a top-level function, parameterized by an argument representing its lexical closure, and simply insert a call to that function.

However, this lifting produces the opposite problem: we may now produce a very large number of trivial functions. In particular, when lifting curried functions that accept many parameters, we will create one function for each partial application, corresponding to each parameter. To limit the copying and lifting, our implementation extends the notion of static values with a *dynamic function*, which is simply a first-order functional analogue to dynamic values. We then add a translation rule similar to D-APP that handles the case where the function is a dynamic function rather than a *Lam*.

Finally, our implementation inlines lambdas with particularly simple bodies; in particular those that contain just a single primitive operation or a record literal. The latter case corresponds to functions produced for partial applications.

6 Empirical Evaluation

The defunctionalisation technique presented in this paper can be empirically evaluated by two metrics. First, is the code produced by defunctionalisation efficient? Second, are higher-order functions with our type restrictions useful? The former question is the easier to answer, as we can simply rewrite a set of benchmark programs to make use of higher-order functions, and measure whether the performance of the generated code changes. We have done this by using the existing Futhark benchmark suite, which contains more than thirty Futhark programs translated from a range of other suites, including Accelerate [4], Rodinia [7], Parboil [32], and FinPar [1]. These implementations all make heavy use of operations such as `map`, `reduce`, `scan`, `filter`, which used to be language constructs, but are now higher-order functions that wrap compiler intrinsics. Further, most benchmarks have been rewritten to make use of higher-order utility functions (such as `flip`, `curry`, `uncurry`, and function composition and application) where appropriate. As expected, this change had no impact on run-time performance, although compilation times did increase by up to a factor of two.

The more interesting question is whether the restrictions we put on higher-order functions are too onerous in practice. While some uses of higher-order functions are impossible, many "functional design patterns" are unaffected by the restrictions. Such examples include the use of higher-order functions for defining a Futhark serialisation library [13, 27] and for introducing the notion of functional images [9], as we shall see in the following section. Higher-order functions also make it possible to capture certain reusable parallel design patterns, for instance, for flattening some cases of nested irregular parallelism [15].

6.1 Functional Images

Church Encoding can be used to represent objects such as integers via lambda terms. While modern functional programmers tend to prefer built-in numeric types for efficiency reasons, other representations of data as functions have remained popular. One of these is functional images, as implemented in the Haskell library Pan [9]. Here, an image is represented as a function from a point on the plane to some value. In higher-order Futhark, we can define this as

```
type img 'a = point -> a
type cimage = img color
```

for appropriate definitions of `point` and `color`. Transformations on images are then defined simply as function composition.

Interestingly, none of the combinators and transformations defined in Pan require the aggregation of images in lists, or returning them from a branch. Hence, we were able to translate the entirety of the Pan library to Futhark. The reason is likely that Pan itself was designed for staged compilation, where Haskell is merely used as a meta-language for generating code for some high-performance object language [10]. This approach requires restrictions on the use of functions that are essentially identical to the ones we introduced for Futhark. In Futhark, we can directly generate high-performance parallel code, and modern GPUs are easily powerful enough to render most functional images (and animations) at a high frame rate. Essentially, once the compiler finishes its optimisations, we are left with a trivial two-dimensional `map` that computes the color of each pixel completely independently. Example images are shown on Fig. 10. The Mandelbrot fractal, the implementation of which is translated from [26], in particular is expensive to compute at high resolutions.

Fig. 10. Images rendered by the Futhark implementation of functional images. The annulus defined by the left-most image is used to overlay grey scale and colorized Mandelbrot fractals. (Color figure online)

7   Allowing Conditionals of Function Type

Given that the main novelty enabling efficient defunctionalisation is the restrictions in the type system, it is interesting to consider how these restrictions could be loosened to allow more programs to be typed and transformed, and what consequences this would have for the efficiency of the transformed programs.

In the following, we consider lifting the restriction on the type of conditionals. This change introduces a binary choice for the static value of a conditional and this choice may depend on dynamic information. The produced static value must capture this choice. Thus, we may extend the definition of static values as follows:

$$sv ::= \cdots \mid Or \ sv_1 \ sv_2$$

It is important not to introduce more branching than necessary, so the static values of the branches of a conditional should be appropriately combined to isolate the dynamic choice at much as possible. In particular, if a conditional returns a record, the Or static value should only be introduced for those record fields that produce Lam static values.

The residual expression for a functional value occurring in a branch must be extended to include some kind of token to indicate which branch is taken at run time. Unfortunately, it is fairly complicated to devise a translation that preserves typeability in the current type system. The residual expression of a function occurring in a nested conditional would need to include as many tokens as the maximum depth of nesting in the outermost conditional. Additionally, the record capturing the free variables in a function would need to include the union of all the free variables in each λ-abstraction that can be returned from that conditional. Hence, we would have to include "dummy" record fields for those variables that are not in scope in a given function, and "dummy" tokens for functions that are not deeply nested in branches.

What is needed to remedy this situation, is the addition of (binary) sum types to the language:

$$\tau ::= \cdots \mid \tau_1 + \tau_2$$

If we add binary sums, along with expression forms for injections and case-matching, the transformation would just need to keep track of which branches were taken to reach a particular function-type result and then wrap the usual residual expression in appropriate injections. An application of an expression with an *Or* static value would then perform pattern matching until it reaches a *Lam* static value and then insert **let**-bindings to put the closed-over variables into scope, for that particular function.

8   Related Work

Support for higher-order functions is not widespread in parallel programming languages. For example, they are not supported in the pioneering work on NESL [3], which was targeted at a vector execution model with limitations similar to modern GPUs. Data Parallel Haskell (DPH) [5] does support higher-order functions via closure conversion, but targets traditional multicore CPUs where this is a viable technique. The GPU language Harlan [22] is notable for its powerful feature set, and it does support higher-order functions via Reynolds-style defunctionalisation. The authors of Harlan note that this could cause performance problems, but that it has not done so yet. This is likely because most of the Harlan benchmark programs do not make much use of closures on the GPU.

A general body of related work includes mechanisms for removing abstractions at compile time including the techniques, used for instance by Accelerate [4] and Obsidian [8], for embedded domain specific languages (EDSLs). These languages use a staged compilation approach where Haskell is used as a meta-language to generate first-order imperative target programs. While the target programs are themselves first-order, meta-programs may use the full power of Haskell, including higher-order functions. As our approach has limitations, so does the EDSL approach; in particular, care has to be taken that source language functions do not end up in target arrays. Other approaches at removing abstractions at compile time include the use of quoted domain specific languages [28], techniques for multi-stage programming, such as [33], and the notion of static interpretation of modules [12], which is also applied in the context of Futhark [2,14] for eliminating even higher-order module language constructs entirely at compile time (before monomorphisation).

Another body of related work includes the seminal work by Tait [34] and Girard [16] on establishing the basic proof technique on using logical relations for expressing normalisation and termination properties for the simply-typed lambda calculus and System F, which has been the inspiring work for establishing the property of termination for our defunctionalisation technique.

9   Conclusion and Future Work

We have shown a useful design for implementing higher-order functions in high-performance functional languages, by using a defunctionalisation transformation that exploits type-based restrictions on functions to avoid introducing branches in the resulting first-order program. We have proven this transformation correct. Further, we have discussed the extensions and optimisations we found necessary for applying the transformation in a real compiler, and demonstrated that the type restrictions are not a great hindrance in practice.

References

1. Andreetta, C., et al.: FinPar: a parallel financial benchmark. ACM Trans. Arch. Code Optim. (TACO) **13**(2), 18:1–18:27 (2016)
2. Annenkov, D.: Adventures in formalisation: financial contracts, modules, and two-level type theory. Ph.D. thesis, University of Copenhagen, April 2018
3. Blelloch, G.E.: Programming parallel algorithms. Commun. ACM (CACM) **39**(3), 85–97 (1996)
4. Chakravarty, M.M., Keller, G., Lee, S., McDonell, T.L., Grover, V.: Accelerating Haskell array codes with multicore GPUs. In: Workshop on Declarative Aspects of Multicore Programming, DAMP 2011. ACM, January 2011
5. Chakravarty, M.M., Leshchinskiy, R., Jones, S.P., Keller, G., Marlow, S.: Data parallel Haskell: a status report. In: Workshop on Declarative Aspects of Multicore Programming, DAMP 2007. ACM, January 2007
6. Charguéraud, A.: Pretty-big-step semantics. In: Felleisen, M., Gardner, P. (eds.) ESOP 2013. LNCS, vol. 7792, pp. 41–60. Springer, Heidelberg (2013). https://doi.org/10.1007/978-3-642-37036-6_3
7. Che, S., et al.: Rodinia: a benchmark suite for heterogeneous computing. In: IEEE International Symposium on Workload Characterization, IISWC 2009, October 2009
8. Claessen, K., Sheeran, M., Svensson, B.J.: Expressive array constructs in an embedded GPU kernel programming language. In: Workshop on Declarative Aspects of Multicore Programming, DAMP 2012. ACM, January 2012
9. Elliott, C.: Functional images. In: The Fun of Programming. Cornerstones of Computing Series. Palgrave, March 2003
10. Elliott, C., Finne, S., de Moor, O.: Compiling embedded languages. J. Funct. Program. **13**(2), 455–481 (2003)
11. Elsman, M.: Polymorphic equality–no tags required. In: Second International Workshop on Types in Compilation (TIC 1998), March 1998
12. Elsman, M.: Static interpretation of modules. In: Proceedings of the ACM SIGPLAN International Conference on Functional Programming, ICFP 1999. ACM Press, September 1999
13. Elsman, M.: Type-specialized serialization with sharing. In: Sixth Symposium on Trends in Functional Programming (TFP 2005), September 2005
14. Elsman, M., Henriksen, T., Annenkov, D., Oancea, C.E.: Static interpretation of higher-order modules in Futhark: functional GPU programming in the large. Proc. ACM Program. Lang. **2**(ICFP), 97:1–97:30 (2018)
15. Elsman, M., Henriksen, T., Oancea, C.E.: Parallel Programming in Futhark. Department of Computer Science, University of Copenhagen, November 2018. https://futhark-book.readthedocs.io
16. Girard, J.Y.: Interpretation Fonctionnelle et Elimination des Coupures de l'Arithmetique d'Ordre Superieur. In: Proceedings of the Second Scandinavian Logic Symposium, pp. 63–92. North-Holland (1971)

17. Henriksen, T.: Design and implementation of the Futhark programming language. Ph.D. thesis, DIKU, University of Copenhagen, November 2017
18. Henriksen, T., Elsman, M., Oancea, C.E.: Size slicing: a hybrid approach to size inference in Futhark. In: Proceedings of the 3rd ACM SIGPLAN International Workshop on Functional High-Performance Computing, FHPC 2014. ACM (2014)
19. Henriksen, T., Elsman, M., Oancea, C.E.: Modular acceleration: tricky cases of functional high-performance computing. In: Proceedings of the 7th ACM SIGPLAN International Workshop on Functional High-Performance Computing, FHPC 2018. ACM, New York, September 2018
20. Henriksen, T., Serup, N.G., Elsman, M., Henglein, F., Oancea, C.E.: Futhark: purely functional GPU-programming with nested parallelism and in-place array updates. In: Proceedings of the 38th ACM SIGPLAN Conference on Programming Language Design and Implementation, PLDI 2017, pp. 556–571. ACM, June 2017
21. Henriksen, T., Thorøe, F., Elsman, M., Oancea, C.E.: Incremental flattening for nested data parallelism. In: Proceedings of the 24th ACM SIGPLAN Symposium on Principles and Practice of Parallel Programming, PPoPP 2019. ACM (2019)
22. Holk, E., Newton, R., Siek, J., Lumsdaine, A.: Region-based memory management for GPU programming languages: enabling rich data structures on a spartan host. In: Proceedings of the 2014 ACM International Conference on Object Oriented Programming Systems Languages & Applications, OOPSLA 2014, pp. 141–155. ACM, New York, October 2014
23. Hovgaard, A.K.: Higher-order functions for a high-performance programming language for GPUs. Master's thesis, Department of Computer Science, Faculty of Science, University of Copenhagen, Universitetsparken 5, DK-2100 Copenhagen, May 2018
24. Hughes, J.: Why functional programming matters. Comput. J. **32**(2), 98–107 (1989)
25. Johnsson, T.: Lambda lifting: transforming programs to recursive equations. In: Jouannaud, J.-P. (ed.) FPCA 1985. LNCS, vol. 201, pp. 190–203. Springer, Heidelberg (1985). https://doi.org/10.1007/3-540-15975-4_37
26. Jones, M.P.: Composing fractals. J. Funct. Program. **14**(6), 715–725 (2004)
27. Kennedy, A.J.: Functional pearl: pickler combinators. J. Funct. Program. **14**(6), 727–739 (2004)
28. Najd, S., Lindley, S., Svenningsson, J., Wadler, P.: Everything old is new again: quoted domain-specific languages. In: Proceedings of the ACM Workshop on Partial Evaluation and Program Manipulation, PEPM 2016. ACM, January 2016
29. Peterson, J., Jones, M.: Implementing type classes. In: Proceedings of the ACM SIGPLAN 1993 Conference on Programming Language Design and Implementation, PLDI 1993, pp. 227–236. ACM, New York (1993)
30. Poulsen, C.B., Mosses, P.D.: Flag-based big-step semantics. J. Log. Algebr. Methods Program. **88**, 174–190 (2017)
31. Reynolds, J.C.: Definitional interpreters for higher-order programming languages. In: Proceedings of the ACM Annual Conference-Volume 2, pp. 717–740. ACM (1972)
32. Stratton, J.A., et al.: Parboil: a revised benchmark suite for scientific and commercial throughput computing. Technical report, University of Illinois at Urbana-Champaign, IMPACT-12-01 (2012)
33. Taha, W., Sheard, T.: MetaML and multi-stage programming with explicit annotations. Theor. Comput. Sci. **248**(1), 211–242 (2000). PEPM 1997
34. Tait, W.W.: Intensional interpretations of functionals of finite type. J. Symb. Log. **32**, 198–212 (1967)

Author Index

Algehed, Maximilian 94

Belikov, Evgenij 1

de Vries, Folkert 20

Einarsdóttir, Sólrún Halla 94
Elsman, Martin 136

Gerdes, Alex 94
Gozillon, Andrew 46

Haeri, Seyed Hossein 46
Handley, Martin A. T. 114
Henriksen, Troels 136

Hovgaard, Anders Kiel 136
Hutton, Graham 114

Jansson, Patrik 94

Keir, Paul 46

Loidl, Hans-Wolfgang 1
López-González, J. 74

Michaelson, Greg 1

Pérez, Jorge A. 20

Serrano, Juan M. 74

Printed in the United States
By Bookmasters